DATE DU

The Parables in the Gospels

A long look from dark eyes, a riddling sentence
to be woven and woven on the church's looms.

James Joyce, *Ulysses*, I

The Parables in the Gospels

History and Allegory

JOHN DRURY

Crossroad • New York

1985
The Crossroad Publishing Company
370 Lexington Avenue, New York, N.Y. 10017

Printed in the United States of America

Library of Congress Cataloging in Publication Data
Drury, John.
    The parables in the Gospels.

    Bibliography: p. 165
    Includes index.
    1. Jesus Christ—Parables. 2. Parables—History and
criticism. 3. Bible. N.T. Gospels—Criticism interpretation, etc.   I. Title.
BT375.2.D78   1985   226'.806   84-27452
ISBN 0-8245-0655-3

ACKNOWLEDGEMENTS
Thanks are due to SCM Press Ltd and Charles Scribner's Sons for
permission to quote from *The Parables of Jesus* by J. Jeremias.
Biblical quotations in this book, unless otherwise stated, are from
the Revised Standard Version of the Bible, copyright 1946, 1952,
1957, 1971, 1973 by the Division of Christian Education of the
National Council of the Churches of Christ in the USA, and are
used by permission.

FOR
THOSE WHO ARE NOT CONTENT
WITH THE STATUS QUO
IN GOSPEL CRITICISM

Contents

Preface

I began the line of criticism which is used in this book with an article in the *Journal of Theological Studies* XXIV called 'The Sower, the Vineyard and the Place of Allegory in the Interpretation of Mark's Parables'. In an essay on 'The Origins of Mark's Parables' in *Ways of Reading the Bible* edited by Michael Wadsworth (Harvester 1981), I explored further into the precedents of Mark's parables; and in a paper read to a conference of the Society of Comparative Literature at King's in 1982 I took stock of my methods. This preliminary work has been incorporated into the present book.

I am grateful to Timothy Jenkins, Ruth Morse and Leslie Houlden for reading the typescript and suggesting many improvements. Practically all of them have been made. Melvyn Ramsden helped me with the rabbinic material.

I owe much in the way of stimulus and support to that growing, if entirely informal, set of people to whom this book is dedicated: particularly Michael Goulder, Gabriel Josipovici, Frank Kermode, Edmund Leach and Chris Rowland.

My thanks to my wife, for her encouragement and understanding, are much more than formal.

JOHN DRURY
King's College, Cambridge
June 1984

Introduction

This book's title and its table of contents are an indication of its aim: having first established the meaning and use of parables which the first Christian writers inherited from Jewish tradition, to understand the parables in the contexts of the books in which they occur. Surprisingly, this second feature has not been the usual way of modern interpretation of the parables. A hundred and fifty years ago F. C. Baur noticed that each New Testament book has a *tendenz*, a theological character and aim of its own. In recent years this insight has been applied to the Gospels in the method known as redaction criticism. By understanding the tendency, or tendencies, of a book we can enter into the milieu in which a subsidiary unit like a parable gets and gives its meaning. It is set in an overall story. It both gets its meaning from it and illuminates it. Dostoyevsky's *The Brothers Karamazov* contains two parables, 'The Grand Inquisitor' and 'An Onion'. It is possible to read them, and get something out of them, on their own and apart from the total narrative. But to understand them fully it is necessary to see them as parts of the narrative development. It matters who tells them to whom and when.

Yet the major books about the gospel parables to have appeared in the past century or so (Trench, Jülicher, Cadoux, Dodd, B. T. D. Smith, Jeremias, Linnemann) have not made this their determining method. They have not sought to establish the functions of parables by reference to the tendencies of the books they are in. Rather, they have emptied them out of the books and their narratives in order to deal with them as a genre on their own. The context for understanding them has usually been a conjectural historical reconstruction of the ministry of Jesus, not the style and purposes of each evangelist. There are powerful reasons for this.

The very character of parables is partly to blame. They are compact and attractive units which, as such, seem to invite detachment from their narrative settings. This often happens with 'The Grand Inquisitor', and still more often with the gospel parables which come to the ecclesiastical listener as units in 'lessons'. He or she is much more interested in what the parable means to him or her than in the prefatory formal announcement of the reader, 'Here begins the fourth chapter of the Gospel according to St Mark.' Yet in that announcement there are indispensable clues to meaning. When the unit is detached from its home ground it has to go somewhere. So the milieu of the meaning will now be one's own experience – if there is a sermon on the lesson it is likely to take it that way – or perhaps in some generalized reconstruction of Jesus' teaching, or both. Not, in any case, St Mark's book. The great exegetes of the parables who have been mentioned shared this procedure, possibly partly because they too were churchgoers. Religious, historical and literary interest combined to make it attractive and satisfactory to them. It is worth looking at these interests in turn.

The religious interest can be divided into two aspects though these may work simultaneously. The first is personal. If religion has meaning it must be meaning, in Luther's phrase, *pro me*, for me, and mesh into my milieu. The second is communal. Religious meaning must mesh with a common or institutional frame of belief; which in Christianity has been above all dogmatic and christological. The religious interest is thus well satisfied if the subjective authority of meaning for me is combined with the objective authority of what Christ, the focus of ecclesiastical authority, meant. This is the combination that Dodd and Jeremias went for. But they went for it by way of historical–scientific method because, for any biblical critic since the eighteenth century, what Christ meant is a question requiring an historical answer.

So they and we are taken into the historical interest. It works on the far side of the text instead of, like the religious interest, on the near side. Thus Dodd:

'We must look first ... to the particular setting in which they [the parables] were delivered. The task of the interpreter of the parables is to find out, if he can, the setting of a parable in the situation contemplated by the gospels, and hence, the application which would suggest itself to one who stood in that situation' (p.26).

Similarly Jeremias: 'to recover the original meaning of the parables' (p.19). The texts are windows upon the world behind them. Interepreters are window-cleaners. It sounds simple. But there is much virtue, and much trouble in store, in Dodd's qualificatory 'if he can'. For the exegete bent on historical reconstruction is confronted by a disabling absence. We do not have the language and parables of Jesus 'except and insofar as such can be retrieved from within the language of the earliest interpreters' (Crossan, p. xiii). The critic who is after the authentic and original parables of Jesus is like a restorer trying to clean an allegedly over-painted canvas by Rubens without having access to a single indisputably authentic Rubens painting or even sketch. The attempts continue because religious hopes die hard. Though the historical Jesus has not been rediscovered, exegesis which holds out some hope of it happening at last, and works according-ly, is much more welcome in Christian circles than that which does not. However, the fact of the matter is that historical inquiry after the actual Jesus has reached an impasse after more than a century of diligent and exacting work. The disabling absence has not dissipated. It has been filled with scholarly conjecture. So Crossan, with a distinct note of desperation, proposes that 'one might consider the term "Jesus" as a cipher of the reconstructed parable complex itself'. With the historical quest in such a pass it is not surprising that Crossan and others have turned elsewhere.

A literary interest in the parables offers, in a relatively time- and history-free way, the discovery of literary structures as the way to find the meaning of parables. Literary preferences were already at work in Dodd and Jeremias whose tastes were against allegory and for realism. But this is something more conscious and sophisti-cated. It also marks a break with traditional method. No longer are the texts treated as windows to see through. They are more like tapestries whose weave can be followed and understood as the way their image is made or their story told. That is refreshing, and very possibly a new lease of life for gospel studies. But these patterns that are discerned – where do they come from? Could they be pictures in the fire, patterns out of our own imagination rather than an evangelist's? If so, we have come full circle and are back with a secular version of the religious interest with which we began. The only hope of breaking the circle is by reviving the historical interest: not, this time, to search for the historical Jesus, but rather for the structures and specifications to which parables were made in the first century and in the neighbourhood of Christianity. For that, there is plenty of evidence around and outside the gospel texts: evidence which has not hitherto been given the weight it should have.

It is that sort of historical inquiry that is proposed here. From modern literary method it takes the hint to look *at* texts rather than through them, to interpret units within them, here parables, by reference to the preceding and consequent story of which they are integral and active parts: 'parables in Gospels'. From modern biblical criticism it takes that historical cast of mind which is interested in what an ancient text meant *then* to 'them' as a counterpoise to what it means *now* to 'us'. Doing that requires not only informaton about what was happening then but also about what they made of it, how they understood the historical process they were in itself. We have plenty of evidence for that because each Gospel is an historical narrative shaped and impelled by a particular view of the significance of history. It is a major part of its *tendenz* which becomes overt in the parables which, as with Dostoyevsky and Kafka, tell the reader what the story is about and what it signifies. In this study the sort of place hitherto occupied by reconstruction of Jesus's ministry and teaching is occupied by the reconstruction of the views of history of the evangelists. To those views Jesus is central. But the reconstruction is much easier to make and to check. The quest for Jesus gets stuck because he is not available to us in isolation from the gospel texts, but those texts and texts in close neighbourhood to them are readily available. Jesus' parables are not isolably accessible to inspection. The evangelists' are, and we know about the evangelists as well as we know about any people who have left books behind them. We cannot get answers to questions of what a particular parable was doing in a particular place in Jesus' ministry because we just cannot get back to that place, and we cannot whistle it up either. We can get answers to questions of what a particular parable is doing in its particular place in a particular book because we can get to that place and, having got there, look about us at the surrounding setting. One evangelist can put the same parable in a different place from another. That raises the question of what was its original place. But the raising of questions holds no guarantee of the certainty of answers. We can only expect the sort of lateral answer which explains why this writer has put this parable here and not somewhere else. Historical knowledge of the views and methods which he used in his history-writing make it possible. So the kind of interpretation done in this book might be called historical–structural and seen as continuous with redaction criticism.

A subsidiary feature of it ought to be noticed in advance because it is unusual. There is no resort here to the hypothesis of Q, the alleged lost source of the material common to Matthew and Luke which is not in Mark. It has not been invoked because the need has not arisen. At the many points where it could have come into play it has threatened problems which were not presented by the competing possibility that Luke used Matthew's Gospel as well as Mark's. He refers in his first verse to 'many' who 'have undertaken to compile a narrative of the things which have been accomplished among us'. The hypothetical Q was not a narrative but a collection of sayings, and whatever Luke's 'many' means it must refer to more narratives than one. I have worked on the assumption of Luke's use of Matthew in two previous books (*Luke* [Fontana 1973] and *Tradition and Design in Luke's Gospel* [Darton, Longman and Todd 1976]). It worked adequately on both occasions. Reviewing the latter book in the *Journal of Theological Studies* XXX, pp. 270ff, Graham Stanton said that it had formidable difficulties, particularly with regard to Luke's 'lack of interest' (his phrase) in Matthew's abbreviations of Mark and his additions to him. With those warnings in mind I have given my theory a further practical test by using it for this book. I can only say that it has not proved formidably difficult. I think Q would have been harder to run. Nor did it disclose the lack of interest on Luke's part in Matthew's abbreviations and amplifications of Mark. Numerous examples of Luke's positive interest in Matthew's editings of Mark may be found in chapter five. They include Luke's consent to points of Matthew's revision of Mark in the grand Marcan parables of the *sower* and the *vineyard*.

Some lesser features of the book can be treated in one paragraph. The titles of the parables have been put in italics for ease of reference, and an index of them put at the back. I have deliberately kept notes and apparatus to a minimum, including them wherever possible in the body of the text. This has been possible because the book is not an addition to the current orthodoxy of parable interpretation, and so does not need to refer to it constantly. Its usual references are much more to the texts themselves, and these are customarily included in the body of the text anyway. They too are given an index at the back of the book. The term 'allegory' which recurs throughout I take to mean a concatenation of symbolic persons, places, things and happenings, which signifies a parallel concatenation in the actual world. Such a structure is distinguished from symbolism in general by having a precise and univocal meaning, to which an interpretation or decoding may provide the key. The allegories dealt with here are, as the reader will find again and again, predominantly historical rather than conceptual. I have considered at least all the obvious parables in the Gospels in the interests of giving my views and methods a thorough testing. But that must at times militate against easy and exciting reading. Indeed, repetitiousness will be an (inelegant but unavoidable) sign of success for the theory and method in coping with the material. This is particularly obtrusive with Luke and his many parables. There is nothing novel to say about the later of them which has not already been noticed in the ones before. Reference rather than continuous reading may be more suitable to the passages about them.

Finally, what is the present relevance of this study? It is a question that needs to be kept at bay for fear of its resulting in yet another Jesus congenial to modern piety, with parables to match and consequent blurring of the historical focus. All the same, the Gospels are still sacred Scripture and the religious reader is likely to ask, like the Lost Boy in *Peter Pan*, 'Am I in this story?' In a sense fundamental to historical study, no. The meaning of most of the parables is tied into a past and particular historical crisis: the emergence of the Christian religion out of the Jewish, and the task of self-definition which it imposed. And yet, if there is any place for passion and imagination in historical study, such a transition must always be of lively interest to people who come long after it has all been settled and yet often feel themselves to be crossing over, to be on a threshold between a certain past and an uncertain future which between them impose a similar task of understanding the self in historical terms. Religion with its rites of passage, with all the ceremonies, stories and doctrines which it uses to steady us as we waver on such thresholds, is still the guardian of these crossings. Its traditional role remains and the gospel narratives are apt to it. It has been given an extra twist by the modern historical study of religion, which has impressed upon us that religions themselves do not stand still, exempt from the ravages and benefits of time. So they do not just help people who pass with time, but are carried along with it (and with them) themselves. To such a radical consciousness of transcience the gospel parables, by virtue of their almost obsessive concern with crisis and change, can speak. They say that the future belongs to those who can adapt to the genuinely new, and use the experience of the past with faith and imagination to do so. And that, in the middle of a reactionary decade confronting awesome novelty with deep misgiving, is worth pondering.

1 Old Testament Parables

The historical study of the New Testament has to work with very fragmentary evidence. The subject is a jigsaw with important pieces missing. One of them has already been noticed: we do not possess an indisputable or undisputed saying of Jesus by which to judge the numerous sayings imputed to him. At the best we have more or less strong probabilities and possibilities which, as such, do not make the best foundations for inquiry. Another is that the New Testament books may, for all we know, be the survivors of a much larger volume of early Christian writings and oral teachings which must also remain a matter of guesswork, such as the Q hypothesis and many other theories about documents which have disappeared or been assimilated into the books we have. Yet another gap is the dating of rabbinic material contemporary with the Gospels. There is plenty of material in the rabbinic collections, Midrash and Talmud, but the difficulties which dog the sayings of Jesus are at least as acute with the sayings of the rabbis of the first and second centuries: the authentic and the imputed cannot be separated with certainty. Further, the influence on the New Testament writers of the Greek and Roman religions of their day is difficult to clarify into detailed certainties. All of these weigh on a study of the gospel parables and handicap the effort to uncover Jesus' own parables, to compare them with those of contemporary Jewish teachers or teachers in other religions.

For all this there is one major piece of the jigsaw, or major group of pieces, which we do possess. It is the Old Testament. It is available to us as it was to the first Christians. Rather, it was more available to them than to us because they had assimilated it more thoroughly. It was their sacred text and worked upon them with a depth of scope which it would be hard to equal today even among the most zealous fundamentalist Christians, whose attention is unavoidably diverted by a mass of other literature and forms of communication. The nearest modern equivalent might be Bunyan's pilgrim, an image of himself, as a solitary man with a book, the Bible, in his hand. But even there we have to notice that this was a bigger book than the literature possessed by first Christians because it included a New Testament which, according to Christian lore, overshadowed the much larger Old Testament. To the first Christians as to their Lord, the Old Testament was the book. Open a New Testament book and one is soon confronted with the Old Testament. Matthew starts with a genealogy which spans it, Mark with resonant quotations from it, Luke with two chapters in its narrative style, John with a version of its beginning. Paul refers to it continually. None of this is mere ornament, tactics or manner. It is fundamental strategy. Moses and all the prophets (which included the narrative books) and the psalms were to be interpreted as concerning Christ (Luke 24. 27 and 44).

A study of parables must first have as clear an idea as possible of what a parable is, because what is included in the study and how it is treated will follow from it. If the study is to be historical then the idea must not be one which suits us but one which suited them, the people of the first two centuries. Parables were part of the way in which they described their world to themselves and understood it. However much religious motives may want that description and understanding to coincide with our own, historical motives work the other way and are ready for strangenesses and differences. The historian will not look at the gospel parables from a subsequent and later standpoint which was not available or formative for them. He will take his initial stand on the other side of them at a previous point, or points, which could and would have influenced the way they are. That includes, above all, the Old Testament. Its definitions, not ours, must be the starting point.

'Parable' is an English version of the Greek word *parabolē*. According to Aristotle (*Rhetoric*, 2.20) parables were used by orators in inductive or indirect proof as a generally recognized means of demonstration and illustration. They are, according to him, of two kinds: true events taken from history, and the more easily invented example such as the fable or the parables used by Socrates in Plato's dialogues. Characteristically, he had a decided preference for the first of these as against the second with its allegorical form. It was a preference which was to appeal strongly and fatefully to modern critics such as Jülicher and Dodd who had had a classical education. But the education of the New Testament writers was different. The Bible, not Aristotle, was their teacher and they possessed it in a Greek translation, the Septuagint. It was full of parables, and the Septuagint translation was usually careful to translate the Hebrew *mashal* by the Greek *parabolē* in spite of the extraordinary range of *mashal*. Since that range is so wide and contains a number of things which would not be called parables nowadays, it is worth setting it out with examples both for reference and as an historical corrective.

1 *A Saying*

1 Samuel 24 has a story about Saul and David. Saul, out hunting for David with his army, turned into a cave to relieve himself. He did not realize that David and his men were hiding there. His men encouraged David to kill Saul on the spot. David, with an amazing mixture of reverence and irreverence towards the Lord's anointed, cut off Saul's skirt instead. Then, when Saul had left the cave, David went out and declared himself to the skirtless king, bowing to the earth and drawing attention to his own reverence and restraint by showing him the piece he had cut off and rehearsing 'the old parable "out of the lawless comes lawlessness"'. But my hand will not be against you.' Here a parable is an old saw. It is not figurative or illustrative. It concerns the relation of inner disposition and outward behaviour. And its context of meaning is a narrative. All four features are worth noting for future reference.

Ezekiel 12.22 is another example of the same usage. Here the parable is 'the days grow long and every vision comes to nothing'. It is a commonplace among the exiled Israelites in Babylon which the prophet is called by God to deny by announcing that 'the days are at hand and the fulfilment of every vision'. Again it is a straight, unfigurative saw set in an historical narrative context which gives it its meaning. Ezekiel is going to emerge as a singularly important figure in the development of parables and this is the first example of the wide range of the genre which he uses.

2 *A Figurative Saying or Metaphor*

Examples are afforded by the same two books.

1 Samuel 10.9–13 tells of an extraordinary alteration in Saul's behaviour after his anointing by Samuel. 'God gave him another heart', and he became an ecstatic prophet. '"What has come over the son of Kish?",' people wondered, '"Is Saul also among the prophets?"' A 'man of the place answered' enigmatically '"And who is their father?" Therefore', the narrative continues, 'it became a parable [RSV 'proverb'], "Is Saul also among the prophets?"' Clearly it is a parable of a figurative sort, applicable when anybody behaves out of character. Again, the narrative setting is integral to its meaning with the extra twist that a distinct historical origin for a parable is posited. It is given an aetiology.

Ezekiel 18.2 is, like the previous Ezekiel 12.22, another popular parable which God rules out of order. '"What do you mean by repeating this parable concerning the land of Israel, 'The fathers

have eaten sour grapes and the children's teeth are set on edge?'
As I live, says the Lord God, this proverb shall no more be used to
you in Israel."' Instead, each individual shall take the consequences of his own sin. The parable is figurative and thus
applicable to any number of appropriate instances in the moral
sphere. But it is striking that its generality is constrained by
history. It is declared redundant, made anachronistic, by a divine
fiat striking into history at this particular point and changing it.

The importance of both these examples is that, while adding a
new usage to the parable's range which looks like loosening its
attachment to the particular narrative context, they actually keep a
firm historical grip: the first by its inquiry into the point of origin
and the second by a similar pinpointing of the precise moment of a
parable's death.

3 *The Enigmatic Allegorical Parable*

Here we move out of the popular realm of the commonplace,
figurative or not, into a more professional world of skilled
contrivance bordering on obfuscation. The difficult parable, the
complicated riddle, appealed as such to those who enjoyed
intellectual exercise for its own sake and as an appropriate genre
for exploring the relation of God to the historical world when it is
felt to be not obvious but puzzling. At Proverbs 1.6, the aim of the
professional wise man or scribe is 'to understand a parable and a
figure; the words of the wise and their dark sayings'. That most
complacently self-regarding of biblical writers, ben Sirach, congratulates himself on his scribal expertise and ability to 'enter in
amidst the subtleties of parables. He will seek out the hidden
meanings of proverbs, and be conversant with the enigmas of
parables' (Ecclesiasticus 32.9).

Ezekiel provides examples of the sort of thing that ben Sirach
spoke about. The prophet is noticeably less complacent than the
scribe about the difficulty inherent in it, complaining bitterly, 'Ah,
Lord God! They say of me, is he not a speaker of parables?' –
meaning that which is barely, if at all, intelligible. The force of the
complaint of Ezekiel's hearers is obvious if we consider his
masterpiece in chapter 17, so intricate that despite its length précis
cannot stand in for full quotation.

> The word of the Lord came to me: 'Son of man, propound a
> riddle, and speak a parable [RSV 'allegory'] to the house of
> Israel; say, Thus says the Lord God: A great eagle with great
> wings and long pinions, rich in plumage of many colours, came

10

to Lebanon and took the top of the cedar; he broke off the topmost of its young twigs and carried it to a land of trade, and set it in a city of merchants. Then he took of the seed of the land and planted it in fertile soil; he placed it besides abundant waters. He set it like a willow twig, and it sprouted and became a low spreading vine, and its branches turned toward him, and its roots remained where it stood. So it became a vine, and brought forth branches and put forth foliage.

But there was another great eagle with great wings and much plumage; and behold, this vine bent its roots toward him, and shot forth its branches toward him that he might water it. From the bed where it was planted, he transplanted it to good soil by abundant waters, that it might bring forth branches, and bear fruit, and become a noble vine. Say, thus says the Lord God: Will it thrive? Will he not pull up its roots and cut off its branches, so that all its fresh sprouting leaves wither? It will not take a strong arm or many people to pull it from its roots. Behold, when it is transplanted, will it thrive? Will it not utterly wither when the east wind strikes it – wither away on the bed where it grew?'

Then the word of the Lord came to me: 'Say now to the rebellious house, Do you not know what these things mean? Tell them, Behold, the king of Babylon came to Jerusalem, and took her king and her princes and brought them to him to Babylon. And he took one of the seed royal and made a covenant with him, putting him under oath. (The chief men of the land he had taken away, that the kingdom might be humble and not lift itself up, and that by keeping his covenant it might stand.) But he rebelled against him by sending ambassadors to Egypt, that they might give him horses and a large army. Will he succeed? Can a man escape who does such things? Can he break the covenant and yet escape? As I live, says the Lord God, surely in the place where the king dwells who made him king, whose oath he despised, and whose covenant with him he broke, in Babylon he shall die. Pharoah with his mighty army and great company will not help him in war, when mounds are cast up and siege walls built to cut off many lives. Because he despised the oath and broke the covenant, because he gave his hand and yet did all these things, he shall not escape. Therefore thus says the Lord God: As I live, surely my oath which he despised, and my covenant which he broke, I will requite upon his head. I will spread my net over him, and he shall be taken in my snare, and I will bring him to Babylon and enter into judgment with him there for the treason he has committed against me. And all the pick of his troops shall fall by the sword, and the survivors shall be scattered to every wind; and you shall know that I, the Lord, have spoken.'

Thus says the Lord God: 'I myself will take a sprig from the lofty top of the cedar, and will set it out; I will break off the topmost of its young twigs a tender one, and I myself will plant it upon a high and lofty mountain; on the mountain height of Israel will I plant it, that it may bring forth boughs and bear fruit, and become a noble cedar; and under it will dwell all kinds of beasts; in the shade of its branches birds of every sort will nest. And all the trees of the field shall know that I the Lord bring low the high tree, and make high the low tree, dry up the green tree, and make the dry tree flourish. I the Lord have spoken, and I will do it.'

There are precedents for this extraordinary parable. Nathan had used a more realistic allegorical story as a mousetrap for David (2 Samuel 12) and Isaiah had beguiled his hearers with a love song about a vineyard (Isaiah 5.1–7). Both attracted their prey by concealing under their agreeable and interesting forms a biting relevance to contemporary events. Similarly, the fabulous glamour and surrealism of Ezekiel serve a sharp and minatory political criticism. This parable is tightly and irremovably tied to the international politics of its time. In that way it is the same as the previous categories, the saying and the figurative saying. But it is more tightly tied to contemporary history than they, simply by virtue of its allegorical structure which makes the fastenings at a series of connected points. The connections however are in the history, or rather the history as the prophet critically sees it. They are in the story behind the parable. The parable itself is wildly improbable and disconnected, all notions of ordinary cause and effect being violated by such entirely fabulous and forced events as an eagle behaving like a gardener and a cedar twig becoming a vine. There is no realism here, only symbolic surrealism. It is fantastic and fabulous, probably owing something to the mytho-logical hybrids, half beast and half human, of Babylonian religious art. But underneath, its basis is in history, as the prophet saw it. It is the 'underneath' which emerges in the subsequent and absol-utely necessary interpretation as the deterministic factor in the making of the parable and the key to its meaning. Ezekiel was a man of extremes and here the stiffest historical grounding supports the most imaginative visionary creativity. It is a precedent for much to come in the development of parables.

It has its precedents too, as we have noticed with Nathan and

Isaiah. But Ezekiel's historical scope and thoroughness are greater and remind us of Pharaoh's dream in Genesis 41 which Joseph interpreted as a revelation of God's plan for fourteen years of history: another symbolic story which embraces a series of historical points. The strategic base for such a major development is vision, the prophet become seer who is shown the workings of that other world which determines what happens in this one. The dream in the night, when the world is as it were turned inside out to be dominated by the powers invisible in daylight, is an obviously appropriate means. So is the fabulous and dreamlike allegory. It is integral to it that the means, the parable, is enigmatic, a riddle for which an interpretation and an interpreter are not optional but necessary. Here are the beginnings of that apocalyptic vision of history which resolves its moral contradictions by resort to a divine elsewhere, where alone sense is to be found. The interpreter is the connection between the two.

There are three further definable uses of *mashal/parabolē* in the Old Testament. They confirm its central function of historical symbolizing.

4 *A Song of Derision*

At Isaiah 14.4 a song of triumph over the fall of Babylon is introduced as a *mashal* (Septuagint, *thrēnos*). The cedars of Lebanon rejoice that they will not be cut down any more; the shades in Sheol welcome one as weak as themselves; Babylon is portrayed as a falling star. Habakkuk 2.6–8 and Micah 2.4 are much shorter examples, and less symbolically rich. But they too have a future orientation, the *mashal* as taunt performing the grand prophetic function of bringing history to a divine crisis which will change its course.

5 *A Byword*

Here the word 'parable' is not applied to the intermediate literary or oral form but directly to the people or person in trouble – or about to be. They thereby 'become parables', and the close connection of the parabolic and the historical is given another twist.

At Deuteronomy 28.37 exile is prophesied in which the nation will 'become a horror' (Septuagint, *aenigma*), a *mashal/parabolē*, 'and a byword among all the peoples where the Lord will lead you away'. The same use is in the same context at Psalm 44.14. At Psalm 69.11 it is used of the lonely and derided righteous individual. At 2 Chronicles 8.20 it is used of the nation again, as at Tobit 3.4.

The prophetic ambience of the Song of Derision is clearly part of this usage. Its distinctive feature is the close interpenetration of the historical and the symbolic whereby the nation or individual *is* a parable. Integral to it also is the sense of enigma and riddle which was noticed in Ezekiel. In Old Testament parable the puzzling is not an unnecessary obfuscation but a part of the life of the thing. The outcast righteous man, the exiled and humiliated people of God – in the face of these, what moral or theological sense can be made of historical process? They are parables, enigmas, which call it in question and make clear that the only answer can come, not from within the historical process itself, but from elsewhere. Here the parable is not so much a resolving theological explanation as the putting of an agonizing theological question which strikes at the root of the accepted understanding of things.

6 *A Prophetic Oracle*

This usage occurs only in connection with Balaam's oracles about Israel's future destiny at Numbers 23 and 24. The narrative context is the advance of Israel into the promised land which threatens Moab. Balak, King of Moab, summoned the prophet Balaam to curse Israel. This, on repeated occasions, Balaam found himself unable to do. As soon as he 'took up his *parabolē/mashal*' he found himself, not cursing, but celebrating Israel's present strength and future victory over all in its path.

This category brings together several features of parable. First, as ever, is the historical context to which it inextricably and vitally belongs. Second is the vision of history as under divine constraint, as driven from outside itself and human cause and effect. This historical supernaturalism was given fabulous expression in the preceding narrative of Balaam's visionary donkey who could see the angel in the path, as his master could not, and tell him about it. When he 'took up his parables' he in turn became a visionary, seeing the supernatural plan and hearing the supernatural words which shape events. So the third feature is the parable as the effect of vision, the utterance of the seer.

> The oracle of Balaam the son of Beor,
>   the oracle of the man whose eye is opened,
> The oracle of him who hears the words of God,
>   who sees the vision of the Almighty,
>   falling down, but having his eyes uncovered.

The only omission from this list of six varieties of usage is the

Book of Job where at 27.1 and 29.1 'parable' is a title for two discourses by Job. It is impossible to attach any distinct or particular meaning to these two uses, though it is tempting to make something of their presence in *the* theologically enigmatic biblical book *par excellence*.

Fortunately there is no need to attempt an arrangement of these categories of use in an historical order. The gospel parables are the goal of this study, and neither the evangelists nor Jesus were concerned with historical biblical criticism: their reading of the Scriptures was shaped by other criteria. Eissfeldt, in *Der Maschal im Alten Testament* of 1913, attempted such an historical arrangement but the results are questionable. Popular sayings, as in our first two categories of the list, do not necessarily precede the more elaborate allegorical parables of the third category. On the contrary, snippets from the sayings of the literary élite often get into common currency subsequently. For what it is worth, it seems certain that the fifth category, byword, must have followed after the first two categories because it is dependent on them for its force. There has to be a genre of parable for a person or nation to be a parable. It is also closely related to the fourth category, derision. In fact, none of the categories, with the possible but weak exception of the two uses in Job, is so singular as to be quite unconnected with all the others. Although 'parable' in the Old Testament covers a different and wider range than in present New Testament commentary (the New Testament itself may turn out to be a different matter), its use is not random or unintelligibly loose. *It describes a distillation of historical experience into a compact instance which is usually figurative and remains strongly embedded in its narrative matrix.* With that centre firm, it can be seen that three other kinds of Old Testament discourse are closely related to the parable if not of its immediate family.

First, the prophets often used figurative or allegorical methods to make *their* sort of historical critical points. The 'case' of the poor man's lamb which Nathan presented to David, and Isaiah's song about the vineyard run wild are examples already noticed. Ezekiel used the same figure of the vine, in a way that shows it to be 'stock' by then, in chapters 15 and 17. The Book of Hosea begins with the prophet's own marriage to a whore, explored in three chapters as an allegory of God's alliance with Israel. Here is an allegory fastened to historical actuality by being presented as allegorical deed rather than word – yet more testimony to the strong historical binding of the material we are considering. Ezekiel transposed this allegory of whoredom and adultery – again a prophetic stock in trade – back into the imaginatively literary in

15

his chapter 16, where Israel's career is a whore's progress, and his chapter 23 where Jerusalem and Samaria figure as international harlots.

Second, parables have been noticed to have a riddling character, being virtually synonymous with riddles at Ecclesiasticus 39.3 and 47.15. The classic biblical riddle is Samson's poser at Judges 14.14,

> Out of the eater came something to eat.
> Out of the strong came something sweet.

The answer is the honeycomb which Samson had found in a lion's carcase. The riddle, like a figurative parable, presents a thing in an appropriate but abnormal way – in code. It is thus a close neighbour of the allegory and, like it, yields to lateral rather than frontal attack. Konrad von Rabenau ('Die Form des Rätsels im Buche Hesekiel', in *Gottes ist der Orient*, [Berlin 1957] Festschrift for O. Eissfeldt) has argued forcibly for its influence on Ezekiel 15 and 17. There is the posing of it: 'what is the vine more than any tree?', 'a great eagle ... came unto Lebanon.' There are the pointed questions: 'shall it prosper?', 'is it profitable for any work?'. There are the answers: 'it shall wither', 'the fire shall devour them'. As in our list of categories, boundaries are not as watertight for prophets and scribes as for critics, and the complex allegorical parable shares territory, method and presuppositions with the more popular riddle. People like puzzles, and puzzles are appropriate to 'higher' religious ends by virtue of requiring engaged commitment with a capacity for being surprised.

Third, there are fables. In *Ancient Hebrew Fables* (Oxford 1973) David Daube has claimed a place for them 'within the wider category of parable, an account of one thing or event throwing light on another'. There are two obvious fables in the Old Testament. At Judges 9.7–15 Jotham satirizes the coronation of Abimelech with a fable about the trees choosing a king. None of the fruit trees wants to forsake its happily productive way of life, so the crown goes to the bramble. At 2 Kings 14.9 Jehoash King of Israel brushes off overtures from Amaziah king of Judah although Amaziah has just had a successful campaign against Edom. He uses a fable. The thistle asked the cedar for his daughter's hand in marriage for his son, but a wild beast comes by and tramples down the thistle. Amaziah's glory is transitory. He should know his station in international affairs, go home and stay there. Daube excludes the parable at Ezekiel 17 from the fold of fable because it distorts nature too violently. That is a strange judgement after these talking trees. Again, the boundaries are not clear. Fables moralize on events and prophetic oracles tease fabulously. And yet again, fables like parables in the Old Testament are closely interlocked with the historical events from which they arise. The hand of the history writers is determinative here too.

Aristotle recognized two kinds of parable, the historically true and the imaginatively fictional, in the context of oratory. He had a decided preference for the first. In the Old Testament the context is history and within it there is a wealth of the second, imaginatively fictional, kind. The balance preferred by the Jewish historians is the opposite of that preferred by the Greek philosopher: the imaginative parable within history rather than the historical parable within oratory. Noticing this is an important preliminary to dealing with New Testament writers who knew their Old Testament Scriptures better than their Aristotle. Two major features of Old Testament parables have emerged from the survey: the imaginative use of figures and disguises together with a tight fit in the narrative setting. Since the prophet Ezekiel has often obtruded himself in the survey, an assessment of it can appropriately take him as a key figure. Historically, he seems to have been a gathering point for previous and current forms and uses of the parables, pressing them into the service of what William Blake called 'the device of raising other men into a perception of the infinite', and what we might call a desire of raising them into a perception of the divine meaning of historical process. It is very likely that as well as being a collecting point for parables, Ezekiel was a creative influence on their future.

As a collector he is formidable. Virtually the entire range of Hebrew *mashal* is to be found in his book. Labelled as parables he has the current unfigurative saying at 12.21–2, 'the days are prolonged and every vision faileth'; the figurative popular saying at 16.44, 'as is the mother, so is the daughter', and at 18.2–3, 'the fathers have eaten sour grapes and the children's teeth are set on edge'; the elaborate historical allegories at chapters 15 and 17 which are complained about as incomprehensible parables at 20.49. This covers the first three categories of our list. At 24.3 the allegory becomes deed when he cooks meat in a rusty pot which represents Jerusalem, 'the bloody city'. There follows upon this the remarkable passage in which he makes his own bereavement into an allegory, which, as such, subserves his prophetic work. And elsewhere he takes the acted allegory to unprecedented lengths, provoking his audience into perception by bizarre performances. Songs of derision are in his book too: the laments over Tyre and Egypt in chapters 27 and 28, 31 and 32. There is no shortage of prophetic oracles. No other book of the Old Testament has such a range of parables. We must wait for the Gospels to find anything like it.

As a shaper of the parable tradition which Jesus and the evangelists inherited he has unequalled importance by virtue of his use of comparative figures in complex allegories which have a determinative historical context. His parables of the vine and the eagle in chapters 15 and 17 have this combination as their essence. So does the cooking episode with the cauldron at 24.1–4. And at 20.45–9 he figures as a fire-raiser. The fire is figurative of divine destruction.

Ezekiel has a disconcerting habit of changing his symbols half way. Chapter 19 is a lament over Israel. In the first part Israel is a lioness whose cubs are captured first by Egypt then by Babylon. In the second part Israel is a vine (shades of Isaiah 5) which once provided wood for the royal sceptre (Zedekiah), but was then torn up and withered and consumed by fire. Under pressure of the conquest of Jerusalem in 586 and the subsequent exile he added further catastrophe although the vine was already dead. It is transplanted into a desert and burned. There is no longer a stem to make a sceptre. And there could hardly be a better example of the force of history on parable, distorting and violent in its effects. Symbols are also switched in the lament over Tyre (chapters 27 and 28) which is first pictured as the wreck of a splendid merchant ship and then as a fallen angel. Egypt (chapters 31 and 32) is first a felled cedar tree and then a stranded sea-monster. The most famous and powerful of all these metamorphoses is the vision in the valley of dry bones in chapter 37. The prophet is caught by the spirit of the Lord, rapt and passive in an ecstatic trance 'in which the prophet's mind is made to serve a reality other than itself' (Zimmerli, *Ezekiel*, p.507). The same thing had happened to him in his house in chapter 8 when he was visited by a being with 'the appearance of a man' but made of fire and brightness, who seized him by the hair and 'brought me in visions of God to Jerusalem' where this being acted as guide and interpreter of the visions. The presence of such a supernatural exegete is important for future developments of parable in which such figures will play a large part, made necessary by the increasingly wide stretch between the earthly and the heavenly in the parabolic form. In the valley of dry bones the interpreter, interrogating and informing the prophet, is the spirit of the Lord anthropomorphically presented as one who leads and speaks. The crux of the 'parabolic event' (Zimmerli's apt label) is the transformation of the bones into a living army. It is followed by an interpretation which fixes it all to future history in the restoration of Israel. It is worth noticing that the interpretation does not quite fit the parable, introducing a slightly different element in which Israel is in graves which God will open, not scattered as unburied bones. This is not an indication of a later or extraneous origin for the interpretation, but rather that *in interpretation creative activity goes on, adorning and amplifying the parable as it does so.* This should be borne in mind when we come to similar gospel parables such as the *sower* where efforts have been made to separate parable from interpretation. Here is a big precedent for their belonging together, and it is not the only one in Ezekiel.

The allegory of sheep and shepherds in chapter 34 is even more clearly a precedent for gospel parables, most numerous in Matthew, and uses the same symbolic figures. The judgement 'between sheep and sheep, rams and he-goats' will be a source of the grand allegory of judgement at Matthew 25.3–46. The image of sheep and shepherd was an old one in Ezekiel's time. He treats it with an elaboration which at every point is made to coincide with Israel's history and destiny. Once again the interpretation (verses 11–16) transcends the imagery of the parable by having the sheep gathered from a *diaspora* among 'peoples and countries' which is unrealistic at the level of the surface of parable, realistic in its relation to the historical reality on which the surface is based. So here too parable and interpretation form a developing unity.

Ezekiel was a man who virtually lived historical allegory, lived parabolically. Not only did he tell parables of unprecedented complexity and power. His parabolic charisma was so strong that he felt it as something objectively working upon him, making a parable of himself as of his people. His utterances are the product of a personality stretched to extremes: of despair and hope, of bold explicitness and riddling obscurity, of tenderness and vigorous asceticism, of a vision of divine transcendence which strains and distorts physical imagery and at the same time a concrete physicality emerging in sensuous wonder and disgust. To hold such extremes together, strong forces of mediation are necessary. Hence the allegorical parable in which every incident and figure, supernatural or surreal in its bizarre nature or metamorphosis, is tightly connected to the details of historical actuality. To fasten the extremes together yet more tightly, lest they explode into the unintelligibility which always threatens such theology *in extremis*, he uses the interpretation and the interpreter to point the connections between the visions and the current events, their past origins and future resolution. History determines vision. But going the other way about – and it is the way which Ezekiel himself preferred – vision determines history. On the literary plane it distorts the materials which it takes from nature and popular culture by the moral and theological force which determines the allegory. The conjunction of vision and history results in a billowing obscurity illuminated by rays of dazzling revelation, as in the great vision of the chariot throne in his first chapter, where concrete images are burned and twisted into indicating transcendent divinity. Ezekiel was a mystery-monger, a fabulist and allegorist, a visionary and a parabolic riddler. He was himself a parable and an enigma to his contemporaries. And he was all this as an interpreter of the history on which every vision, and every detail in it, bore. 'Riddler' is in the end too homespun a term for him. He was the father of apocalyptic, that ultimate biblical solution to enigmatic history which lives on allegory. He was also the father of the allegorical historical parable which is the commonest kind of parable in the Gospels. He provides a much better point of departure for the historical investigation of parables than Aristotle or the prejudices of critics to whom allegory is an embarrassment.

2 From Ezekiel to Paul

Parable and Apocalyptic

Ezekiel worked out his view of history in the hard times of the Babylonian exile. Uprooted spiritually as well as physically, deprived of the historical initiative by becoming subject to strangers in a strange land, it was no longer possible for reflective Jews to read off from the actuality of history an unproblematic theology. History was no longer, as it had comparatively recently been for the Deuteronomic historians, so morally intelligible as to be one great and continuous moral illustration of theology. If it was not to be abandoned it had to be approached with a new emphasis on the invisible power behind it which could only be spoken of in symbols. After the exile there was a revival of older notions of history by the Chronicler who forced his material, much to its impoverishment, into rigid priestly categories; and by ben Sirach whose 'praise of the fathers' is marked by a celebratory complacency which falls short of serious historiography. Both efforts, as is common with revivals which do not fully face the effects of an intervening catastrophe, were well below the standards of the older books edited and bowdlerized by the Chronicler or glowingly rehearsed by ben Sirach. In the still harder times of the persecution of Antiochus Epiphanes from 167 to 163 BC Ezekiel's symbolic and parabolic view of history, with its capacity to embrace perplexity and calamity, came into its own.

> The Jewish people, sorely tried, fighting desperately for their sanctuary, their law, and the faith of their fathers, now needed *a new interpretation of history* which went beyond the glorification of the past in the 'praise of the fathers' or in the work of the Chronicler and was displayed in God's hidden plan with his people and the powers of the world, to encourage and comfort the oppressed so that they would continue to persevere in an apparently hopeless world.
>
> (M. Hengel, *Judaism and Hellenism* [SCM 1974] I, p. 194)

The resolution of the appalling mess must be elsewhere. It must be in a hidden design, a design which could be grasped only by special revelation in symbolic or parabolic form and by

> the oracle of him who hears the words of God,
> who sees the vision of the Almighty,
> falling down, but having his eyes covered.
>
> (Numbers 24.3–4)

The element of secret knowledge which had always been part of the structure of prophecy came to dominate it. The prophet became a wise man, a dreamer and visionary, an interpreter of dreams like Joseph in his affliction and exile. As such he held the clue. He knew the meaning of the symbols, he had been taken behind the scenes. 'J'ai seul la clef de cette parade sauvage', 'I alone hold the key to this wild parade' (A. Rimbaud, *Illuminations*, IV).

With the Book of Daniel the 'I' is still more complex than with Ezekiel. Ezekiel was complex enough, passionately indirect and parabolic in his style of utterance. But he did address his hearers and readers in his own person. The author of Daniel hides behind a mask of pseudonymity, taking upon himself the person of a past hero of legend. Added to this, his understanding of the visions is indirect too. The archangel Gabriel or 'one having the appearance of a man' (Daniel 8.15; an Ezekielesque approximation!) interprets the historical meaning of the allegorical visions to him. Both as himself and as Daniel, the author has become yet more passive than the Ezekiel who was swept about by divine spirit. Daniel's passivity (or, the author's) has become more settled and predictable as an invariable part of the narrative structure. The *locus* for understanding history is, without qualification, on the divine and not the human side. Congruently with this, the material is not parables which the prophet-seer contrives or symbolic actions which he performs but visions which he is shown. A powerful trait in Ezekiel has become an indispensable stock-in-trade in Daniel. The intervening layers of hermeneutic are thicker – author, Daniel, angel, vision – and as such testify to an increased opacity of the historical. It is more intractable to human understanding and more secret in its significance. Daniel himself is remote from the events with which he is concerned, which are for later times. There is comfort in this. What is now happening was foreseen, as it had been fore-ordained, long ago. It would be resolved in a not-too-distant future which, too, the legendary worthy had been shown in vision and had interpreted to him by an angel. The negative present was set in the frame of a positive past and a positive future. So the Jewish allegiance to history as theology was saved. But at a price. Now it could only be utterly riddling and parabolic.

Daniel's visions are not called parables as Ezekiel's were. Like Joseph's they come in dreams and waking dreams, so testifying to the power of the divine over the human. But their sustained, even forced, historical allegory, their content whatever their label, fixes them in the same category of parables with the same alliances with fable, oracle and riddle. The dream of the great tree in Daniel 4.10–37 has Ezekiel's tree visions as its source. It exploits it by Ezekielesque metamorphosis: the tree stump becomes a man, and the man is given the heart and grazing habits of a beast. In the visions of chapters 7 and 8 metamorphosis is ceaseless, the hybrid beasts changing and succeeding one another, growing horns which speak, with terrible and bewildering surrealism. But there is method in it all, a method like Ezekiel's but more tightly and pervasively articulated. Every symbol stands for something in international history, every metamorphosis of a symbol for a development or change in that history. It is the still stronger historical foundation which supports the still more bizarre parabolic superstructure. Obscurity was a torment to Ezekiel: 'Ah Lord God, they say of me, is he not a speaker in parables?' (20.49). To Daniel it is matter for celebration:

Blessed be the name of God for ever and ever,
    to whom belong wisdom and might.
He changes times and seasons;
    he removes kings and sets up kings;
he gives wisdom to the wise
    and knowledge to those who have understanding;
he reveals deep and mysterious things;
    he knows what is in the darkness,
    and the light dwells with him.
To thee, O God of my fathers,
    I give thanks and praise,
for thou has given me wisdom and strength,
    and hast now made known to me what we asked of thee,
for thou hast made known to us the king's matter.
                (Daniel 2.20–3)

The author of Daniel is more settled in to the allegorical interpretation of history than Ezekiel, his source and master. There is less of the urgency of a man thinking, or 'seeing' on his feet; less tension, for all the piling up of the horrible and the fantastic. But there is tension, and it is eschatological: 'Shut up the words, and seal the book, even to the time of the end' (12.4). This precise eschatological orientation is big with consequences for the future of parables.

Eschatology, but with much less precise reference to history, dominates the Book of Enoch. Its Book of Parables may well not be a part of its original form. The book is in any case treacherously composite and much in it may be too late to be, strictly, background for the Gospels. But that would not reduce the parabolic character of the whole, which is pervasive and settled to the point of dissolving the tension which would come from preoccupation with history like Ezekiel's or Daniel's. Enoch is another legendary figure summoned up from the remote past to unlock the future's secrets. He tours heaven in a pedestrian way, being shown its mysteries. The resolution of moral injustices at doomsday is mixed with the unveiling of astrological secrets. Enoch's understanding of what he sees is feeble and is corrected and amplified by his angelic guide who explains them to him. For all its weakness, the book confirms the strong alliance of parabolic imagery with the task of making sense of the world in an eschatological perspective, and the angel testifies to the predominance of revealed knowledge over weak human capacity. These are not parables as we understand them. They are scientific and historical secrets. The difference is valuable and warns us to adjust our intellectual receivers in order to hear biblical parables.

2 Esdras is a better book altogether. Once again a past hero is recalled, this time the fifth-century reformer and scribe. Tension returns. The book is a series of agonized broodings upon the destruction of Jerusalem in AD 70, which brings us into contemporaneity with the Gospels. Actual historical disaster revives both the sense of history and that of moral urgency which got lost in the ramblings of 'Enoch'. There is a theological concern with humanity at large and a depth of sensitivity which is reminiscent of the Book of Job. Ezra (Greek, 'Esdras') is shown the eschatological solution of his problem, the affliction of the righteous, in response to an urgency of hope far more highly strung and darkly threatened than with 'Enoch'. As a result, the parables have power greater than the interpretations given to them by the angel Uriel. Once again, parable and interpretation belong together indissolubly, but here the parables have the upper hand. A notable shift takes place. Here the angel is not just an interpreter of parables but also a maker and teller of them. It is a further projection away from the human capacity for wisdom, a line which runs from Ezekiel in the sixth century, through Daniel in the second century, to this book. Now there is not only pseudonymity to play down the part of the actual author, not only emphasis on his weak intellectual capacity where the things which matter in

history are concerned. The very making of parables has, by a further literary contrivance, been taken from his hands and given to supernatural agency. The parable is on the way up in the great chain of being, the hierarchy of power and authority, which makes the apocalyptic world. This too matters for our understanding of the gospel parables. For all their basically popular haggadic nature and function (*haggadah* is in rabbinic terminology the way to get religion to the masses, and so a lower activity than the more élitist and legislative *halakah*, and the more natural home of parables), parables have become a proper way for the most exalted religious authority short of God himself to explain history. If an angel can use them, so can the Son of God, for parables are the clues to the highest theological knowledge.

The angel Uriel's first parable is a riddle:

> Weigh me a pound of fire, measure me a bushel of wind; or call back a day that is passed.   (2 Esdras 4.5)

It is a 'vicious' riddle, unanswerable and totally negative in its function which is to show up human theological and historical incompetence in the face of divine mystery made impenetrable by actual historical disaster. 'If you cannot understand things you have grown up with, how can your small capacity comprehend the ways of the Most High? A man corrupted by the way of the world can never know the ways of the incorruptible' (4.10–11). There is more than an echo of the Book of Job at its most radically pessimistic.

The second of the angel's parables is a fable like Jotham's of the trees:

> I went out into a wood, and the trees of the forest were making a plan. They said, 'Come, let us make war on the sea, force it to retreat, and win ground for more woods.' The waves of the sea made a similar plan. They said, 'Come, let us attack the trees of the forest, conquer them and annex their territory.' The plan made by the trees came to nothing, for fire came and burnt them down. The plan made by the waves failed just as badly, for the sand stood its ground and blocked their way. If you had to judge between the two, which would you pronounce right, and which wrong?   (2 Esdras 4.13–18, NEB)

So the parable turns out to be a fable-cum-riddle, and again an insoluble riddle which is correctly recognized by Ezra as such when he answers that both parties are wrong and each ought to keep to its proper place as Jotham's trees preferred to do. Put bluntly, the right interpretation of the parable is to say, 'It is all nonsense.' It is an answer which comes perilously near to saying that history is bunk, since allegorically the trees and the waves stand for conflicting historical forces which cause unintelligible suffering. Perhaps it even does say that – but only as an unspoken prelude to the conclusive moral, which is that earthly understanding is severely limited to earthly things. Questions of value and meaning, religious or philosophical questions, can be dealt with only at another and higher level: 'Only those who live above the skies can understand the things above the skies.' For all the similarity, we are far from Jotham's fable which is intelligible to commonsense. The form may be the same, but here it is pressed into the service of apocalyptic with a vengeance, apocalyptic which refuses to reveal as its opening gambit. The modern reader may feel himself uncomfortably near to the appalling parable of alienation told to Joseph K in the cathedral in Kafka's *The Trial*, chapter 9. Kafka is near 2 Esdras when he has the priest say, in the course of argument about the parable's meaning, 'The Scripture is unalterable, and the opinions are often merely an expression of despair on the part of the commentators.'

But Ezra persists: 'Why have I been given the faculty of understanding? My question is not about the distant heavens, but about the things which happen every day before our eyes. Why has Israel been made a byword among the Gentiles; why has the people you loved been put at the mercy of godless nations?' (4.22–3). 'Byword' – the presence of that most concretely historical sense of *parabolē* is telling. What, Ezra wants to know, is God going to do about this denial of theology by history? What is his solution to this all-too-concrete enigmatic parable? At last the angel tells him a parable which has some positive moral and historical meaning, for all that it is set in a commanding eschatological frame.

The present age is quickly passing away; it is full of sorrows and frailties, too full to enjoy what is promised in due time for the godly. The evil about which you ask has been sown, but its reaping is not yet come. Until the crop of evil has been reaped as well as sown, until the ground where it was sown has vanished, there will be no room for that which has been sown with the good. A grain of evil seed was sown in the heart of Adam from the first; how much godlessness has it produced already! How much more will it produce before the harvest! Reckon this up: if one grain of evil seed has produced a crop of godlessness, how vast a harvest will there be when good seeds beyond number have been sown! (2 Esdras 4.26–32, NEB)

The parable is full of indications that it belongs to a Judaism close to the New Testament. The most obvious is its similarity to two major gospel parables, the *sower* (Mark 4.3–20) and the *wheat and tares* (Matthew 13.24–30). The basic images are the same: sowing, an intermediate period of perplexity, then harvest. The allegorical pattern has the same points of reference, the seeds standing for supernatural powers good or bad, and the ground in which they are sown standing for the human heart as the secondary base (the supernatural being the primary) of moral operations. The reference is not general but historical, to a particular and sharp crisis in events, the fall of Jerusalem, which is seen between a mythical time in which it originated (Adam) and a mythical time in which it will be accomplished and resolved (harvest). As usual, a strong apocalyptic eschatology is held together with a concern about origins, the intervening tension being the experience of the reader or hearer in an age quickly passing away but concealing in itself and its dying the age to come. It is in this intervening phase that the parable belongs and from which it looks back and forward over the whole range of history from start to finish. Its scope is thus greater than Ezekiel's and is indebted to Daniel at least in its preoccupation with doomsday, which it shares with Enoch. Enoch, by virtue of its protagonist, takes us back into Genesis where Enoch is part of the antediluvian descent from Adam. Ezra's angel goes back further still and to the earliest possible *terminus a quo* for human history in the Jewish mould – Adam. This extended *recherche du temps perdu* was in line with much apocalyptic thinking at the time such as is found in *The Book of Jubilees*, *The Life of Adam and Eve* and *The Apocalypse of Moses*. It is most familiar to Christian readers from St Paul who twice, in Romans 5 and in 1 Corinthians 15, recalls Adam as the original point of human alienation from God. At 1 Corinthians 15.42ff. there is a further parallel to the 2 Esdras parable of sowing. Adam's body was 'sown in dishonour' and 'weakness', 'a physical body'. It will be raised as 'a spiritual body' by the causality of the 'last Adam', Christ, who 'became a life-giving spirit'. Present life is strung in tension between the two. Paul and the writer of 2 Esdras share this apocalyptic historical schema which, with its dependence on figures who 'stand for' religious forces and realities in the manner of myth, is already historically allegorical.

The big parable of sowing at 2 Esdras 4.26–52 is referred to twice later in his book. 'Referred to' is not quite the right expression. What happens is that it returns once as a much smaller parable, once again as a little figure-parable.

In chapter 8 Ezra is worrying about morals and eschatology. 'The righteous, who have many good works laid up with Thee, shall receive their reward in consequence of their own deeds' (8.33). But what of original sin, what of the universal and essential wickedness of man whereby 'in truth there is no one among us . . . who has not transgressed' (8.35). Will God be merciful? The angel tells him that he is, on the whole, right. God will not concern himself about 'those who have sinned, or about their death, their judgment or their destruction' (8.38). He will rejoice over the righteous. That will be his concern.

> For just as the farmer sows many seeds upon the ground and plants a multitude of seedlings, yet not all that have been sown will come up in due season and not all that were planted will take root; so also those who have been sown in the world will not all be saved.   (2 Esdras 8.41)

Still Ezra worries. Some of 'the farmer's seed does not come up because it has not received rain in due season, or if it has been ruined by too much rain it perishes' (8.43). He is bidden to trust in divine love and justice.

At 9.31 the giving of the law at Sinai is put in the figure of sowing. 'Behold I sow my law in you, and it shall bring forth fruit in you.' Yet some of the 'fathers' of those days did not keep the law. Yet again, in the end, there is the fruit of the law. It does not perish, for all its failure in some quarters. There is eschatological hope.

The parable of the *sower* in Mark 4.3–9 has a very similar message. It is noteworthy that in 2 Esdras as in the Gospels a big parable of sowing is followed by smaller ones which are related to it. Mark's *seed growing secretly* at 4.26–9 is clearly like Esdras' seed: in a way which men do not know it will bear fruit. And 2 Esdras' endless concern with the *corpus mixtum*, the moral mixture of good and bad which is humanity, is also dominant in Matthew's *wheat and tares* (Matthew 13.24–30).

Paul is little esteemed as a writer of parables. At Romans 11.24 there is a notorious example of his performance in the genre. He likens gentile Christianity to a slip cut from a wild olive tree and grafted into a cultivated olive tree. This is contrary to nature. But at least he himself admits it. The figure is forced in the sense of being unrealistic and this, for Paul, is its point. Nor will the reader who has been taken through the fables of Jotham and Jehoash, the wildly unnatural parables of Ezekiel, Daniel and Enoch and the riddles put to Ezra, feel that there is anything startlingly novel about such strangeness. Strangeness is integral to the exercise. If Paul lets the message distort the medium in his parables, there is ample precedent for it. This is one reason for giving Paul something better than his usual marginal position in the study of parables. Another is that he provides us with the major part of our extant material for understanding that period of Christianity which comes between the life and death of Jesus and the writing of the Gospels. Paul never uses the word parable. But he uses parables and parabolic methods.

At Galatians 4.21–31 he deploys allegory on what he believes to be history in order to establish the credentials of Christianity. Since many parables in the Gospels also have this motive of confirming Christianity's inheritance of the sole divine right, to the exclusion of Judaism, and do it by allegorizing history, this passage of Galatians is of importance and significance. 'Now this is an allegory: these women are two covenants.' Both women bore sons to Abraham, the archetype and criterion for Judaism of true religion. The first, prior in time, was Hagar who bore Ishmael. But she was a slave woman and slavery is for Paul the subjected religious existence of man under law. The second woman was Sarah who bore Isaac: historically junior to Ishmael but theologically superior because he and his mother were not slaves but free. And freedom is for Paul the religious existence of man under the Christian gospel. This reversal of historical/temporal by theological value was by divine fiat: '"Cast out the slave and her son; for the son of the slave shall not inherit with the son of the free woman"' (4.30). The allegory is, incidentally, compounded by reference to Mount Sinai and Jerusalem, a second allegorical layer explaining and complicating the primary point. It betrays yet again the primacy of theological over realistic considerations which marks all allegorical compositions and which has made it so many enemies in modern times. Paul's starting point is that Christianity is divinely appointed freedom, Judaism a state of bondage which God has superseded. To establish this he resorts to history as the court where all claims of this sort are settled. But it is not to the surface of history that he goes, as to a record of old and far-off things. He penetrates it to disclose its kernel or heart of meaning which is not confined to its historical point of origin, but, as an insight into the divine purpose, is true for all times. Allegorical interpretation was aready, in Paul's time, a widespread resource for making ancient Scripture, law or narrative, relevant to the present. His contemporary Philo was a master of it. This allegory, of two sons with the younger superseding the elder, was a telling ploy in the deadly serious game of connecting young Christianity with old Scriptures to the exclusion of its senior sibling. So it is not surprising to find it cropping up elsewhere, and it does so triumphantly in Luke's parable of the *lost son* in chapter 15 of his Gospel.

The same concern with the legitimacy of Christianity informs Paul's parabolic use of widowhood at Romans 7.1–4. It too is meant to establish the legitimate authority of a new and apparently discontinuous way of living. Why do Christians not subject themselves to the law? The short answer is that God has himself killed the law. It is dead. So, allegorically again, the law is the husband who dies, the Christian the wife who survives and is thus free for a new liaison which would previously have been legally culpable but is now permissible. Because of the law or because there is no law? Paul is not clear. Like the allegory of the sons, this allegory is obfuscated by its exegesis. 'Likewise, my brethren, you have died to the law through the body of Christ, so that you may belong to another, to him who has been raised from the dead in order that we may bear fruit for God.' The Christian is the widow. That is clear. But immediately confusion sets in. The Christian is the one who died 'to the law through the body of Christ'. Christ is the new husband. That is clear. But again it is followed by a confusion which compounds the previous one. Christ died – and rose again. Insoluble as this is within the terms of the parabolic illustration itself, it is not difficult to see how it has come about. The parable is no sooner uttered than it is distorted and overwhelmed by the theology which is its *raison d'être*: in this instance Paul's central theological pattern of the death and resurrection of Christ as an historical end and beginning in which believers share by the mystery of baptism. It is in this frame that the Christian 'dies' incorporate in the death of Christ. This is what matters to Paul more than any parable or anything else on earth. The parable suffers accordingly. Once again we notice that an interpretation which not only fails to fit its parable but actually distorts it is not necessarily secondary because of it. The energetic mind goes on creating while it interprets. The theology which gave rise to the parable in the first place has the whip hand in the second place and drives it according to its will. The parable is its servant and not its master.

At 1 Corinthians 3.1–5 Paul uses a parable to correct partisanship in the Corinthian congregation. It fares better than the previous parables we have considered, being less forced and complicated by theology. But not entirely. The parable is overshadowed by Paul's theological contempt for the 'fleshly', is thoroughly allegorical within the frame of the history of the Corinthian church, and undergoes a metamorphosis at its end where a field turns into a building and a second, parallel parable begins. Here too parables are decidedly instrumental, taken up, pushed and discarded as theology in an historical framework requires. Some people in the Corinthian church say that they belong to Paul, some that they belong to Apollos. In the parable, Paul planted, which seems to argue that he was historically prior, and Apollos watered. But – and here the theological concern establishes its dominance – 'neither he who plants nor he who waters is anything, but only God who gives the growth. He who plants and he who waters are equal': that is, in their secondariness which under theological pressure overcomes the order of priority hinted at before. So Paul returns to himself and Apollos, but this time with their pay in mind rather than their work. 'Each shall receive his wages according to his labour'. What is the wage, the reward? It could be heavenly and eschatological as at the conclusion of the subsequent parable of the building (3.14,15). It could be material as at 9.3–12 where Paul animadverts bitterly on his and Barnabas' apparent ineligibility for material reward, literally 'reaping material things'. Money was, for Paul, a topic fraught with embarrassment and annoyance because of his wish both to have a right to it and to be innocent of having insisted on it. The right is argued for by a series of little cases used as parables at 9.7. 'Who serves as a soldier at his own expense? Who plants a vineyard without eating any of its fruit? Who tends a flock without getting some of the milk?' The innocence is protested at 9.12. 'We have not made use of this right, but we endure anything rather than put an obstacle in the way of the gospel of Christ.' So it is not surprising that Paul is not explicit about the nature of the reward at 3.8. He moves on to the interpretation of the allegory. He and Apollos are God's fellow-workers. The Corinthians are 'God's farm, God's building'. And so, by implication, not Apollos' or Paul's.

The first parable of the farm or field and its workers has obvious affinity with several gospel parables, most noticeably Matthew's *wheat and tares* (Matthew 13.14–30) and his *labourers in the vineyard* (Matthew 20.1–16). The next parable of the building, its foundations and its fate of eschatological fire, is as clearly similar to the parable of the *two houses* at Matthew 7.24–7. The Matthean houses suffer by water. Fire was the fate of the tares in 13.24–30. Field, crop, labourers, house, foundations, fire – the apparatus of Jesus' parables in the Gospels in general, and in Matthew's in particular, is present in Paul too. Paul comes after Jesus and before the evangelists, so what we make of this common imagery will depend on how we evaluate the gospel parables. If they are Jesus' work, then Paul could be drawing on it. If they are the evangelists' work, then they could be drawing on Paul, or this could be a coincidence in using a common stock of images. In any case, the Gospels and Paul's epistles are not so separate from one another as is often presupposed.

The parable of the building (1 Corinthians 3.10–15) is subjected to stronger theological pressure with consequent surrealism. It starts realistically enough. Paul as mastermason laid down the foundations, the actualized ground plan. With that done, as in the first phase of the building of King's College Chapel when Reginald of Ely realized the entire plan to six feet above the ground, subsequent work was controlled enough to be left to others, for a while at least. But the immediate interpretation of the foundation as Jesus Christ signals the allegorical nature of the parable and the possibility, always such a lively one with allegory, of bizarre developments which subserve the intellectual scheme. The possibility is soon realized. This is no ordinary, worldly, building. On the foundations people may build in gold, silver, precious stones, wood, hay, stubble. Of these materials only wood is realistically plausible, possibly precious stones if they are understood as denoting marble, which is highly unlikely in the context. Otherwise the sort of building envisaged is surreal: either a fairy tale palace of jewels (as in Isaiah 53.11 and Revelation 21.18f) or a house of straw or stubble (as, less relevantly, in the children's story of the wolf and the three little pigs). In any case, apocalyptic imagery supervenes at the end of the parable. The fire, as in Matthew's *wheat and tares*, is the fire of doomsday. And beyond the fire is the doomsday allocation of rewards and punishments. Good builders will get a reward, bad ones a fine. C. K. Barrett in his commentary on 1 Corinthians offers an interpretation in terms of historical allegory:

> To abandon the metaphor, and say plainly what Paul appears to have had in mind: if Judaizing Christians, such as the disciples of Peter, attempt to build their old Jewish exclusivism into the structure of the Church (cf. Gal. ii. 11–14) they will fail; this rotten superstructure will perish. They themselves, however, will not be excluded from salvation, though the destruction of their work will involve them in pain and loss.
>
> (*Commentary on 1 Corinthians* [Black 1968], pp. 89f)

So both these parables, the field and more obtrusively the house, are allegories, dominated by an apocalyptic historical scheme which triumphs at the end of each with a scene of judgement. The imagery suffers distortion and switches which are dictated by the underlying ideas.

At 1 Corinthians 5.6 Paul uses the same parabolic proverb as at

Galatians 5.9: 'A little yeast leavens the whole lump.' This is just the sort of figurative saying which was second in the list of Old Testament usages of parable (p.9). In the context leaven (i.e. yeast) is bad: first by reference to the corrupt church member who ought to be excommunicated, and secondly by reference to the Passover rites to which Paul refers on the other side of the proverb. Yeast is also an image of badness at Mark 8.15 (parallel Matthew 16.6 and Luke 12.1). It is the leaven of the Pharisees. But Matthew has a little parable at 13.33, paralleled at Luke 13.20–1, in which leaven is good, a simile for the mysteriously expansive power of the Kingdom of heaven. This is a remarkable turn-about for an evangelist noted for his rabbinic cast of mind. We cannot decide here whether Jesus or Matthew is the changer of the value of yeast. We can only note again the presence in Paul's correspondence of a figure used in gospel parable. In this instance the context of meaning is Jewish. By contrast, there are two parables in 1 Corinthians which have a decidedly gentile context and so illustrate the hybrid, cross-cultural character of Pauline Christianity.

The first of these is the parable of the athletic contest at 1 Corinthians 9.24. Here Paul, the erstwhile Pharisee, uses as a metaphor for Christian life an aspect of hellenistic culture abominated by Pharisaic Jews, the games. Typically enough it switches its purpose and direction several times in a short space. Paul's first ploy is to encourage religious effort by comparison with the efforts of athletes to win the prize which 'only one receives'. This prize only for one has a very bad fit with Christian asceticism, and a sense of its ineptness may well motivate Paul's switch from athletics as competition to athletics as training and discipline: 'Every athlete exercises self-control in all things.' Then an interpretative note points to a heavenly meaning which makes the aptness of the parable secondary to its other-worldly and eschatological subject: 'They do it to receive a perishable wreath, but we an imperishable.' Once again, the real point of a parable transcends it and is elsewhere rather than being inextricably immanent within it. The earthly picture has a heavenly meaning. Paul ends this parable with more general and unfocused reference to athletic activities. His running is not aimless, his boxing is not beating the air. Here again there is a weird twist: he is boxing himself, pummelling his own body into subjection.

The second parable of markedly gentile character is of the body and its parts at 1 Corinthians 12.12f. The best known and most elaborate of all Paul's efforts in this field, it has a wealth of precedent and parallel in Greek and Roman literature so great as to make less convincing appeals to Old Testament anthropology unnecessary. Besides, an apostle who can liken Christian discipline to the games could have no objection to a stock pagan parable which, while perhaps slightly offensive to the strictest Jewish tastes on account of its mention of the genitals, is far less stridently obnoxious.

In *Protagoras* 330 A, Plato has Socrates argue for virtue as a single entity comprised of various parts such as wisdom (the greatest) and courage. Each is distinct from any other and has its particular and inalienable function, yet all cohere in 'virtue'.

> 'Just as, in the parts of the face, the eye is not like the ears, nor is the function the same; nor is any of the other parts like another, in its function or in any other respect: in the same way, are the parts of virtue unlike one another, both in themselves and in their functions?'
>
> 'Yes, they are so, Socrates.'

The figure is similar, though Paul uses the whole body and Plato only the face. The point is the same, diversity in unity, though Plato is concerned with virtue and Paul with church order. Xenophon in *Memorabilia* II.iii.8 has Socrates resort to a similar metaphor in dealing with a quarrel between brothers.

> 'What if a pair of hands refused the office of mutual help for which God made them, and tried to thwart each other, or if a pair of feet neglected the duty of working together for which they were fashioned, and took to hampering each other? That is how you are behaving at present.'

The context is more overtly social than in Plato. The presence of the same parable in both accounts of Socrates argues for its being a part of Socrates' discourse before Plato or Xenophon wrote their books. It also has a rich subsequent history.

The body parable was much used by the Stoics, to illustrate their vision of a cosmos filled with *pneuma* (spirit, air), whose function is the coherence of matter, the contact between all parts of the cosmos in a coherent physical world. Clement of Alexandria reports them as believing that

> the virtues are each others' mutual cause in such a way that they cannot be separated because of their interdependence. They are like the stones of a vault which are each others' cause for staying in place. (*Stromateis*, 8.9)

Cicero uses the parable in a context of political order which is close to Paul's context of church order. Dwelling on the evils of theft he says:

> Suppose that each of our bodily members should conceive this idea and imagine that it could be strong and well if it should draw off to itself the health and strength of its neighbouring member, the whole body would necessarily be enfeebled and die; so if each one of us should seize upon the property of his neighbours and take from each whatever he would appropriate to his own use, the bonds of human society must inevitably be annihilated.   (*de Officiis* III.v.22)

Like Paul he argues against the threat of anarchy and for stable interdependence. For him the disruptive force is theft. For Paul, characteristically, it is boasting – religious self-righteousness and independent self-aggrandisement.

The most famous example of the parable occurs in Livy II.32. It is not more relevant to Paul than the preceding examples, but is of interest for biblical parables generally because it shows how, in the hands of an historian, a parable which served philosophers as an illustration of permanent and timeless truth becomes an historical allegory closely tied in to its temporal context. More, the context is popular, and so similar to *haggadah* in Jewish teaching. The scene is the secession of the plebs in 494 BC. The Fathers of Rome sent Menenius Agrippa to win them back. He told the following tale 'in the quaint and uncouth style of that age'.

> In the days when man's members did not all agree among themselves, as is now the case, but each had its own ideas and a voice of its own, the other parts thought it unfair that they should have the worry and the trouble and the labour of providing everything for the belly, while the belly remained quietly in their midst with nothing to do but enjoy the good things which they bestowed upon it; they therefore conspired together that the hands should carry no food to the mouth, nor the mouth accept anything that was given it, nor the teeth grind up what they received. While they sought in this angry spirit to starve the belly into submission, the members themselves and the whole body were reduced to the utmost weakness. Hence it had become clear that even the belly had no idle task to perform, and was no more nourished than it nourished the rest, by giving out to all parts of the body that by which we live and thrive, when it has been divided equally among the veins and is enriched with digested food – that is, the blood. Drawing a parallel from this to show how like was the internal dissension of

the bodily members to the anger of the plebs against the Fathers, he prevailed upon the minds of his hearers.

(*History*, II.32)

The point of contact with Paul is in the bizarre details of allegory, the parts of the body behaving like the people they represent, voicing their feelings and stating explicitly their misguided intentions. In a more subdued form the same motif was present in Xenophon and Cicero. Paul is not careful for realism. All in all, the gentile world is clearly the source of Paul's body parable, with a particular debt to the Stoic idea of the coherence-making *pneuma*. Paul prefaces his parable with a reference to the 'one spirit' into which all Christians were baptized. He follows it with a tightening christological ecclesiology: 'Now you are the body of Christ and individually members of it.' Then comes a listing of ecclesiastical functions followed by a recommendation to 'desire the higher gifts' which has its transcending climax in the hymn of love in chapter 13. Stoic generalities are baptized into Pauline Christology, ecclesiology and ethics. It is not a forced or difficult baptism. But it has to be said that nothing like 1 Corinthians 12.12–31 occurs in the Gospels, whereas in Paul it has neighbours in the parables of the Church as field and as building in 1 Corinthians 3. It is a testimony to the gentile affiliations of one nurtured in the Jewish rabbinic context. His stock of imagery is as cross-cultural as his gospel. Paul's championing of gentile Christianity is more than skin deep and gets into his most vital thinking in a parable which is quite without apocalyptic colour for all its rich and strange allegory.

It is different with the parable of seeds in 1 Corinthians 15.35–50. Characteristically, it moves far from its starting point into Pauline Christology, but it has obvious similarities with Mark's parable of the *sower*, its synoptic parallels and 2 Esdras. The closest similarity is with the parable of seeds and harvest in 2 Esdras 4. The scope and scheme are apocalyptic, from Adam to the end of time. The figure of growth connects the two: from seed time to harvest. Ezra was told of 'evil seed sown in the heart of Adam'. For Paul, in the interpretation which follows his parable (the two are done simultaneously in 2 Esdras), Adam's body is itself a seed, the seed of life after the flesh and of doomed physicality. As in 2 Esdras, Paul contrasts this bad seed and its bad harvest with good seed and a good outcome. But he is able to do so with more sharply precise symbolism because he has Christ as an embodied individual counterpart of Adam. He has, in fact, a transforming symbol. It adds a clearer and more substantial note of optimism than there was in 2 Esdras' vaguer note of 'good seeds without number'. It also disrupts the shape of Paul's parable. There is not the continuity amounting to inevitability which there was in 2 Esdras. Instead there is a radical discontinuity between seed and grown plant. So in Paul's parable 'what you sow is not the body which is to be, but a bare kernel, perhaps of wheat or of some other grain. But God gives it a body as he has chosen, and to each kind of seed its own body' (15.37f). God is for Paul the God of the eschatological miracle of resurrection. So in his interpretation: 'Just as we have borne the image of the man of dust [Adam] we shall also bear the image of the man of heaven. I tell you this, brethren: flesh and blood cannot inherit the kingdom of God, nor does the perishable inherit the imperishable' (15.49f). Not for the first time, Paul's parable-making suffers from the weight of his theological vision. He knows that seed and plant have a sequence in which there is some continuity: 'As was the man of dust, so are those who are of dust; and as was the man of heaven, so are those who are of heaven' (15.48). But he holds as a central belief the transformation of the human condition by the death and resurrection of Christ. He is realistic enough about this to see it in terms of the transformation of human bodies. And it is integral to his parable.'What you sow does not come to life unless it dies' (15.39). 'So it is with the resurrection of the dead. What is sown is perishable, what is raised is imperishable. It is sown in dishonour, it is raised in glory. It is sown in weakness, it is raised in power. It is sown a physical body, it is raised a spiritual body' (15.42–4). It is as if Ezra's parable has been invaded by the transforming symbol of Christ's death and resurrection; as if this, dropped into the middle of an ordinary parable of predictable natural events, had jerked it all into a far more positive and apocalyptic vision of historical process, making it at the same time odder and stronger. The gospel parallel is, rather than with the *sower*, with the *seed growing secretly* of Mark 4.26–9 with its greater unpredictability, surprise, discontinuity, and sense of mystery:

'The kingdom of God is as if a man should scatter seed upon the ground, and should sleep and rise night and day, and the seed should sprout and grow, he knows not how. The earth produces of itself, first the blade, then the ear, then the full grain in the ear. But when the grain is ripe, at once he puts in the sickle because the harvest has come.'

The most obvious feature of Paul's parables is also, by now, the least unexpected. They are allegorical. In each and all of them every physical detail has a metaphysical counterpart. The second major feature is also something with which Old Testament and inter-testamental examples have made us familiar. Most of Paul's parables are historical. He uses them to establish the historical credentials of Christianity as the heir to the sacred history in Scripture and as superior to the Judaism it supersedes. He uses them to expound the true significance of the founding and development of the Christian church at Corinth, its history. He uses them to interpret the entirety of human history from Adam to the end of time. All this is in the mainstream of biblical parable-making as we have traced it and will continue vigorously in the Gospels. But Paul's energetic theological mind is not confined. His own financial anxiety gets sharp parabolic expression: a theologian reaches for a parable when he is particularly keen to be under-stood. In a more generally interesting cause he also breaks the bounds of his own biblical Pharisaical tradition and gets onto hellenistic ground. The parable of the athletic games uses a decidedly gentile figure of comparison for Christian asceticism, while turning it to an eschatological end and treating it in a strange and confused way. The parable of the body is a stock-in-trade of Stoicism and of general discourse – philosophical, scientific and political. It serves the end of church order easily, only needing to be set in the context of Paul's Christ-centred theology of the Church to do its work as tellingly for him as for Cicero or Livy's Menenius Agrippa. It is an allegory, but not primarily Jewish or primarily historical. Paul is eclectic.

3 Mark

PARABLES IN MARK

2.17	Physician
2.19f	Bridegroom and 'Sons of Bridechamber'
2.21	Clothes
2.22	Wineskins
3.25–7	Divided Kingdom } Divided House } riddles Strong Man
4.2–8	Sower
4.9–13	Mystery of Parables
4.14–20	Interpretation of Sower
4.21	Lamp
4.26–9	Seed Growing Secretly
4.30–2	Mustard Seed
4.33–4	Parables Generally
7.14ff	Digestion
7.17ff	Interpretation of Digestion
7.27	Children's Bread
9.50	Salt, and Interpretation
10.25	Camel and Needle
12.1–10	Vineyard
13.28	Fig Tree
13.34–7	Servants

Introduction

'"Do you not understand this parable? How then will you understand all the parables?"' (Mark 4.13). It is a crucial question in the context of modern biblical criticism as well as in the context of Mark's Gospel. The parable in question is the _sower_ and with it the baffling assertion by Jesus at verses 11 and 12 that

> To you [those who were about him with the twelve] has been given the secret [*mustērion*/mystery] of the kingdom of God, but for those outside everything is in parables; so that they may

indeed see but not perceive, and may indeed hear but not understand; lest they should turn again, and be forgiven.

A very startling answer to this question of the understanding of parables which are deliberately obscure, and even to many people impenetrably obscure, is given by Jeremias (p. 18). Mark, he says, was 'misled by the catchword *parabolē* which he erroneously understood as "parable"'. That is why he 'inserted' this baffling assertion by Jesus 'into the parable chapter' which originally existed without it. If the meaning of 'parable' in this passage of Jeremias is obscure, the implications are plain. Jesus never uttered this assertion of intentional obscurity; it came from somewhere or someone else; Jesus' parables were accessible and clear. These convictions are fundamental to Jeremias' whole work. But someone has to pay the price, and it is Mark. He did not understand, as the modern critic does, what constitutes a parable. He was 'misled by the catchword *parabolē* which he erroneously understood as "parable"', and so gave an illegitimate twist to the parables in Mark 4 with fatal results which it takes form-criticism to unravel and put right.

But form-criticism as Jeremias practised it has an Achilles heel. It is very like the restoration of old pictures, removing subsequent layers of overpainting to reveal the pristine original. It is essential in such work to have access to what is indisputably original. A painting by Rubens cannot be correctly restored without constant reference to unassailably genuine work by Rubens. A parable by Jesus cannot be restored without constant reference to unassailably genuine work by Jesus. This necessary criterion we do not have. Jeremias thinks we do: in parables in Luke's Gospel such as the *prodigal son* and the *good Samaritan*, for example, which he treats as such. Our judgement on this criterion will have to wait for the consideration of the parables in Luke's Gospel. My previous studies of Luke (see my *Tradition and Design in Luke's Gospel*, pp. 75ff) convinced me that the parables in it have a decided Lucan character which puts their use as a decisive criterion of authenticity in question. But let us deal with what we have here: Jeremias' assertion that Mark was 'misled by the catchword *parabolē*' and thought wrongly that it meant the same thing as 'parable'. Hence Mark's disorienting belief in the deliberate obscurity of parables. *Parabolē* is a misleading 'catchword', according to Jeremias. 'Parable' is the thing to go by. The surprising, and even rather shocking, thing here is that an ancient meaning associated with an ancient word, a meaning contemporary with Mark, is being dismissed and a modern word, no doubt associated with a modern meaning, is being instated. The tendency of the present investigation is set against this. We have gone through the evidence of parables in the Old Testament, the intertestamental literature and Paul, in order to establish the ancient category of parables, as it existed up to and including Mark's time. It has come out clearly and strongly enough to be able to resist its being shrugged off as a misleading aberration. There is no need to replace the ancient meaning of an ancient word with a modern substitute. Mark meant what he wrote.

Rather than start from a theory agreeable to modern expository requirements, we have started from the tradition of parables which was available to Jesus, the evangelists and Paul. This tradition was not just available to them. They had absorbed it devoutly. Unencumbered by the multiplicity of books which besets the modern Christian, yet as intelligent and receptive as we, they gave to their tradition and above all to their holy Scripture, the Old Testament, a dedicated and rapt attention which it requires an effort of historical imagination to recapture. It is that most routine and unimaginative of early Christian writers, the author of the Pastoral Epistles, who says to his pupil:

> From childhood you have been acquainted with the sacred writings which are able to instruct you for salvation through faith in Christ Jesus. (2 Timothy 3.15)

To establish this vital general connection in the particular field of parables we need look no further than Mark 4.11 and 12, the ostensible obscurity of which led Jeremias into doubt and restoration. It is a quotation, with abbreviation, of Isaiah 6.9–10. The prophet, called by God to speak for him to his people, is told that he will be met with obdurate resistance to his message. So he is to say to them:

> 'Hear and hear, but do not understand; see and see, but do not perceive.' Make the heart of this people fat, and their ears heavy, and shut their eyes: lest they see with their eyes, and hear with their ears, and understand with their hearts, and turn and be healed.

The peoples' unreceptivity is thus pre-empted by being presented as a thing foreseen, and even ordained, by God. So it was when God sent Moses to be his spokesman to Pharaoh, at the same time hardening Pharoah's heart so that he paid no attention (Exodus 7—11 *passim*). The quotation is apt, not forced, and represents a decided trait in the Old Testament's reflection upon the ways of God with men and the fate of spokesmen for the divine. We have seen enough of Old Testament parables – and particularly of Ezekiel, their greatest proponent, and ben Sirach, the expert at penetrating their labyrinthine obscurity – to see that it fits the parabolic tradition behind the New Testament. Ezekiel's hearers could not understand him, Balak did not heed Balaam, the apocalyptic writers were confronted with parables which they could not understand without supernatural hermeneutical help. And all this was no unfortunate accident, no being misled by a misapprehension of the nature of parables, but something integral to their world as they understood it. They would have had no quarrel with the presence of Isaiah 6.9–10 in a context of parables. Rather, it would have struck them as an apt and illuminating piece of scriptural interpretation, however perverse it may seem to the modern critic. Mark makes it a part of the scene or setting of chapter 4. After telling the parable of the *sower* in public, Jesus is seen alone with 'those who were about him with the twelve' (4.10). To them, he says, 'has been given the secret [mystery] of the kingdom of God, but for those outside everything is in parables'. And again at the end of the series of parables at 4.33f Mark notes that

> with many such parables he spoke the word to them, as they were able to hear it; he did not speak to them without a parable, but privately to his own disciples he explained everything.

The implication of the scene-setting is clear: parables are spoken in public, their meaning is got only within the inner circle of discipleship. Jesus stands to the disciples as the angel stood to Ezra in 2 Esdras. The change of scene is a topographical realization of the two aspects of parable in its belonging at the same time both to secrecy and revelation, hiddenness and openness. If it is appropriate to the biblical sense of parable at large, it is particularly apt to Mark's Gospel with its well-known emphasis on the secrecy of Jesus' nature, the mystery at the heart of the Gospel's dramatic theology .

It is their dramatic, their narrative, context which gives Mark's parables their power. That is itself a major reason for quarrelling with Jeremias' form-critical method. It prises the parables out of their narrative context and then seeks explanations and restorations of them which are not in *its* terms but in the terms of a modern existential Christology used to reconstruct the parables' 'original' sense, such as Jeremias declares in the 'Conclusion' of his book. It is not entirely inappropriate to them, and when it is appropriate it contradicts Jeremias' previous work. 'All the parables of Jesus compel his hearers to come to a decision about his person and mission. For they are full of "the secret of the kingdom of God" (Mark 4.11), that is to say, the recognition of an eschatology that is in process of realisation' (p. 230). It is striking, and unfortunately typical of his unstable criteria, that Jeremias should invoke at the triumphant conclusion of his book the very verse, Mark 4.11, which he had told his readers to set aside as a misleading insertion in the exegetical body of the work. It is as if Mark's theology of parables is reasserting itself *malgré lui* as much stronger than he thought. We can take our cue from this mishap and let Mark's theology speak for itself at a much earlier stage in the investigation. We will do it by looking at the parables within their narrative context and seeking explanations within it. It has major advantages in clarifying the reading of Mark and the understanding of early Christian historical narrative.

Mark's Parables in their Places

Mark establishes Jesus' theological identity early and resounding-ly. Prophesied by Old Testament Scripture and John the Baptist, he is declared 'my beloved Son' by the divine voice at his baptism and the Spirit descends upon him, he is tempted, declares his gospel and enlists four disciples, all in the course of twenty verses. But as he sets to work in a series of miraculous healings, his identity and his deeds become more and more a matter of dispute among men rather than of unambiguous revelation from God. They do not fit established frames of theological reference: the sabbath, for example, and the forgiveness of sins. They are too direct in their conjunction of divine power with human incapacity. After a miracle which raises the question of Jesus' theological credentials with particularly divisive sharpness, the healing of the paralytic at 2.1–12, Jesus enlists the tax-gatherer Levi as a disciple and sits at table with him, other tax-collectors and his disciples. 'The scribes of the Pharisees' ask, in hostile bewilderment, why. Jesus replies, 'Those who are well have no need of a physician, but those who are sick; I came not to call the righteous, but sinners' (2.17). Here is the first parable in Mark's Gospel. It fits the second of the categories in our Old Testament list (p. 9), the figurative saying such as 'The fathers have eaten sour grapes and the children's teeth are set on edge', and 'Is Saul also among the prophets?' Like them it is set in a particular context of historical confrontation: prophet with people, people with charismatic king, but has a resonance reaching into any number of similar situations which gives it the force of general truth. The figure of the physician is immediately followed by its own interpretation which narrows its general plausibility so as to focus it on the particular issue which obsesses the narrative, who Jesus is and why he is behaving as he does: 'I came not to call the righteous, but sinners' (2.17). In its very brief compass it contains the essentials of allegory: Sick people = sinners such as tax-collectors, healthy people = the righteous, physician = Jesus. Further, it is a miniature allegory set in, and explanatory of, an historical occurrence. And it is the first of a series of four such; all brief, all figurative and all proffered as explanations of the historical crisis, *the* crisis for the understanding of history, brought about by Jesus and his activity.

The next in the series responds, likewise, to a question. 'Why do John's disciples and the disciples of the Pharisees fast, but your disciples do not fast?' (2.18). It is a question about religious customs, about asceticism. But the answer is in terms of history from which religious practice should take its cue as effect following upon cause. 'Can the wedding guests (literally 'the sons of the bridechamber') fast while the bridegroom is with them? As long as they have the bridegroom with them, they cannot fast. The days will come, when the bridegroom is taken away from them, and then they will fast in that day' (2.19f). The basic parable is a riddling and figurative question followed by its answer. But, as with Ezekiel's sour grapes, the basic parable does not tell the whole story because the situation to which it refers is to be superseded. It belongs to a finite and transient time, 'As long as the bridegroom is with them they cannot fast'. This brings to mind the possibility of another time with things otherwise. 'The days will come, when the bridegroom is taken from them, and then they will fast in that day.' The source of the image is Isaiah 62.5, a prophecy of deliverance in which

> as the bridegroom rejoices over the bride, so shall your God rejoice over you.

Paul had spoken of Christ as bridegroom and Church as bride at 2 Corinthians 11.2 and the image recurs at Revelation 19.7ff and 21.9. So it was a symbol available to Christians in their Scripture and exploited by them in their own writings between the death of Jesus and the writing of the Gospels. This is worth noticing, because as the basic image is developed it becomes clear that the historical standpoint from which it is deployed is outside the ministry of Jesus and in the time after his death. Unlike the basic parable, the historical perspective of the development is *ab extra*, outside the immediate historical context. As a result it excites the imagination by its intimation of sorrow impending, of the wider frame of destiny within which a pernickety question finds its answer. To the less literarily excitable form critic it is, however, he chance to posit a disjunction between the basic parable and the developments of it which spoil its realism with improbability and allegory. Yet the allegory was there from the outset: Jesus = bridegroom, disciples = sons of the bridechamber (the exact translation making the allegory better than the RSV's 'wedding guests'). Also the improbability is implicit in the basic parable with its touch of the riddle, its invocation of the incongruous: 'Can the sons of the bridechamber fast while the bridegroom is with them?' The form critics may be right. We cannot tell. But the parable can look after itself and play its part as an interpretation of a narrative within the narrative as a whole without their speculative analysis – and better without their dismemberment of it. In justice, though, it must be noticed that this implies conceding the major point of all form criticism: the creative hand of the early Christians in the shaping of the Gospels both overall and incident by incident. The historical point of view of the whole bridegroom parable is, if we keep it whole, the ministry of Jesus in its totality which was only available for reflection after his departure. Conservative readers may prefer the form critics' supposed palimpsest of the authentic and the secondary to such a radical view. The fundamental reason for the more radical view, however, is that we are trying to explain parts of Mark's book by reference to the whole book which contains them, and Mark is famous for the way in which the shadow of its end is cast across the whole of Jesus' life in advance. He uses his liberty as an historical narrator; that is, his standing outside the events which his *dramatis personae* stand within, his knowing of their outcome better than they – to shape his story to its end. That grand strategy is presented in the smaller tactical area of this parable. It is, after all, a leading feature of biblical parables. They illuminate the tales in which they are set.

The last parables of this series are about *clothes* and *wineskins*.

No one sews a piece of unshrunk cloth on an old garment; if he does, the patch tears away from it, the new from the old, and a worse tear is made.
And no one puts new wine into old wineskins; if he does, the wine will burst the skins, and the wine is lost, and so are the skins; but new wine is for fresh skins. (Mark 2.21f)

Again, history is the subject. Both parables are about the relation of Jesus' work, of Christianity indeed, to traditional Judaism. So, like the preceding parable of the bridegroom, they have a standpoint outside the narrative from which its significance can be seen as a whole. They tell us what it is all about.

As in Hebrews 1.10–12 (quoting Psalm 102.25–7) the image of an old garment is used for the old dispensation in its totality. Mark has a particular interest in clothes as an image of change: Jesus' garments at the transfiguration 'glistening, intensely white, as no fuller on earth could bleach them', the young man who lost his clothes in the garden of Gethsemane, the very deliberate play with Jesus' clothing at his trial and execution, the white robe of the young man at the tomb. It is an argument for this parable being integrated with the Gospel rather than an insertion from outside it. Closer examination confirms the view that it deals with the total historical significance of Christianity. The old and the new cannot be cobbled together. The relation of Christianity to Judaism is treated with the same bold radicalism as by Paul in the battle with the conservative opposition to him which resounds through Galatians and Romans. Here in Mark is the same sharp-edged conviction that Christianity is a new force which the old ways cannot contain. It was the great historical question, the question of destiny, of the early Church. Mark's answer to it is the same as Paul's but without the continuity-saving convolutions of Romans 9—11. It is energetically implicit in his whole Gospel, Jesus having a negative attitude to Jewish law and customs so aggressive that both Matthew and Luke demurred at it and toned it down (e.g. their omission of the master-stroke, 'the sabbath was made for man, not man for the sabbath', when they retail the controversy in the cornfield of Mark 2.23–9). Subsidiary to this major interest in the transforming historical crisis which is the root of Christianity, is the form the parable takes. It is, like the bridegroom, a figurative saying enlivened with the paradox of the riddle. An absurd course of action is envisaged in order to rouse perception of the particularity of the time.

The same features mark the immediately subsequent parable of the *wineskins*. It too is a figure coloured by the absurdity of riddle. It too is a condensed presentation of the historical significance of Christianity in line with the radicalism of Paul. As such it recurs in John 2.1–11 where, as in Mark, wedding and wine are associated.

The tendency and function of this group of four little parables – *physician, bridegroom, clothes* and *wineskins* – is clear. It posits, in appropriate traditional images, the historical significance of Christianity in terms of its origin, the ministry and destiny of Jesus. It contains strong and inalienable elements of riddle and allegory. From a standpoint outside the narrative, allowed by the break in narrative which is always made by a parable, it clarifies the narrative's overall thrust.

✴ The next group of parables is a threesome at Mark 3.23–7: *divided kingdom, divided house, strong man* plundered. In the interval between it and the previous group Jesus twice flouted the sabbath, once in the cornfield and once in the healing of a man with a withered hand. He was followed by a large and motley crowd, not of Jews only but of people from gentile Tyre and Sidon as well as from the betwixt-and-between region of Galilee. He healed many and unclean spirits acknowledged him as Son of God, though he told them to keep it secret. He went up into 'the mountain' (3.13: the RSV's more realistic, but less symbolically resonant, 'the hills', is false) and chose twelve apostles: the symbolism of Moses and the twelve tribes of Israel indicating a bid for authority on the part of Jesus and the Church at least equal to that of the old dispensation. Then 'he went home' (3.19) only to be thronged and have his friends attempt to seize him in the belief that he had gone mad, and the scribes come down from Jerusalem to accuse him of wielding demonic power. 'He is possessed of Beelzebub, and by the prince of demons he casts out demons' (3.22). In answer to this charge comes the group of parables, labelled as such.

If one thing is clear about the narrative which has led up to it, it is its hectic and accelerating pace. It starts provocatively enough with the two polemical sabbath incidents. From then on it is breathlessly episodic, pressurized by the crowds to the point where explosion threatens – and bursts violently in the accusations that Jesus is mad and evil. In the middle of this comes the august tableau of authority, Jesus on the mountain choosing twelve apostles to be with him, to preach, and to exorcize: the founding of the new Christian community in terms of the geographical and numerical typology of the old. The sense of historical crisis could hardly be more urgent than in this narrative which sets the establishment of the Church in the pressure of bitter conflict: Jesus against sabbath customs, diseases, demons and religious functionaries; religious functionaries, friends and family (3.31) against Jesus; and the crowd adding a less decided but as urgent forcing of the issue. For the issue is being forced, the issue of the whole Gospel: who Jesus is in the light of what he has done. To this pressure, no longer to be contained, the group of parables is addressed.

> He called them [the scribes who say he is evil] to him, and said to them in parables, 'How can Satan cast out Satan? If a kingdom is divided against itself, that kingdom cannot stand. . . And if Satan has risen up against himself and is divided, he cannot stand, but is coming to an end. But no one can enter a strong man's house and plunder his goods, unless he first binds

the strong man; then indeed he may plunder his house.'

(Mark 3.23–7)

Which side is Jesus on, God's or the devil's? He is cornered in the house by the crowds and his hostile family and has to answer. So he does: but in parables. The dominant meaning of parable here is 'riddle'. A riddle seizes the initiative, allows the one put on the spot to put his interrogators on the spot. By resort to absurdity it pin-points the absurdity of the opposition. Riddle is the most aggressive kind of parable: little, hard and menacing. The figures in these parables come from the Old Testament, baiting the trap with familiar reference. The divided kingdom or house evokes the historic division of Israel and Judah after Solomon with all its dismal consequences familiar to Bible readers. The strong man recalls Isaiah 49.24f:

> Can the prey be taken from the mighty,
>   or the captives of a tyrant be rescued?
> Surely, thus says the Lord:
>   'Even the captives of the mighty shall be taken,
>   and the prey of the tyrant shall be rescued.'

Also, it was prophesied of the delivering servant of God at Isaiah 53.12 that he would divide the spoil with the strong because he had poured out his soul unto death and been numbered with the transgressors. Very possibly there is also reference to the dispossession of the heathen by Israel as it entered the promised land. All of which serves to make this string of figures resonant of the tragedy and hope of biblical history.

In a further way this group has an even wider historical field than the previous one. There is a strong eschatological note in the basic theme of Satan rising up against himself. He is coming to an end; literally 'he has an end'. And the end can be no other than the end of history as a battle between good and evil; the world's end, which is the beginning of the Kingdom of God which Jesus' first words in Mark proclaimed imminent (1.15). The implied narrative scope has broadened from the crisis in the 'middle of time', which was the subject of the previous set of parables, to include the end of present historical conditions. The focus has narrowed into Christology: who is the one stronger than the strong? And once again it is by parables that the reader's, or hearer's, historical consciousness is raised and concentrated. We are learning that the historical context which was so determinative of Old Testament parables holds good for Mark in no uncertain manner. It is a lesson which we need to hold on to as we approach the critical parable of the *sower* and the others in its group.

The Sower and its Group

This third group of parables includes the *sower*, the *lamp*, the *seed growing secretly* and the *mustard seed*. It is set with an unprecedented solemnity and deliberation. The previous groups have sprung out of incidents and debates. Here Jesus is to teach *sua sponte*, and not as a rejoinder to criticism.

> Again he began to teach beside the sea. And a very large crowd gathered about him, so that he got into a boat and sat in it on the sea; and the whole crowd was beside the sea on the land. And he taught them many things in parables, and in his teaching he said to them... (Mark 4.1f)

The pressure of the crowd is removed by Jesus getting into a boat. More, he sits – on the sea. Sitting denotes the settled authority of the teacher. To sit on, or over, the sea is to be like God who sits enthroned over the sea (Psalm 29.10). All of which leads us to expect more studiedly reflective and freely authoritative teaching than we have had before. We will not be disappointed, above all in the theology and purpose of parables. But first, the very deliberate scene setting for this major and central group of parables constitutes a broad hint that it occurs at a consciously planned point in the book as a whole. All commentators agree that Mark as editor shows his hand in the first two verses of chapter 4. What, as narrator, does he intend?

The usual function of speeches within biblical narrative is reflection on past, and future, action. The chief monument of this kind in the Old Testament is the book of Deuteronomy, the great speech of Moses as he stands on the threshold of the promised land reminiscing about the past and looking into the future with warnings and promises. Artificial though this convention is, it also has verisimilitude. Human beings cannot take very much actual history, particularly if it is bewildering and fraught, without making some discursive sense of it. Mark's narrative is nothing if not fraught and shot through with bewilderment. We have already seen him reflecting on its meaning in two groups of brief parables told by Jesus. We are about to see him do the same thing in a more majestic and leisurely manner. So it is reasonable to suppose that, whereas the previous groups of parables made sense of the narrative briefly and *en courant*, and in the setting of brisk debate, this group will do so in a more thorough manner something like Deuteronomy. It takes stock of the entire story so far and sets up what is to come.

The story so far may be divided into four blocks:

1   1.1–15   Revelation of who Jesus is. Proclaimed by John as the expected Christ, by God as his beloved Son, he is tested and proclaims the imminent Kingdom of God.

    1.16–20   He calls four disciples.

2   1.21—2.12   Jesus's identity is worked out in a series of miracles, the last surrounded by hostile controversy.

    2.13f   He calls Levi.

3   2.15—3.12   A series of heated arguments about Jesus' evangelistic conduct, with the *first group of parables*. A hectic resumé of his activity.

    3.13–19   He calls twelve and gives them authority.

4   3.20–30   The grand controversy about Jesus' conduct and identity including the *second group of parables*.

    3.31–35   A reappraisal of who really belongs with him.

This lands us at this third group of parables. It is a point at which there is much scope and more need for some kind of accumulative and ordered reflection. Mark has shown that the gospel is about, even is, Jesus the Son of God (1.1). It, or he, strikes into the public world by a proclamatory sentence (1.15), the calling of four disciples, and instantly effective miraculous power. This triggers a reaction of hostility and dispute which returns to the original question of who he is in the second block of controversy. Then he calls Levi. And so the rhythm goes on, deeds with arguments about their propriety and significance which include the telling of parables in blocks 3 and 4, followed or punctuated by three intervening notes about disciples being summoned and a final note about those who are not disciples or associates of Jesus. The central and major concern is Jesus – or, Christology. He is known, after his baptism, by what he does and says. Disciples join him, Pharisees and scribes oppose him. The parables of chapter 4 are fundamentally structured by the same forces that have driven the narrative: Jesus is the agent of the gospel power which, thrown into the historical world, is denied and opposed on the way to ultimate achievement.

Achievement in the face of denial and opposition: it is an antinomy which not only fixes and explains what has happened in the narrative already, but also points towards death and resurrection as the climax to which the whole story drives. Chapter 4 is an integrating point for the entire book. But there is more to it than that. Ancient literary art, as seen for instance by Robert Alter in his *The Art of Biblical Narrative* (George Allen & Unwin 1981) is not slapdash or content only with general connections. It rejoices in integration of narrative by very minute historical particulars. We might think, by way of illustration, of a Greek country church. To the West European eye its mural paintings are 'primitive'. Yet they are worked out in terms of a tight scheme by which every prophet and apostle, every historical incident, has an exactly predetermined place in relation to the others and the whole. Such art is sophisticated and exact in ways we do not expect, with contrivances which are strange to us. So it is in Old Testament narrative.

So here in the parable of the *sower*. We naturally think that the different kinds of soil signify different attitudes of mind in a general fashion transcending particular incident. We are interested in attitudes generally. But there are distinct signs in this parable that Mark, while not denying our interest, is more historically particular about it. What has been put before us in the *sower* parable is going to happen in the story yet to come. The Gospel is history, not psychological generality. Mark does his historical particularizing work in the interpretation of the parable in verses 14–20 which is far more exact than is generally supposed. The birds which take away the word-seed on the path, or way, are Satan: 'Satan comes and takes away the word sown in them' (4.15). Now, Peter will be on the way with Jesus as his disciple at 8.27. But at 8.32 he will try to remove Jesus' prophecy of the doom, death and resurrection, of the Son of Man: to take away that word. It amounts to a cancellation of the gospel at its christological base. So Jesus will rebuke him with the words 'Get behind me Satan! For you are not on the side of God, but of men' (8.33). The parable's prophecy is fulfilled. Next in the interpretation comes the shallow and rocky ground which is said to represent those who 'when tribulation or persecution arises on account of the word, immediately fall away' (4.17). This too will get its precise historical fulfilment. At 14.43 tribulation will arise as Judas and his posse come to arrest Jesus in the garden, and at 14.50 Mark says, 'they all [the eleven] forsook him and fled'. The third category is 'the ones sown among thorns; they are those who hear the word, but the cares of the world, and the delight in riches, and the desire for other things, enter in and choke the word, and it proves unfruitful' (4.18f). At 10.17 Jesus will be accosted by a rich man eager to inherit eternal life. He tells him, 'Go, sell what you have, and give to the poor, and you will have treasure in heaven; and come, follow me.'

At that saying [*epi tō logō* = on account of the word] his countenance fell, and he went away sorrowful; for he had great possessions.

The word of discipleship, 'follow me', was spoken to him. But it was strangled at birth by wealth.

So each occurrence in the parable has, via its interpretation, an exact equivalent in the narrative of the book. There is one striking exception, the good soil with its abundant crop. No one in the narrative reaches that happy condition. Mark would seem to be looking beyond his book, with its famously abrupt ending, to the life of his church; hoping for better things after the resurrection than happened before it. He is looking to that *eschaton* which lies beyond his book yet dominates it.

So much for the setting of the parable in the book. But the book also has a setting in a tradition of imagery. An appreciation of it will illuminate our understanding of the parable. In Old Testament Scripture seed and plant growth had long served as images of religious and moral development.

> Sow for yourselves righteousness,
>   reap the fruit of steadfast love;
>   break up your fallow ground,
> for it is the time to seek the Lord,
>   that he may come and rain salvation upon you.
>   (Hosea 10.12)

> Break up your fallow ground,
>   and sow not among thorns.
> Circumcise yourself to the Lord,
>   remove the foreskin of your hearts.
>   (Jeremiah 4.3f)

Second Isaiah had likened God's word to the power of plant growth,

> making it bring forth and sprout,
>   giving seed to the sower and bread to the eater.
>   (Isaiah 55.10)

Ezekiel told elaborate allegories of vines and trees. Daniel dreamed of a fast-growing tree (4.10–12). The closest neighbour and contemporary to the *sower* is the parable of seed at 2 Esdras 4.27–32 (see p. 26). It shows us the imagery of sowing in the apocalyptic context within which parables in general flourished. Its similarities with Mark's *sower* do not need to be laboured: the divine agency of sowing, the eschatological bent, the contrast of good and bad. At 2 Esdras 8.41 the imagery recurs in a briefer parable, much as Mark's *sower* is followed by the shorter (one verse) parable of the *seed growing secretly*:

> For it is just as the farmer sows many seeds upon the ground and plants a multitude of seedlings, and yet, not all that have been sown will come up in due season, and not all that were planted will take root; so also those who have been sown in the world will not all be saved.

And at 2 Esdras 9.31:

> Behold I sow my law in you, and it shall bring forth fruit in you.

The figure is developed to show that the law remains and triumphs in spite of human disobedience. 2 Esdras and Mark are obviously very close to one another. Certainly Mark's book is a through-going narrative which 2 Esdras is not. Yet the latter is a meditation upon history. And Mark's story is shot through with apocalyptic ideas and themes: the secret divine plan for history to be suddenly revealed, the persecution and trial of the elect, the Christ, the eschatology, to name but some. Of particular relevance is the apocalyptic view of human morality, nature and destiny which Mark and the writer of 2 Esdras shared. The *raison d'être* of apocalyptic was a collapse of confidence in the human historical and moral continuum as the place where things could come out right. It had not been so in the more prosperous days of King Solomon when the Joseph narrative and the Succession Narrative were written. Then God worked his purpose out within the twists and turns of history and within the vagaries of ambivalent and ambiguous human characters. For the apocalyptic mind that is no longer a possible story of salvation. Events had contradicted it too strongly. Salvation could only be at the end of history and by means of some victoriously annihilating divine act from without, the *dies irae*. To correspond with this, apocalyptic vision sees people as predestinately set in their ways. 'The time is near. Let the evildoer still do evil, and the filthy still be filthy, and the righteous still do right, and the holy still be holy' (Revelation 22.10f). Thus the John of the Apocalypse. With the end impending, leisure for repentance is short or non-existent. The same determinism informs the parable of the *sower*. As people are, so they must and will be. And so it is all through Mark. Some hear and see, God knows why. More, God knows why, do not. And they all do it by sudden, and – from the human historical point of view – virtually motiveless reflex. We are back with the crux of

Mark 4.12, not as an aberrant intrusion in its chapter, but as integral to its thought and thoroughly appropriate. It may baffle humanistic and realistic exegetes. Within Mark it makes sense.

Having seen how the *sower* parable and its interpretation belong within Mark's Gospel on grounds of theme and argument, historical ideas and the connections of narrative, it remains to examine vocabulary and syntax. Jeremias has already and convincingly shown that the interpretation belongs with the vocabulary of the early Church, not with Jesus. We need only see the Marcan vocabulary and style in the parable itself – which Jeremias did not attempt – in order to judge Matthew Black's claim in his *An Aramaic Approach to the Gospels and Acts* (Oxford 1967) that 'here we may speak with confidence of a literal translation Greek version of a parable of Jesus' (p. 45).

Sir John Hawkins (*Horace Synopticae* [Oxford, 1909] pp. 12f) lists as words characteristic of Mark those 'which occur at least three times in Mark and which either (a) are not found at all in Matthew or Luke or (b) occur more in Mark than in Matthew and Luke together'. The more severe Pryke (*Redactional Style in the Marcan Gospel* [Cambridge 1978] pp. 136–8) wants them to occur five times in not less than 50% of the whole. In the verses which make up the parable (nobody disputes that the three introductory verses are by Mark) the distinctively Marcan vocabulary is:

verse 3   Hear!
           Behold!
    5   Suddenly
    6   Dried out
    7   Rose up
    8   Bore
    9   Hear!
           To hear

A fair total and a very fair spread. For syntax, Pryke lists fourteen characteristic constructions of Mark's of which four or five (one overlaps his categories) happen here.

1 Mark uses the parenthetical clause, 'a loosely constructed sentence which appends a phrase as an afterthought to clarify a previously obscure statement', though this is often not exactly clarifying but 'leads the author astray'. We get:
   verse 5: because it had no depth of earth
   verse 6: because it had no root.

2   He has participles replacing verbs. We get this at:
    verse 8: coming up and increasing

This is also Mark's characteristic 'juxtaposition of similar or contrasting words' in 'a rhythmic thought process'.

3   He very frequently uses 'suddenly' (v.5).

4   He uses redundant participles as at v.8 and v.3, 'The sower went out to sow'.

5   He uses two or more participles together before or after the main verb as at v.8 where the main verb is 'gave (fruit)' followed by 'coming up and increasing'.

The last example is the overlap (no.5 with no.2). Again a fair total, four or five out of fourteen, and a fair spread. On these grounds of vocabulary and syntax it seems that if we have here 'a literal translation Greek version of a parable of Jesus' then we have it in a literal translation Greek version of a book by Jesus – an exciting possibility if it were not preposterous.

A very different view of the *sower* parable from Jeremias' is emerging. Instead of a parable of Jesus inserted in a narrative, we are beginning to see a parable of Mark's (it may be Jesus' too by some undiscoverable route of tradition – we cannot tell) firmly and intricately set in the narrative as an elucidation of it. If elucidation is too coolly rational a word, that too is apt for Mark as a whole and not just this parable or its interpretation. Elucidation in the apocalyptic context is always, and at the same time, mystery. And that brings us to a final point of contention with Jeremias who sees the parable, not as mysterious, but plain and everyday. That is the message of a memorable and attractive passage at the beginning of his book.

> The pictorial element of the parables is drawn from the daily life of Palestine. It is noteworthy, for instance, that the Sower in Mark 4.3–8 sows so clumsily that much of the seed is wasted; we might have expected a description of the regular method of sowing, and that, in fact, is what we have here. This is easily understood when we remember that in Palestine sowing precedes ploughing. Hence in the parable the Sower is depicted as striding over the unploughed stubble and this enables us to understand why he sows 'on the path': he sows intentionally on the path which the villagers have trodden over the stubble, since he intends to plough the seed in when he ploughs up the path. He sows intentionally among the thorns standing withered in the

fallow because they, too, will be ploughed up. Nor need it surprise us that some grains should fall upon rocky ground; the underlying limestone, thinly covered with soil, barely shows above the surface until the ploughshare jars against it. What appears to the Western mind as bad farming is simply customary usage under Palestinian conditions.

(The Parables of Jesus, pp.11f)

This is not so much an interpretation of the parable as a recognizably different version. And the differences are the realistic details which Jeremias adds at every point. A lot of material which is absent from the parable is imported into it, drastically changing its character – perhaps for the better to the 'Western mind' with its love of realism and historical relativity which is so ill at ease when it reads Mark's Gospel. But it is spurious. Mark does not tell us that the sower 'comes striding over the stubble', nor that the path has been 'trodden over the stubble' by the 'villagers', nor that the sower sows them 'intentionally', nor (above all) that he intends to 'plough in'. Neither does he tell us that the thorns are standing withered in the fallow. Neither does he have anything of the ploughshare jarring against a limestone substratum. However refreshing it may be to read such earthy and vivid details in a book of New Testament criticism, we have to remember that we are not reading Mark when we read this passage of Jeremias. We are, in fact, reading something quite different.

The greatest difference which Jeremias makes turns on his theory, presented as fact – and fact which we ought to be able to remember – that in Palestine sowing precedes ploughing. Jeremias' immediate source for this idea, as for the rest of the vivid detail in the passage quoted, is an essay by Dalman in the *Palästina Jahrbuch* for 1926 entitled 'Viererlei Acker'. Speaking of broadcast sowing Dalman says that it entails 'most of the seed being cast on the unploughed land so that, of course, by ploughing it can be covered over by the topsoil' (p. 122). For Jesus this would have gone without saying, *selbstverständlich gelten* (ibid.). It is not at all clear that Dalman himself saw this happening. His visit to the Palestinian countryside was in May and the ploughing he refers to was done in the late autumn. The photograph which he adduces is quite inconclusive and obviously posed (p. 121). 'Of course' or *'selbstverständlich'*, like Jeremias' 'when we remember', acts as a substitute for the production of real evidence by making the reader feel that he would be obtuse or ignorant to question the almost offhand assertion of a very unusual and improbable method of sowing.

The best evidence for it, the real evidence behind Dalman's speculation, is not in modern Palestinian agriculture but in the Mishnah. At *Shab*. vii.2 the work which is forbidden on the sabbath is particularized in a list which reads 'sowing, ploughing, reaping, binding sheaves, threshing, winnowing'. Clearly the list is in chronological order and incontrovertibly sowing comes before ploughing in it. That is the one piece of evidence that supports Dalman and Jeremias. They do not, however, mention the perplexity it has caused to commentators on the Mishnah. The Babylonian Talmud at BT *Shab*. 73B wonders how this can be, since definitely ploughing is done first. Why, then, does it not say 'ploughing then sowing'? The objection is left suspended by the conclusion that there has been a tradition that in Palestine they sow first and after that they plough. Utterly improbable as that seems to the Talmudic commentator, he has to admit that it is there in the Mishnah and move on. Rashi, the eleventh-century writer of the normative commentary on the Talmud shares its perplexity at the Mishnah's description of a method unknown in the whole world. His conclusion is that the ground is so hard that the land was ploughed after sowing *as well as* before in order to bed the seed in, and that the two ploughings are spoken of as one. Bertinora in his seventeenth-century commentary on the Mishnah says the same. Contemporary with the Mishnah and the repository of material not used in it is the Tosefta *Berakoth*. It uses the list of labours in the Mishnah for the blessing of food but, as Dalman and Jeremias notice, in the Vienna manuscript of it the order is reversed to the conventional ploughing and sowing.

Dalman and Jeremias also invoke the legend of Abram's invention of bird-scaring and the seed drill in Jubilees 11, though that is scarcely of a genre to provide earthily trustworthy agricultural information. The story goes that when the farmers were sowing, the evil angel Mastema sent ravens to devour the seed before it could be ploughed in. Abram redeems the situation by running at the birds and shouting 'Descend not: return to the place whence ye came.' Apparently bird-scaring had not occurred as a possibility to the farmers, least of all in so grandiloquent a style. Then Abram contrived a drill fixed to the plough which hid the seed in the earth immediately. If this legend has any agricultural realism in it, then Rashi's theory of a *second* ploughing after sowing copes with it adequately. Also sowing before ploughing is represented in the tale as a method in the very remote past and superseded by Abram's ingenuity. So only the Mishnah supports Dalman and Jeremias and its evidence was a problem to its interpreters.

If the rabbinic evidence for ploughing after sowing is too problematic to form the base of interpretation which Dalman and Jeremias make it, the Old Testament evidence is against it. Isaiah 28.24 asks, 'Does he who ploughs for sowing plough continually?'. Hosea 10.12 has the usual order of sowing, reaping, then ploughing up the fallow ground. And Jeremiah 4.3 is unambiguous: 'Break up your fallow ground, and sow not among thorns.' So it is not surprising that when K. D. White challenged Jeremias' theory in the *Journal of Theological Studies* XV, pp.300f, Jeremias was forced in an essay in *New Testament Studies* 13, pp.48–53, to concede ploughing before sowing in Palestine, but without revoking his theory. But does the theory work as an interpretation of the parable anyway? If the farmer ploughed up the path he was too late because the birds had eaten the seed. Seeds planted on shallow ground do not in fact spring up 'immediately'. A farmer who does not know the whereabouts of the limestone substratum in his familiar little plot is too ignorant to be credible. If he ploughed up the thistles he either killed them by doing so, which spoils the parable: or ploughed in *their* seed with the sad results which fit the parable but make his husbandry so ineffective as to be incredible. We are either being presented with a farming method so inefficient that no one in his senses would use it for long, as Rashi and the Babylonian Talmud noticed, or the *sower* is a parable which resorts to the bizarre nonsense of riddle in order to jolt the hearer into perception, not of agriculture but of the mystery of the gospel. The latter is decidedly the more appropriate to Mark.

The *sower* parable, its interpretation, and the note about the function of parables which comes before them, have been seen to belong together as a coherent entity within the coherence of the narrative. Beyond that, the belonging together of parable and its interpretation, hinging upon the deliberate obscurity of parables, was a marked feature of apocalyptic parabolic method from Ezekiel onwards with strong roots in previous tradition. There is no need to prise them apart and attribute them to different sources.

After the interpretation comes a series of four little parables each introduced by 'and he said...'. They too are part of the mechanism of the whole. The first is the *lamp*.

> Is a lamp brought in [literally, 'does a lamp come?'] to be put under a bushel or under a bed, and not on a stand? For there is nothing hid, except to be made manifest; nor is anything secret, except to come to light.   (Mark 4.21f)

It has the riddling character, the reference to absurdity, of previous parables including the *sower*. It is immediately followed by an explanation: 'For there is nothing hid...'. And it is finished off with the same words as close the parable of the *sower*: 'He that hath ears to hear, let him hear.' It is a thoroughly Marcan little parable then, not least in its juggling of secrecy and revelation. This ground-theme of apocalyptic which makes the *lamp* a part of the interpretation of the *sower*, also marks it as a parable about opposite extremes which presents the Kingdom of God as mystery made manifest. Out of the bizarre and frustrated sowing came a final harvest. Out of the dark riddle of a lamp hidden under a bushel or a bed comes, in the end, illumination.

The next parable turns upon another familiar apocalyptic theme, 'The time is near. Let the evildoer still do evil... and the righteous still do right' (Revelation 22.10f) – with an added twist of increase:

> Take heed what you hear; the measure you give will be the measure you get, and still more will be given you. For to him who has will more be given; and from his who has not, even what he has will be taken away. (Mark 4.24f)

It fits the saying about the function of parables at verse 12. It fits the predestinate view of human nature in the *sower*.

Between them these two little parables have interpreted the bigger one by reiterating two of its major doctrinal features: revelation and predestination. Next comes the *seed growing secretly*:

> The kingdom of God is as if a man should scatter seed upon the ground, and should sleep and rise night and day, and the seed should sprout and grow, he knows not how. The earth produces of itself [literally, 'automatically'], first the blade then the ear, then the full grain in the ear. But when the grain is ripe, at once he puts in the sickle, because the harvest has come.
> (Mark 4.26–9)

The dramatic movement from the hidden to the invisible is here again. The parable relates to the *sower* as the smaller seed parables of 2 Esdras related to the earlier and bigger one: a briefer reiteration emphasizes a point or two from the parent parable. It takes the beginning and the end of the *sower*, and emphasizes the mystery of the time between. The end gets an extra boost by the resonant quotation of Joel 3.13, 'put in the sickle for the harvest is ripe' – also quoted at Revelation 14.15, where it is spoken by an angel. The doomsday theme in apocalyptic has emerged *fortissimo*, confirming and reinforcing the eschatological drive of the end of the *sower* parable.

The final little parable of the group ends with similar apocalyptic force. The quotation this time is from Daniel 4.12, Nebuchadnez- zar's dream of a tree which sheltered birds and beasts – an image going back to Ezekiel.

> With what can we compare the kingdom of God, or what parable shall we use for it? It is like a grain of mustard seed, which, when sown upon the ground, is the smallest of all the seeds on earth; yet when it is sown it grows up and becomes the greatest of all shrubs, and puts forth large branches, so that the birds of the air can make nests in its shade. (Mark 4.30–2)

Once again Mark's agricultural and botanical knowledge is wrong. He is not realistic or naturalistic. The mustard seed is not the smallest of seeds, its plant far from the greatest of shrubs. Jeremias (p. 147) here concedes 'features of the parables which transcend the bounds of actuality' and 'are meant to tell us that we have to do with divine realities'. As the absurdity holds, so does the apocalyp- tic vision. Putting in the sickle proclaims the moment of escatologi- cal harvest. Here is an image of the eschatological state or kingdom, a tree full of birds. Eschatology, of a decidedly futuristic sort, as we would expect in the context, triumphs and has the last parabolic word before the editorial conclusion:

> With many such parables he spoke the word to them, as they were able to hear it; he did not speak to them without a parable, but privately to his own disciples he explained every- thing. (Mark 4.33f)

So the section ends, with an obviously editorial note which is sometimes thought to be a revocation, or an amendment, of the tough saying at 4.12 ('so that they ... may indeed hear but not understand'). It is not. 'They' and 'them' in this passage refer to the crowd in contradistinction from the disciples. 'As they were able to hear it' then refers to precisely the sort of hearing of which they were capable, a hearing which is uncomprehending. 'But privately to his own disciples he explained everything.' It is an epistemology integral to apocalyptic. Because the end of which it speaks has not yet publicly come, the knowledge of it, and of the true meaning of the events leading up to it, is a secret known only to the few to whom it has been revealed by a supernatural agency of explanation. This fits into narrative by virtue of being a persuasion, based in gloomy meditation upon historical process which allows the story to go on, the secret to be kept. So we note finally that this whole collection of little parables following the

sower is a part of the interpretation of the *sower* which is given to
the disciples: and that parables thus fulfil precisely the function of
hidden disclosure which is needed to maintain narrative tension.
The *sower* is not understood for the good reason, among others,
that it has not yet been fulfilled historically. It signals events to
come. And more narrative.

Various Little Parables

After chapter 4 it is a long time before we meet another parable.
Jesus' next teaching session is at chapter 7.1–23. It is about purity,
honouring parents and defilement. Throughout it, Jesus appeals to
the heart and its disposition rather than the head of ritual
tradition: a typically prophetic appeal reinforced by a quotation of
Isaiah 29.13 at 7.6f. The parable of *digestion* occurs within it at
7.14f. It is followed, in true Marcan style, by Jesus withdrawing
into 'the house' where he tells his uncomprehending disciples that
it means. Here is the whole section:

> And he called the people to him again, and said to them, 'Hear
> me, all of you, and understand: there is nothing outside a man
> which by going into him can defile him; but the things which
> come out of a man are what defile him.' And when he had
> entered the house, and left the people, his disciples asked him
> about the parable. And he said to them, 'Then are you also
> without understanding? Do you not see that whatever goes into
> a man from the outside cannot defile him, since it enters, not his
> heart but his stomach, and so passes on?' (Thus he declared all
> foods clean.) And he said, 'What comes out of a man is what
> defiles a man. For from within, out of the heart of man, come
> evil thoughts, fornication, theft, murder, adultery, coveting,
> wickedness, deceit, licentiousness, envy, slander, pride, foolish-
> ness. All these evil things come from within, and they defile a
> man.' (Mark 7.14–23)

The editorial stage-management is pointed. Jesus calls the people
to tell them the parable – previously he has been arguing with
Pharisees – and begins, 'Hear me all of you and understand'. In
this public setting it resembles the *sower*, but now Jesus apparently
hopes for understanding from the general public. We are not told
whether he got it, but it would seem that Mark intends a wider
reception of Jesus' teaching than before. However, he immediately takes things the other way, having Jesus in the house
expound the parable in privacy to his disciples. So the first and
public setting was no more than an indication of the sort of

thoroughly public parable speaking which we get only with the final parable of all, the *vineyard* at 12.1–12. Here, however, Mark revokes the clarity he had momentarily adumbrated. The secrets are not yet out.

The meaning of the parable is plain. The digestive system can look after itself. It is an efficient cleansing apparatus. The food that people take in cannot defile them. It goes into their stomachs, not their hearts, which are the centre and source of religious activities, and the stomach has its way of cleansing it. Excrement, on the contrary, does defile. And the heart has its excrement, the list of vices which all come out into the world from the human interior and poison humanity. Historically, the parable is set at the parting of the ways between Christianity and Judaism, marked, for this evangelist, by an antinomianism more unambiguous than Paul's. For Mark there is no doubt about the irrelevance of Jewish dietary laws. In the aside, 'He said this making all foods clean', he gives the parable the force of a mandate. Yet still it remains secret. The narrative reason for this could lie partly in Mark's historical consciousness. The mandate is for the disciples as representatives of the Church which does not yet exist. The secret is not yet out. The religious reason for it could be that for Mark Christianity is an inward as well as an historical religion. We can only be tentative and say 'could be' because the deployment of secrecy in Mark's gospel has proved so successful as to defy the clarifying efforts of modern criticism. There are things we can be more definite about. The parable belongs with primitive church discipline – or lack of it – set in Jesus' ministry. It is not allegorical, which is rare for Mark, but it is a riddle, which is usual for his short parables. As such it needs interpretation, and parable and interpretation belong together as tightly as with the *sower*.

A riddle occurs in the subsequent incident of the Syro-Phoenician woman's daughter. Jesus first brushes her off with 'Let the children first be fed, for it is not right to take the children's bread and throw it to the dogs' (Mark 7.27). There is an allegorical element here, children = Jews and dogs = Gentiles, which the woman apparently understands well enough to make the smart rejoinder, 'Yes, Lord; yet even the dogs under the table eat the children's crumbs.' Jesus immediately relents and the girl is cured. A parable has been understood! But we must notice straightaway that this has happened in gentile territory, the region of Tyre and Sidon. The secret of the gospel cannot be understood within Judaism. But this gentile woman, and the centurion at the crucifixion (15.39), can break it and get through: she by her quick wits and he by revelation. Gentile Christianity and the Christianity of the cross are for Mark true Christianity. It is hard not to think that he owes much to Paul. Even the disciples are left behind in Mark's radical view of things. At 8.14–21 occurs the enigmatic dialogue about bread as they go with Jesus by boat back into Jewish territory. It is irreducibly obscure. But we can see that Jesus is speaking parabolically when he says, 'take heed, beware of the leaven of the Pharisees and the leaven of Herod'. He does not mean yeast but some spreading evil force such as yeast symbolized. And the usual language about not perceiving and not understanding, associated with parables in Mark, recurs. It is, at any rate, appropriate that Mark's least intelligible passage should have strong parabolic connotations: appropriate to his view of parables, that is, however surprising to modern presuppositions about them.

Two more small parables occur before we get to the major one of the *vineyard*: about *salt* at 9.50 and about the *camel and the needle's eye* at 10.25. After the transfiguraton and the exorcism of the boy which follows it, Jesus teaches his disciples about their discipleship. The instruction is at the same time liberal and severe. To receive a child is to receive Christ and God (9.36f). Anyone who does good in Christ's name belongs to him regardless, apparently, of ecclesiastical credentials. Yet anyone who causes a 'little one' to stumble would be better drowned, and all impediments must be ruthlessly cut away (9.42–8). Anyone who demurs and prefers his own comfort and well-being will be thrown into the Gehenna 'where their worm does not die and the fire is not quenched'. As a pendant to this ferocious instruction Mark puts a collection of parabolic sayings about salt.

> For every one will be salted with fire. Salt is good; but if the salt has lost its saltness, how will you season it? Have salt in yourselves, and be at peace with one another.   (Mark 9.49f)

The connection with the previous section is by the word 'fire'. But only the word. The fire here operates differently from that at verse 48. It purifies rather than torments or consumes. Whether it is the fire of divine spirit or of persecution or of the last days, we have no means of knowing. At all events, the Christian will not escape fire, as Paul had warned the Corinthians (1 Corinthians 3.13–15). Now 'salt' becomes the connecting word, and it stands for something essential to Christian discipleship, some irreplaceable preserver of all else which must no more be lost than the 'life' of the preceding verses 42–8. It is presented as a riddle: what is the use of saltless salt, of an absurdity? In the second half of the saying it is seen as the bond of peace among Christian disciples. Discipleship is the theme here as in the preceding teaching. The movement is a stepping from symbol to symbol, or rather, from symbol under one aspect to symbol under another: fire as consuming, fire as purifying, salt as purying, salt as preserving. This is a form of wit and instruction more esteemed by the ancients than their modern exegetes – whose attempts to make some *other* sense of it in their commentaries (see Vincent Taylor's ad loc.) have had no success at all.

The little parable about the *camel and the needle's eye* at 10.25 is not in the least obscure, but it is deliberately absurd in a way which has attracted efforts to make it realistic for a very long time: e.g. by suggesting that there was a gate in Jerusalem through which camels could just squeeze, that *kamelos* (camel) should read *kamilos* (cable). The latter was aired by Theophylact, an eleventh-century Byzantine exegete, showing that the realistic approaches of Dodd and Jeremias to the gospel parables have precedents – which get into as grave difficulties with the ineluctable strangeness of the texts, when they are pressed, as did the realistic interpretation of the *sower* parable.

The Vineyard

But the real nemesis of that approach comes with the parable of the *vineyard* at Mark 12.1–12. Jeremias recognizes this candidly and instantly, and then protects the other parables from its influence by cordoning it off with the word 'unique': 'This parable, linked as it is with the song of the vineyard in Isaiah 5.1–7, exhibits an allegorical character which is unique among the parables of Jesus' (p.70). In no sense does allegorical character make the *vineyard* parable unique, as we have seen and shall go on to see more. But when Jeremias says that 'the whole parable is evidently pure allegory', he is entirely right. Exegete after exegete has found it impossible to understand in any other way. The 'man' is God, the vineyard Israel, the tenants the Jews or Jewish authorities. All that is known from Isaiah 5. The servants are Old Testament worthies and prophets, often called such in the Old Testament. The son and heir is Jesus, here, as at Mark 1.11 called the 'beloved' Son. The 'others' are the Gentiles. The catastrophe is the destruction of Jerusalem. All this being so, it is very difficult to accept as a parable of Jesus an historical allegory whose historical vantage point is quite clearly later than Jesus, whose death, as son and heir to the vineyard, forms the climax and turning-point of the story in a way so integral to it as to forbid its being treated as some addition by the earlier Church to an original version by Jesus. The

parable is an indivisible whole with Jesus' death and the subsequent transfer of divine favour to the Gentiles as inalienable parts
of it. Its wholeness is based on the historical material which it
treats – it is about the entire history of Israel from the beginning to
(what Mark saw as) the end, from Israel's election by God to its
rejection by him in favour of the Gentiles. Condensed historical
resumés of this sort were common in Old Testament literature.
They could be straightforwardly historical as in the well known
Deuteronomic 'creed' beginning, 'A wandering Aramean was my
father' (Deuteronomy 26.5–11). The prophets often presented
them figuratively or allegorically, Hosea and Ezekiel picturing
Israel's history as courtship or marriage. One of these prophetic
allegorizations has already been noticed as a basis of this parable,
Isaiah's Song of the Vineyard at Isaiah 5.1–7. It includes the
prophetic allegorical motif of courting by being a love song. It is
also a passage on which Ezekiel had drawn for his historical
allegorizing and from which descend the numerous rabbinic
parables of Israel as a farm or garden. It could be for this reason
that Mark's *vineyard* parable is presented without interpretation:
the figures used are immediately recognizable by reference to
Scripture and contemporary events. 'They perceived that he had
told the parable against them.' But people in Mark are extraordi-
narily and invincibly uncomprehending, not least of parables. It
would in principle not have been beyond him to say that the
meaning of this parable escaped them as had the meaning of the
sower. We may even, by now, almost expect it.

It is the narrative scheme that dictates otherwise. We are
nearing the end of the story, approaching the final rejection of the
Son of God on which the parable itself turns. Throughout, Mark
has hinted that here the mystery of the gospel, the meaning of all
that Jesus had done and said, would be revealed in death and
resurrection. This double reversal of expectation is authenticated
by the text about the stone from Psalm 118, rejected by the
builders but become the headstone of the corner – the integrating
point of historical architecture according to its divine plan. The
climax of the book is the death of Jesus outside the city. It is
marked by two momentous occurrences. The veil of the Temple is
torn in two from top to bottom. It is the destruction of that ancient
sacred order which marks off the holy. This catastrophically
negative symbolic event is immediately followed by an equally
catastrophically positive one, an eucatastrophe.

When the centurion, who stood facing him, saw that he thus
breathed his last, he said, 'Truly this man was the Son of
God'. (Mark 15.39)

The sacral boundaries of Judaism are broken. The revelation of the gospel mystery is given to a Gentile. The congruence of the *vineyard* parable with the passion story is a vivid instance of the function of a parable within narrative. Like a programme note to a drama, it outlines the points in it which are most integral to its meaning. It points its symbolic values. But it prefers to do so by keeping to narrative form rather than by discursive argument. So another narrative form than the directly historical is required, and the best will be that which, while still narrative, is more overtly symbolic, which relates its own masked characters and events indissolubly to the real characters and events of the larger historical tale which it explicates. It is allegory. The parable of the *vineyard* is not only entire in itself in a way which defies efforts to strip off some parts of it as secondary – as Jeremias (p. 71) somewhat desultorily tries to do with the reference to the prophets and their fate in verse 5. It is also thoroughly integrated within the Gospel of Mark. The beloved son, on whom all turns, is, as we have seen, the one first designated as such by God at the baptism which was his first narrative appearance. His death, as his last narrative appearance (Mark has no resurrection appearances) is the precise point of the destruction of ancient religious order and the beginning of the new revelation with the gentile centurion – the first character in the book other than Jesus to grasp entirely its essential gospel.

The parable alerts the reader to the significance of what has happened and of what will happen on either side of it. It is a key which belongs with its lock. The book is its setting. By contrast, if one invokes the historical evidence in support of a realistic reading, familiar problems reappear. The economic conditions of first century Galilee do not support the theories of Dodd and Jeremias. Dodd referred to 'large estates ... often held by foreigners' in Galilee, but the historical evidence for them in Jesus' time is lacking. According to Rostovtzeff (*The Social and Economic History of the Roman Empire* [Oxford 1957] vol. i, p.270) the major landowners were not foreign but Jewish, including Herodian royalty. The only foreigners to have estates in Palestine were the Roman emperors and their families: as had the Ptolemies (M. Hengel, *Judaism and Hellenism* [SCM 1974] I.39 – the Ptolemaic vineyard at Beth Anath). There could well be reference to them in this parable. But if so, it is more allegorical than realistic. For any band of Jewish tenants to suppose that they could alienate an imperial estate would be unrealistic in the extreme and there is no record of such a *coup*. What did happen was the revolt of AD 66–70 which was an attempt to liberate the entire land. That revolt could

well have been in Mark's mind if we take 13.14–23 as referring in
tones of hushed horror ('Let the reader understand') to the events
of that time, and particularly the advance of the Roman army on
Jerusalem. It is reasonable to do so because Jesus' advice to run
without looking back, to pray that it may not happen in winter, fits
local war better than some apocalyptic event from which there
could be no escape. So does the lament for those who are pregnant
or nursing. The history behind this parable is not some local
fracas. It is the whole of the history which concerned Mark as the
origin and authentication of his religion. It extends from the
beginnings of Israel to the fall of Jerusalem in AD 70 and the rise of
gentile Christianity.

The Fig Tree and the Servants

There remain only two more parables in Mark to be considered.
They occur at the end of Jesus' apocalyptic discourse in chapter 13
and serve to confirm the view and findings we have built up. The
first is the *fig tree* at 13.28f.

> From the fig tree learn its parable [RSV 'lesson']: as soon as its
> branch becomes tender and puts forth its leaves, you know that
> summer is near. So also, when you see these things taking place,
> you know that he is near, at the very gates.

'He' is the Son of Man of the preceding verse 26, coming as the
herald and dispenser of doomsday, the gathering of the elect to
which the apocalyptists looked forward. Once again, we are
standing outside the immediate and apparent historical/narrative
context of Jesus' ministry. The text makes sense if we imagine that
we are with a Christian congregation after his first coming and
going, waiting for his second and conclusive coming. The two are
linked by Jesus' apocalyptic prophecy. In just the same way
Daniel, as a figure from the past, spoke to the future from the
ground of prophetic vision; and his text makes sense in the context
of Antiochus Epiphanes and his persecutions. 'From the fig tree
learn its parable'. The fig tree in its season, the spring, is an
indicator of historical season, the springtime of the messianic age
which is the *dénouement* of all history. Attention to this little point
within time, the fig tree in spring, opens the visionary eye to its
environing context – the whole temporal process and its goal. This,
not agricultural or botanical matters of fact, is the milieu which
determines and reveals the parable's meaning. It is interesting that
Jesus does not actually tell a parable here. He points to the fig tree
which is, or tells, its own parable. It is an indicaton of the

pervasiveness of the apocalyptic outlook on the historical world that for it everything becomes parable indicative of other and greater things. To it, *alles vergängliches ist nur ein Gleichnis* (Goethe, *Faust*, II.v): every transient thing is but a parable. The fig tree does not tell us about ordinary but about doomsday weather.

Last of all is the parable of *servants* at 13.33–7. Matthew and Luke both give fuller versions in their parables of *talents* or *pounds* (Matthew 25.14–30‖Luke 19.11–27). This one is sketchy, shorter on moral exhortation and entirely oriented on doomsday. Once again, its milieu is unmistakably the Church waiting for the second coming of its Lord. Hence its unrealistic quality: an actual householder would scarcely leave his home without some indication of when he would come back. But Mark is only secondarily and parabolically concerned with household management. The end of the world is his prime concern and he has just told us (verse 32) that 'of that day or that hour no one knows, not even the angels in heaven, nor the Son, but only the Father': a fine example of that integral secrecy which limits apocalyptic knowledge and thus gives an air of mystery to the parable. It is essential to the parable, but somewhat at variance with its homely imagery. It is, of course, essential to Mark's whole theology and method too. Once again we have the three Chinese boxes: the parable fits into Mark's book and Mark's book fits into an environing pattern of history.

The character of Mark's parables has emerged so clearly that only a brief resumé is needed to recapitulate it. Their first major feature is their continuity with preceding parabolic tradition. This had reached its climax with Ezekiel and the apocalyptic writers after him. They used parables to explain history and their parabolic method was the concatenation of symbolic figures in allegory. The meaning of history was a divine secret beyond it, not to be had by direct historical knowledge but by vision. To the apocalyptists history, while still of utmost importance, was not as morally and theologically transparent as it was to the historians of Solomon's court or of Deuteronomy. Clarity was elsewhere. The allegorical parable thus became a prime vehicle of historical explanation. And so it is in Mark. Of his two biggest parables, the *sower* gives the key to what is really going on in the ministry of Jesus, the *vineyard* gives the key to what is really going on in salvation history at large, including time before Jesus' ministry and time after it. Neither is as solidly realistic as, say, Luke's *prodigal son* or *good Samaritan* – but that, and the reasons for it, will be another story.

As well as the highly articulated allegory of which Ezekiel was the grand master, parables also came as brief and pithy sayings of which the riddle is a common variety. Ezekiel had these too, and so does Mark. The group in Mark 2 fall into this category: the *physician*, the *bridegroom*, the *clothes* and the *wineskins*. To these can be added the *divided house*, the *divided kingdom* and the *strong man despoiled* in chapter 3. Both sets consist of little riddles or conundrums. Yet again, to get the answers to them, to see what they mean, is to get the clue to history, to understand the historical significance of Jesus and early Christianity as a new and divinely powerful force which turns history towards its end. Another set of such little parables follows on the *sower* in chapter 4 and reinforces its theology of revelation. In chapters 7, 8 and 9 other little parables point up questions of purity and discipleship. The final pair, the *fig tree* and the *servants* in chapter 13, appropriately open the mind to the end of history. As with their Old Testament precedents, even the little parables are closely tied into the historical narrative which they illuminate. There is concern with ethics, but it is nothing like Matthew's, to whom we now turn as an evangelist converting Mark's theology and parables to more everyday and practical concerns.

4 Matthew

PARABLES IN MATTHEW

3.7	Snakes	(John the Baptist)
3.10	Tree and Fruit	
3.12	Threshing	

Sermon on the Mount

5.13	Salt	Mark
5.14–16	Light	Mark
5.25	Judge	Q
6.24	Two Masters	Q
7.3–5	Eye	Q
7.6	Pearls	
7.7–8	Asking and Knocking	Q
7.9–11	Loaves and Fishes	Q
7.13–14	Two Roads	Q
7.15	Sheep and Wolves	
7.16	Grapes and Figs	
7.17–20	Tree and Fruit	Q (Matt. 3.10)
7.21–3	Doomsday	Q
7.24–7	Two Houses	Q

Disciples

8.20	Foxes and Birds	Q
8.22	Burying the Dead	Q

Eating with Sinners

9.15	Bridegroom and Attendants	Mark
9.16	Clothes	Mark
9.17	Bottles	Mark

Crowds

9.36	Sheep and Shepherd	Mark
9.37	Harvest	(Matt. 3.12)

Apostles' Mission

10.16	Sheep and Wolves	Q	(Matt. 7.15)
	Serpents and Doves		

John the Baptist

11.7	Reed	Q	
11.16f	Children's Games	Q	

Beelzebub

12.29	Strong Man	Mark	
12.33	Tree and Fruit	Q	(Matt. 3.10)
			(Matt. 7.17–20)
12.35	Treasures	Q	
12.43–5	Empty House	Q	(Mark 9.25)

Sermon by the Sea

13.3–9	Sower	Mark
13.10–17	Theory	Mark
13.18–23	Interpretation of Sower	Mark
13.24–30	Wheat and Tares	
13.31f	Mustard Seed	Mark
13.33	Leaven or Yeast	Q
13.34f	Parable and Prophecy	Mark
13.36–43	Interpretation of Wheat and Tares	
13.44	Treasure	
13.45f	Pearl	
13.47f	Net	
13.49f	Interpretation of Net	
13.51f	Householder	Mark 13
13.53	End of Parables	

Vain Tradition

15.13	Plants	
15.14	Blind Guides	
15.17	Digestion	Mark
17.25	Kings and their Sons	

Discipleship

18.12–14	Lost Sheep	Q	(Matt. 7.15 10.16)
18.23–5	Two Debtors		
20.1–16	Labourers in Vineyard	Mark 12	
	(Disciples and Israel)		

71

Disciples, John Baptist and Israel

21.18–22	Fig Tree		(Mark 11.12–21)
21.28–32	Two Sons in Vineyard		Matt. 20.1–16
21.33–43	Vineyard		Matt. 21.1–16 (Mark 12)

Disciples and Israel

22.1–14	Marriage Feast	Q	(Mark 2.19f, 12)

Eschatology

24.42–4	Thief	Q	(1 Thess. 5.2)
24.45–51	Servant	Q	(Mark 13.34)
25.1–13	Ten Virgins		(Mark 2.19f)
25.14–30	Talents	Q	(Matt. 24.45–51)
25.31–46	Sheep and Goats		(Matt. 18.12–14)

Matthew 1—12

Matthew's Gospel is much longer than Mark's because it includes a great deal more teaching. It is to be expected that the additional teaching will include yet more parables. Mark, to whom Matthew is heavily indebted, presented Jesus' teaching as decidedly and deliberately parabolic. This was in keeping with the apocalyptic writings of the Old Testament and the intertestamental literature, which were the native soil of Christianity and had the same character. So Matthew had every reason for making his wealth of additional teaching of Jesus include many more parables. It would be capricious to doubt that Jesus himself taught in parables. But he was far from being the only teacher of his time to do so. Paul shows us that a Christian writer was capable of making up parables to illustrate his doctrine, even when he had as modest a natural talent for the work as Paul.

It has often been noticed that Matthew's additional teaching material clusters about four major concerns: Christian discipleship, Judaism, eschatology and Christology. He has much to say about the ethics of discipleship, both individual and corporate. He is concerned with the running of a Christian church, the conduct and spirituality of its members both on their own and within the Christian group. The Sermon on the Mount and the teaching in chapter 18 including the parable of the *lost sheep* are famous examples. He is also much concerned with the relation of new Christianity to old Judaism. In chapters 21 and 22 the two interests overlap, Christian discipleship being described in relation to the traditional religion and status of Israel. Parables about a vineyard, an accepted symbol of Israel since Isaiah at least, fix and illustrate it: the *labourers in the vineyard* and their wages (20.1–16), the *two sons* called by their father to work in the vineyard (21.28–32), and Mark's parable of the *vineyard* (21. 33–43). To these can be added the parable of the *marriage feast* at 22.1–14. Matthew's third major concern is with eschatology. To his version of Mark's eschatological chapter 13 he adds a catena of increasingly elaborate parables from the *thief* at 24.42–4 to the great doomsday scene of *sheep and goats* at 25.31–46.

The most important thing to notice from this rapid preview is the strong influence of the historical framework on all this didactic material. It may look time-free: ethical injunctions for any time and all times. In fact it is set firmly in history. For Matthew is editing Mark and Mark's historical-narrative bent is the major force in his parables. It carries over to Matthew who does not write a book of teaching like Proverbs or the hypothetical Q source. In spite of his didactic facility he writes a narrative of which the teaching is a part. He writes teaching which is always set in narrative to clarify and interpret it. More than that, his interest in the relation of the Church to Judaism is fundamentally a concern with an historical question or cluster of questions. To whom does the sacred past belong, Church or Synagogue? To whom will the sacred future belong, Church or Synagogue? And between these two questions: what did Jesus do and say to his disciples and to his compatriots, and who was he, that these questions should arise and that the answer to both should be 'Church'? The parables in chapters 22, 24 and 25 turn around these questions. More, Matthew's placing and handling of the *sower* complex from Mark 4 in his chapter 13 has been shown by J. D. Kingsbury to have an enhanced historical force by becoming the point at which Jesus turns from frustrated mission to Israel to fresh fields and pastures new – a sort of Matthean 'middle of time'.

Chapters 3–12   Figures, Metaphors and Similes

With the *sower* complex postponed until Matthew 13, we have to wait a surprisingly long time for Matthew to present us with a full-scale parable – meaning by that the kind of complex allegory which was the third of our Old Testament categories and of which Mark's *sower* and *vineyard* were examples. There are narrative reasons for this delay which we have glanced at (the function of the *sower* as a commentary on the mid-point of the story) and which we will explore more fully. Meanwhile, there are plenty of examples of the second of the Old Testament categories, the figurative saying or metaphor. John the Baptist uses them in his preaching. The Sermon on the Mount is full of them and on several occasions they are long enough to border on the more elaborate form of parable. Jesus uses them to justify his eating with sinners and his exorcisms, in sending the twelve on their mission and discussing the role of John the Baptist. The list at pp. 70–2 gives some idea of their number and character. Little as they are, they still give indications of Matthew's purpose and method with parables which are the best possible way of establishing a point of view for understanding the bigger parables from chapter 13 onwards. So they are worth some careful attention.

The appearance of John the Baptist on the historical scene is a charged historical moment which Matthew inherits from Mark. His contribution is to add explicit teaching by the Baptist to compound the sense of historical crisis. His gives him a replica of Jesus' eschatological summons at Mark 1.15: 'Repent, for the kingdom of heaven is at hand' (3.2). And in 3.7–12 John has preaching of his own which is not in Mark.

> But when he saw many of the Pharisees and Sadducees coming for baptism, he said to them, 'You brood of vipers! Who warned you to flee from the wrath to come? Bear fruit that befits repentance, and do not presume to say to yourselves, "We have Abraham as our father"; for I tell you, God is able from these stones to raise up children to Abraham. Even now the axe is laid to the root of the trees; every tree therefore that does not bear good fruit is cut down and thrown into the fire. I baptize you with water for repentance, but he who is coming after me is mightier than I, whose sandals I am not worthy to carry; he will baptize you with the Holy Spirit and with fire. His winnowing fork is in his hand, and he will clear his threshing floor and gather his wheat into the granary, but the chaff he will burn with unquenchable fire.'

It contains twenty words listed by Goulder as semi-Matthean, that is 'they occur twice as often in Matthew as in Mark *and* more often than in Luke; or they are inserted redactionally by Matthew into an agreed Marcan context or OT citation' (M. D. Goulder, *Midrash and Lection in Matthew* [SPCK 1974] p. 476). This suggests that John's preaching may in fact be Matthew's own composition. If not, it is a very Matthean version of Q. The figures used are agricultural or natural and all are turned to the eschatological purpose which is a strong Matthean trait, particularly in conjunction with ethics. He speaks of snakes, fruit, stones, axe, tree, fire and winnowing. Behind it stands the prophecy of Malachi 4.1:

> Behold a day comes burning as an oven ... and all that do wickedly shall be as stubble: and the day that is coming shall set them alight ... and there shall not be left of them root or branch.

Fire, which had been a prophetic stock image since Amos, is taken up enthusiastically by Matthew who uses it seven times after this and always in the context of doomsday. Tree and fruit were also commonplaces of prophetic imagery. The use of them here is paralleled later in Matthew at 7.17–20, where Jesus uses it towards the end of the Sermon on the Mount. There is a case for Matthean authorship which is strengthened by the setting: 'Pharisees and Sadducees' at verse 7 is a phrase peculiar to Matthew who uses it five times. But the whole content of John's preaching and its manner show typical tropes of Matthew's which will become more familiar as we go on. John, like Jesus in his preaching, uses metaphors. The preaching concentrates ethics upon the vision of the end which is definitively divisive between good and bad. In the same perspective Judaism is put into historical crisis, the Pharisees and Sadducees being part of a 'generation' facing doom. For the Messiah is about to come upon it to divide, with his winnowing-fan, wheat from chaff: one for the barn, the other for the fire. History, ethics, Christ and eschatology are the main ingredients of John's teaching, and they are of Matthew's too.

With the Sermon on the Mount we meet another of his leading themes – discipleship. After the beatitudes come the similes of salt and light. The *salt* comes from Mark 9.49f. (see p. 63). The Marcan obscurity and complication are relieved by the omission of the saying, 'have salt in yourselves and be at peace with one another', and some of its force is assimilated by Matthew's much more explicit note that 'you (the disciples) are the salt of the earth'. Likewise, though Mark's 'every one will be salted with fire' disappears, some of its tone is present since the immediately preceding verses have been about disciples under persecution. The motif of throwing out shows that Matthew is at work: the note of exclusion which it adds to the Marcan source is very much in his line and will feature powerfully at the end of many of his parables. Matthew makes plain what was implicit in Mark: that the disciples are the salt of the earth. And he stresses Mark's negative: unsalty salt is thrown out.

Matthew clarifies again in the very next verse with 'You are the light of the world'. The metaphor comes from the riddle at Mark 4.21 'Is a lamp brought in to be put under a bed...?'. The use of the metaphor of *light* is neatly indicative of the tendencies of each of the New Testament Gospels. For Mark it is the light of revelation and its form is the riddle, the question; for Matthew it is the light of true discipleship which illuminates 'all in the house', all in the Church: he adds straight metaphor to Mark's riddle. For Luke (8.16 and 11.33) it is a light to guide those entering a house and so serves his interest in the growth of the Church by the entry of new members. And for John at 8.12 it is Jesus himself ('I am the light of the world'), with John engaged in his overall strategy of packing up and tightening his Christology. The metaphor is an Old Testament commonplace, notably in Psalm 119. At Philippians 2.15 as in Matthew, Christians are lights in the world. The two verses Matthew 5.15–16 contain six Matthean words and six of Goulder's semi-Matthean ones: an unmistakable sign of a strong editorial hand. The metaphor is enriched and complicated by Matthew inserting in the middle of it the additional metaphor of a city set on a hill. Twice more he will pair house and city in a Marcan context where there is no such pairing, at Matthew 10.14 and 12.25. The motif of hiddenness which Matthew associates with the city, and which he derives from Mark and makes more explicit again, will reappear in his chapter 13. It does not obtrude here. What does obtrude, and powerfully, is his added emphasis on discipleship. It is there at the beginning with, 'You are the light of the world'. It is there at the end in the thoroughly Matthean verse 16:

Let your light so shine before men, that they may see your good works and glorify your father which is in heaven.

So the light metaphor, and how he develops it from his Marcan material, is a clear indication of Matthew's editorial policy and interests: Christian discipleship in an ecclesiastical context manifested in good works which glorify the heavenly father. He will use the metaphor again at 6.22f in the Sermon in the context of individual discipleship: 'the light of the body is the eye'.

The rest of the Sermon is full of metaphors as the list makes plain. They all come in pairs, a pattern characteristic of Matthew: *two masters* (6.24), birds and flowers (6.26–30), logs and specks (7.3–5), dogs and pigs (7.6), *asking and knocking* (7.7–8), *loaves and fishes*, stones and snakes (7.9–11), *two roads* (7.13–14), *sheep and wolves* (7.15), *grapes and figs,* thorns and thistles (7.16), good *trees and fruit* with bad trees and fruit (7.17–20, strongly reminiscent of 3.10), *two houses* (7.24–7). It is a simple scheme, this working by twos, which will dominate Matthew's grander parables when he gets round to them. They work by the deployment of two different sets of people or by two contrasted individuals. Even where he has more than one group he likes to fine them down to two (the *labourers* and the *talents*). The method testifies to a strong moral dualism which is deeply set in Matthew's mind, sorting people out, *sub specie* of eschatology, into good and bad with a confident simplicity which contrasts with Luke's more nuanced and developmental view of human nature. We can pick out from the list three examples where the dualism works by contrasting two things of the same sort: two masters, two roads, two houses. They show how firm and clear it is. Three other examples bring in an element of complication by introducing a contrast: sheep and wolves, grapes and thorns, figs and thistles. Here is the deliberate and provocative nonsense of the riddle. The complication is absurdity, so Matthew's simple and severe dualism is vindicated. There are no good people who do badly or bad people who do well. However complex life may seem now, in the end all will be solved with an unequivocal yes or no. It is the old apocalyptic hope in the midst of perplexity, though one has to admit that Matthew only glimpses perplexity in order to dispel it. He is not *in tormentis* as Mark was, or 2 Esdras, or Ezekiel were, and his congregation need never have complained of the lack of a clear moral lead from him.

Between the end of the Sermon and the beginning of chapter 13 metaphorical parables are less frequent. Narrative dominates. But there are metaphorical parables, well integrated with narrative, and concerned with history and time like the earlier metaphors of John the Baptist's. Two groups, and a single parable lying between them, claim and repay attention.

The first group is the three in 9.14–17: the *bridegroom*, the *clothes* and the *wineskins*. Their context is the question by disciples of John, 'Why do we and the Pharisees fast, but your disciples do not fast?' Jesus' answer is that times have changed – critically and decisively. But he gives it in the form of these three little parables. They all run parallel with Mark 2.18–22, Matthew having been busy with editing Mark's narrative since the end of the Sermon. As in Mark, they serve to bring out what is significantly going on within and underneath the train of events. They give the key to the history. The editing of Mark here is so slight and sparing that we need not work over them again. It need only be noted that believers in Q are embarrassed by the agreement of Matthew with Luke to omit as redundant the second half of Mark 2.19, 'as long as they have the bridegroom with them, they cannot fast'. But this very slightness of editing is important because it shows that Matthew is every bit as concerned as Mark with forging a Christian understanding of history, with the ministry of Jesus forming the determinative crisis which changes its course and conditions. And Matthew follows Mark in using parables to explain it.

The parable of *children's games* at 11.16–17 is a particularly neat example of parable as historical allegory. As H. B. Green correctly observes, 'Matthew uses it to illustrate his own view of sacred history. The Jews have rejected not only their Messiah, but along with him the authentic representative of the old Israel. Hence their own rejection by God' (*The Gospel according to Matthew* [Oxford 1975] pp. 117f). In common with Jeremias and many others Green believes Matthew to be using an existing parable of Jesus. An argument for this is that it accurately reflects Palestinian wedding and funeral customs: men danced at weddings, girls wailed at funerals. Against this, as against all such arguments that Palestinian detail indicates the authorship of Jesus, it must be said that such details were *ex hypothesi* available to Matthew and thousands of other people. Another argument, used by Jeremias at p. 160n, is that rhyme is got by retranslation into Aramic. The previous argument applies again here: a lot of people spoke Aramaic, probably including Matthew. Also, as Goulder (p. 357n) notes, 'suffixes always yield rhyme when antitheses are as neat as Matthew's.' The further argument that the parable takes a high view of the status of John the Baptist is simply not true. It is inattention to John, not his status, that the parable is about, and that is something which the Old Testament prophets had suffered too – an historical reflection which both Mark and Matthew use in their parables (the *vineyard*, the *marriage feast*). Matthew is emphatic that the rejection of Jesus was precedented by, and continuous with, the rejection of his prophetic predecessors (Matthew 5.12; 23.31 and 37). The parable looks as Matthean as Matthew 21.32 which Jeremias accepts as Matthew's:

> For John came to you in the way of righteousness, and you did not believe him, but the tax collectors and the harlots believed him; and even when you saw it, you did not afterward repent and believe him.

Further, the marriage imagery in this parable is a favourite of Matthew's, who adds to Mark's parable of Jesus as bridegroom the *ten virgins* and the *marriage feast*. The pattern of twos is characteristic of him too: piping for dancing, wailing for mourning; John neither eating nor drinking, Jesus eating and drinking; John as a demoniac, Jesus as a glutton and drunkard. Since it also fulfils the major requirement of a parable by illustrating the evangelist's own view of sacred history it can be sufficiently understood as an integral part of Matthew's Gospel.

The second group is at Matthew 12.29–45 and includes the *strong man, tree and fruit* (again!), *treasures* and, after a passage about signs at verses 38–42, the *empty house*. The context is the question of the source of Jesus' power, which the Pharisees say comes from Beelzebub. The first metaphor, the *strong man*, is copied from Mark virtually word for word. The second, *tree and fruit*, is enjoying its third appearance in the Gospel (previously at 3.10 and 7.16–19) and holds no surprises for us in its obsessive but proper hatred of hypocrisy. The third, good and bad *treasures*, is as thoroughly Matthean. Of its nineteen words one is Matthean and nine are semi-Matthean. It is shaped by clear contrast of good and bad, with the 'bringing out' (literally 'throwing out') motif exhibiting yet again Matthew's concern with inner and outer as well as with dualistic sorting-out. Treasure is a favourite figure of Matthew's. It has already appeared in the Sermon: 'Where your treasure is, there will your heart be also' (Matthew 6.21), which is clearly apposite to this metaphor. It will appear again in the parable of the *treasure* hidden in a field at 13.44 and the concluding parable of chapter 13 about the scribe converted to the Kingdom of God who is like a householder bringing out of his treasure things old and new. At 19.21 the rich postulant is promised treasure in heaven if he will sell up and follow Jesus. This is a borrowing from Mark, and possibly the source of the treasure figure which Matthew uses more, and more parabolically, than his source. The *talents* at Matthew 25.14–30 is its grandest development. So, of this group of three metaphors, one, the *strong man*, is a faithful retailing of Mark. For the origin of the other two, *tree and fruit* and *treasure*, we need look no further than Matthew with the *treasure* having Marcan precedent. The answer to the calumny of the Pharisees is first historical: Jesus is the stronger man who despoils the strong man. The times have changed. The metaphor is a little allegory of Jesus, Satan and Satan's household of evil spirits. Then comes a moral answer in terms of Matthew's conviction of the congruence of inner and outer: good can only come of good, evil of evil.

In this trio the more historical parable comes from Mark. But the parable of the *empty house* does not. At least, not as a parable: at Mark 9.25 Jesus expelling a demon from a boy saying, 'Come out of him and never enter him again' may have prompted this parable.

It has long perplexed commentators, as being psychologically telling and haunting yet difficult to explain in terms of Jesus' precise purpose. It is separated from the previous metaphorical parables by a passage (Matthew 12.38–42) of invective against the 'evil and adulterous generation' which seeks a sign but ignores the sign it is given: Christ. Christ, like Jonah, was three days entombed (Jonah in the fish's belly, he in 'the heart of the earth'). Christ like Jonah preached repentance, He got repentance from the Ninevites, whereas Christ preaching it to Israel met with no such success. The Queen of Sheba came to hear Solomon's wisdom but Israel ignores the wisdom of the Christ greater than Solomon. There can be no mistaking that Matthew is dealing in history, and in terms of the crisis of decision brought to Israel by Christ, the negative response of Israel and the positive response of Gentiles. Nor can there be any mistaking that in all this, as in Mark's vineyard parable, the most likely standpoint or point of view is retrospective and in subsequent church history beyond Christ's death and resurrection. All this precedes the parable of the *empty house* and immediately after it comes the definition of those who belong with Christ: not his natural kin but 'whoever does the will of my father' (Matthew 12.50). This is the parable's setting: the doom of Israel. The frame is historical. So it is worth taking up the suggestion of the setting and seeing whether the parable too might refer to the fate of Israel as seen through the eyes of early Christian historiography. There is a hint that this is so in the reminiscences of the Exodus in the picture of the wanderer, like Israel in the wilderness, going through dry places seeking rest, not finding it, and longing to return to the point of departure. Hebrews 3 and 4 are about the failure of Israel to enter the rest ordained for the Church, and Matthew 11.29 has promised rest to the obedient disciple of Christ. Could the empty house which the man finds on his return be the empty and subjugated land left behind by the Roman armies after AD 70? The suggestion is offered tentatively, though it is supported by the common Old Testament use of 'house' for the Temple. But the conclusion of the parable gives it weight. 'The last state of that man becomes worse than the first.' The juggling of last and first is used by Matthew at the end of the parable of the *labourers* at 20.16, and at 19.30 in the context of eschatological judgement (following Mark 10.31). In the *labourers* parable, 'the last will be first, and the first last', indicates the standing of late-come Christianity over long-standing Judaism. In this *empty house* parable, by the same token, the man whose last state is worse than his first could aptly represent traditional Judaism. It is addressed to the scribes and Pharisees. Its last words give further weight to such an historical-allegorical interpretation: 'so shall it be also with this evil generation'. The parable would then fit into Matthew's major theme of the doom of Israel. As we are now on the threshold of his version of Mark's

80

sower, which he will treat and sharpen precisely in terms of this historical theme, the suggestion seems highly plausible. Matthew's hand in the parable can be seen in the fifteen Matthean or semi-Matthean words in its three verses. The phrase 'worse than the first' is also used at 27.64 in a passage peculiar to Matthew where the chief priests and Pharisees represent to Pilate their fear that the dead Christ's disciples will invent a resurrection 'and the last fraud will be worse than the first'. With such signs of Matthew's work in the parable it is sensible to look for congruence with his ideas. The very important idea of Israel's supersession and desolation recommends itself both by the setting of the parable and by the major features of its content.

Matthew 13

With chapter 13 Matthew goes into a higher parabolic gear. Up until now he has used figures and metaphors. They have only rarely been long enough to qualify for membership of the third and grandest of the Old Testament categories, the allegorical historical parable. The *two houses* at the end of the Sermon on the Mount and the *empty house* at the end of the chapter 12 are the strongest candidates: two 'house' parables. Mark, incidentally, had no house parables, but used Jesus in the house with his disciples as a recurring image. Parables have been loosened from Mark's theory of secrecy by Matthew and have been used simply to explain and clarify. On both these counts things will be different now: parables will come bigger and darker. But there is continuity. The metaphors which we have seen so far exhibit traits which are maintained in chapter 13. Matthew has shown himself to be much concerned with discipleship. The metaphors in the Sermon on the Mount were about it. So were two in chapter 8 (*foxes and birds* at 8.20 and *burying the dead* at 8.22) and the metaphors of *sheep and wolves*, *serpents and doves* which were included in the charge to the twelve apostles at 10.16. But this concern with true discipleship is often sharpened by contrast, embedded in Matthew's strong moral dualism. The *two masters, two roads* and *two houses* in the Sermon examplified it. A third feature of the metaphors to date is the concern with history. It marked those in the preaching of John the Baptist in chapter 3. It was there in the three metaphors in 9.15–17; *bridegroom, cloth* and *wineskins*, which all came from Mark. It was there in the simile of *children's games* at 11.16–17 which explained the historical significance of John the Baptist. It was there in the metaphor of the *strong man*, following Mark, in the Beelzebub argument at 12.29; and at the conclusion of that argument it seems to have shaped the parable of the *empty house*. These three features – discipleship, dualism and history – will be strong in chapter 13 as Matthew sets himself to give his version of Mark 4, that chief and central passage for the study of gospel parables. But here, at long last, Matthew turns to the editing and composition of full-dress parables and to give us his theology of them. It will emerge as monumentally historical in its focus on the historic significance of Christ, in a way of which we have so far had only strong hints.

Let us briefly survey what is in front of us to get our bearings. First, Matthew gives a reasonably faithful version of Mark's *sower* parable, prefacing it with a more precise note of time: in 'that same day' (13.1). Then comes Mark's theology of parables. Its strong negative tendency is balanced by a positive consideration added by Matthew: the disciples are blessed because they see and hear what prophets and good men had longed for (Matthew 13.16f). Mark's distinction between insiders and outsiders is, in effect, changed to Christians and Jews. The interpretation of the *sower* is only slightly edited. Then comes the parable of the *wheat and tares* (Matthew 13.24–30), an elaboration of Mark's *seed growing secretly*. It is followed by the parables of the *mustard seed* (Mark) and the *leaven* (not Mark). A note about the historical significance of Jesus' use of parables follows: it fulfils prophecy and uncovers things hidden from the beginning of time (Matthew 13.34f). The parable of the *wheat and tares* is then interpreted as the *sower* has been. Three similes follow, not called parables as the previous examples were: *hidden treasure*, the precious *pearl* and the drag *net*. A further simile, about parabolic method, concludes the collection. At verse 53 we are told that Jesus 'finished these parables' and, coming into 'his own country', was rejected.

Matthew is being very deliberate. Particularly, he is tidying up Mark's tangle of dark mystery by historical reflection which draws on the Old Testament and resorts to further parables which amplify the historical framework of Mark's paradox of secrecy and revelation. Mark's single mystery becomes plural mysteries – teachings rather than a riddle. He is just as thoroughly deliberate in having his version of Mark 4 at this particular point of his narrative.

The discoverer of the narrative strategy of Matthew 13 was J. D. Kingsbury.

The function of chapter 13 within the ground plan of Matthew's gospel is to signal the great 'turning point'. By definition, the great turning point has to do with the flow of events in the ministry of Jesus as recorded by Matthew in dependence on Mark. Thus, Matthew depicts Jesus as coming to the Jews with a ministry of teaching, preaching and healing (4.17, 23; 9.35; 11.1). In addition, Jesus empowers and dispatches his twelve disciples to undertake an identical mission (10.1–8). But, in spite of such activity, the Jews on all sides reject Jesus as the Messiah and inaugurator of God's eschatological kingdom (Chapters 11—12). In reaction to this, Jesus himself turns against the Jews. He charges them with being a people that is deaf, blind and without understanding in regard to God's revelation to them (13.13), and he lends substance to this charge by speaking to them, not openly as before, but in parables, which are enigmatic forms of speech (13.10f, 13). The reverse of this is that Jesus addresses his disciples as the true people of God (13.10–17). This phenomenon, namely Jesus' turning away from the Jews and towards his disciples, is what is meant by the great 'turning point'.

(*The Parables of Jesus in Matthew 13* [SPCK 1969] p. 130)

Kingsbury is right and his thesis only needs amplification. Chapter 11 consisted of teaching about history: John the Baptist's place within it and Jesus', the parable of *children's games* to satirize the mugwumpery of 'this generation', the doom of Chorazin and Bethsaida for not noticing 'the mighty works', the revelation to babes of what is hidden from the wise by the Son who alone knows the Father and reveals him. In chapter 12 miracles are followed at 12.17 by an Old Testament quotation showing Jesus to be the promised servant of God; quiet and humble, destined for the Gentiles. Matthew further makes several additions to Mark's account of the Beelzebub controversy which point up its historical significance *vis-à-vis* Israel. 'If I by Beelzebub cast out devils, by whom do your sons cast them out?' (12.27). 'He who is not with me is against me' (12.30). The 'generation of vipers' is attacked in 12.34–7 after the added metaphor of *tree and fruit*. The addition to Mark at Matthew 12.40–5 is entirely concerned with historical crisis in terms of two ancient precedents, Jonah and Solomon, and includes the (arguably) historical *empty house* parable.

All this generates a sense of ominous historical crisis as the setting of chapter 13. The Christ was not accepted by his generation. Two reasons for it have emerged. It was because they were deeply wicked and perverse, fundamentally incapable of good – the theme of the editorial additions we have just noticed. It was also because the Christ was unobtrusively revealed – the theme of the christological addition from Isaiah at 12.17. Here

Matthew has elucidated Mark's grand theme of the secrecy of Christ's theological nature in terms of the obduracy of his hearers and of Christ's character – but note that the character of Christ is entirely scriptural. The Messiah, though public – or because public – is hidden before he is revealed. The perversity of the nation and the nature of christology are the reasons for the failure. Its effect is two divisions. There is a division of history, falling between John the Baptist and Jesus (11.11–15), between the old dispensation and the new (12.38–42). There is also a division between people as believers or unbelievers (11.20, 25ff; 12.30 and 35). 'He who is not with me is against me' (contrast Mark 9.40).

Mark's doctrine of history, which structured his parables, Matthew confirmed and illustrated by ethics: the bad tree cannot yield good fruit. All this is gathered into chapter 13 by its first words, 'in that same day'. It is the same day as the christological quotation of Isaiah and, more precisely, of the Beelzebub controversy. After the parables Jesus is rejected in his own country. The historical setting could hardly be more thorough or polemical.

When we looked at Mark 4 we considered the wider historical setting as well as the setting in the book: what view of historical process as a whole informed the parables? We will do the same here. The key text comes when all the parables have been uttered (that is, the parables labelled by Matthew as such) and before the parable of *wheat and tares* is interpreted. It is 13.34f:

> All this Jesus said to the crowd in parables; indeed he said nothing to them without a parable. This was to fulfil what was spoken by the prophet:
> 'I will open my mouth in parables,
> I will utter what has been hidden since the foundation of the world.'

The first sentence of this quotation is an exact rendition of the Septuagint. The second is not. The Septuagint has, 'I will declare problems from the beginning' (*phthenxomai problēmata ap' archēs*). Matthew has literally, 'I will find out hidden things from the foundation' (*ereuxomai kekrummena apo katabolēs*). Reference to the *katabolē*/foundation is found elsewhere in the Gospels only at Matthew 25.34, in the parable of *sheep and goats* where the just are bidden to inherit the kingdom prepared for them from the foundation of the world. So what Jesus tells in parables has its origin in the dark, backward abysm of time, the beginning of creation. It will have import for the end of time. And this Jesus who tells parables is the one who has been described in the highly important Matthew 11.25–7: the Son who shows things hidden by

84

the Father from the wise to babes, who alone knows and reveals the Father. It is a text akin to John's Christology, perhaps helped to form it. But it is central to Matthew too and not an alien intrusion into his work. Indeed, it is essential to his tripartite historical scheme. What was hidden at the foundation will be finally revealed at doomsday. But at the critical point between the two stands Jesus, speaking in parables which combine the hiddenness of the beginning with the revelation of the end. Jesus' revelation is under the semi-propitious and ambivalent conditions in which parables are thoroughly apt. In mythological views of history such as Matthew inherited, end and beginning are both simple. In the transition between the two there is mixture, as Matthew knew so well in his own church congregation. This transition from hiddenness to clarity is the centre of Matthew's theology of history and forms the basic movement of the parables in this chapter. Parables hold, and even *are*, the axis of the historical turning point by virtue of their very nature and method. To put it in a diagram:

CREATION   JESUS   DOOMSDAY

Hidden   → Hidden/Revealed in Parables → Revealed

Such is the scope of the scribe converted to the Kingdom of God, Matthew himself, who brings out of his treasure things new and old. It is, decidedly and obviously, an apocalyptic scheme in which visions of ancient origin connect to visions of future destiny through the midpoint of a problematically critical present. At this point what has long been hidden is uncovered – but in adverse and penultimate conditions which make it the sign and beginning of the ultimate and unconditioned uncovering of doomsday rather than that day itself. Matthew would say, more succinctly, that it is revealed 'in parables'. We have had to work hard to recover what he meant by that, because modern ideas of parable do not dispose us towards it.

Having got hold of this scheme with its axial turning point we can see Matthew's strategy in chapter 13 with fresh eyes. The 'stage directions' give broad confirmatory hints.

The parable of the *sower* is told in public to great crowds. This setting holds right through to 13.34–6 where Matthew tells us clearly and laboriously that Jesus spoke to the crowds in parables but now leaves the crowds and goes into the house. Within the public setting which holds up to this point, belong the *sower* (1–9), the theology of parables (10–17), the interpretation of the *sower* (18–23), the parables of *wheat and tares*, *mustard seed* and *yeast* (24–33). But the public nature of this section is not absolute. After the telling of the *sower* parable 'the disciples came and said to him "Why do you speak to them in parables?"'. Matthew seems to have forgotten that Jesus is in a boat. If he has, it is because other interests have preoccupied him, and especially his dominant interest in Christian discipleship. So for verses 10–23 there is within the public scene an inner circle of disciples being addressed by Jesus who is temporarily oblivious of the crowds. To them he gives a version of Mark's theology of parables. They are baffling not *so that* (Greek *hina*) people *should* not understand them. They are baffling *because* (Greek *hoti*) people *will* not understand them – a perversity of which the preceding chapters 11 and 12 have given plenty of illustrations. To this negative judgement Matthew adds happier teaching of the blessedness of the disciples in seeing and hearing: the historically privileged position they occupy is better than anyone's in the Old Testament! Then Jesus tells the disciples the interpretation of the *sower*, after which he addresses 'them'. Who are 'they'? Consistently in this chapter the pronoun is reserved for the Jewish crowds. They get three more parables, each introduced as such: *wheat and tares, mustard seed* and *leaven*. They are all about an intermediate state of confusion, littleness, hiddenness; the confusion will clarify, the littleness grow, the hidden be seen.

So the first scene is public with an intimate interlude for disciples in the middle of it. It closes with the note about the historical significance and function of parables which we have looked at, after which Jesus 'left the crowds and went into the house' (Matthew 13.36). With the change of setting (once again Matthew seems to have forgotten the boat) all sense of concealment is abandoned. The parable of *wheat and tares* is interpreted with maximum stress on the traditional secrets of the apocalyptic 'close of the age'; angels, fire, and a loose quotation of Daniel 12.3 about the triumph of the righteous. Three similes follow. In the *treasure* simile the emphasis is on its finding, digging up and purchase rather than the preliminary hiding of it – a marked change of emphasis from the previous and similar 'hiddenness' parable of *yeast*. The same trait is noticeable in the similes of *pearl* and *net*. It is in the final outcome of finding and purchase, catching and sorting out that the significance lies. And so it is too with the concluding simile of the householder bringing out of his treasure things new and old. It is the bringing out which counts, no matter how the things got there. The shift of significant emphasis from hiddenness to discovery is entirely appropriate to the change of scene and audience. In the house, or Church, is gathered the eschatological and enlightened community of Christian disciples, heirs of ancient

86

tradition and of Kingdom come. They can see and hear what prophets and righteous men had longed to see and hear. What has been hidden since the foundaton of the world is shown to them.

The drama of the chapter, in stage directions and didactic content, presents in miniature the drama of the gospel story from beginning to end. Within this majestic framework it only remains to notice some features which have so far been neglected, but confirm our findings. To take them in order and as a list:

1   By having omitted the word 'parables' at 12.25 when he retailed Mark's *divided kingdom* figure (Mark 3.23), Matthew makes 13.3 his first use of the word. It occurs twelve times in chapter 13 and five times later on. So it is reserved for that latter half of the book which begins with chapter 13 and in which tension is tighter than before.

2   Matthew has used Mark's parable of the *light* already in the Sermon on the Mount where he applied it to disciples. But he kept the saying appended to it there, 'to him who has will more be given: from him who has not will be taken what he has', and puts it in his section on the theology of parables at 13.12. There it proclaims the division brought about by parables, amplifying Mark's material about the disciples who have been given the mystery (Matthew 'mysteries') of the Kingdom and those outside who only get parables. In the same context, Matthew's disciples are not just 'given' the mystery. they are given to *know* it. Mark's dualism is made more balanced and more intelligible by Matthew's ending.

3   In the parable of the *wheat and tares*, 43 words out of 137 are Matthean or semi-Matthean. But in it there are words also featuring in, and important to, Mark's parable of the *seed growing secretly* which has otherwise disappeared: man, sleep, grew up (*eblastēsen*), plant (*chortos*), fruit, harvest. This suggests that Matthew's full-blown parable is a much amplified version of Mark's little one. In the simile of the *treasure* there are 12 Matthean or semi-Matthean words out of 30, in the *pearl* 10 out of 23, in the *net* 30 out of 71, in the *householder* 13 out of 22. Few scholars dispute the Matthean authorship of the interpretation of the *wheat and tares*, which is conclusively demonstrated by Jeremias (pp. 81ff). Yet it contains a slightly lower proportion of Matthean and semi-Matthean words, some 37 out of 156, than these examples. If it is full of 'Matthean thought and theology to the very core' (Kingsbury, p. 95), 'the work of Matthew himself' (Jeremias, p. 85), then the same ought to apply to these other parables.

4   In the similes of *treasure* and *pearl* a major part is played by the inner/outer duality which informed so many of Matthew's previous similes. To the apocalyptic mind of Matthew this contrast holds the eternal secret behind the historical and ethical dualism of the chapter. There is scope for later gnostic development here, and the *Gospel of Thomas* has the *treasure* at §109 with a world-denying interpretation, the *pearl* at §76 with a spiritual interpretation. But Thomas eschews the *net*: for Matthew, however concerned with the human moral interior, is no gnostic but traditionally eschatological. Divine action in judgement has the last word.

Christians and Israel   Matthew 15—22

Matthew next uses parables in Jesus' debate with Pharisees and scribes from Jerusalem at 15.1–20. He here follows Mark 7.1–23 as he has been following Mark since the end of chapter 13, and controversy with the leaders of traditional Judaism is an attractive topic. But at the same time the subject of this argument embarrasses him. Mark's text is a straight and energetic attack on the oral tradition which rabbinic teaching added to Scripture as exposition of it. Matthew upholds it. At 23.2 he has Jesus say, 'the scribes and Pharisees sit on Moses' seat: all things therefore whatsoever they bid you, do and observe'. It is not an injunction which has lodged in subsequent Christian policy, but it is all the more striking for its singularity. Matthew believed in the authority of Jewish oral and expository teaching and thought that the Church should submit to it. Here in Mark he is confronted by a text which denies it, while supplying useful ammunition for his preoccupying denunciation of Jewish obduracy. So he alters the text in various ways to suit his more traditionalist, but still polemical, viewpoint.

Jesus finishes his Marcan critique of tradition with the saying about defilement: nothing which enters a man defiles him, but rather what comes out of him. At this point Matthew introduces a protest and answer before Jesus' exposition of the saying:

> Then the disciples came and said to him, 'Do you know that the Pharisees were offended when they heard this saying?'
>
> (Matthew 15.12)

Jesus rebuts it with a saying in the form of a parabolic metaphor:

> 'Every plant which my heavenly Father has not planted will be rooted up.'   (Matthew 15.13)

It clearly recalls the parable of *wheat and tares*, and by virtue of being a string of Matthean words ('heavenly Father', 'rooted up', and 'plant/planted' (*phuteia/ephuteusen*) which occurs only here in the Gospels) seems to be a Matthean recapitulation of that Matthean parable. Its effect is to postpone the resolution of the argument to a later historical event, either the future destruction of Jerusalem or doomsday. For the present, Jesus' advice is 'Let them alone' – with another parabolic metaphor:

> 'Let them alone; they are blind guides. And if a blind man leads a blind man, both will fall into a pit.' (Matthew 15.14)

It is dominated by the Matthean words 'blind' and 'guide' as noun and verb; it refers to Leviticus 19.14 'You shall not put a stumbling block before the blind'; and the 'let them alone' (Greek *aphete*) recalls the previous *aphete* concerning the *tares* at 13.30. It again leaves the resolution of the controversy to the course of events. Another stroke of Matthean editing follows. Mark 7.17 reads:

> And when he had entered the house, and left the people, his disciples asked him about the parable.

'The parable' is the immediately (in Mark, but not Matthew) preceding saying about digestion whereby the body cleanses itself of waste. Matthew has instead

> But Peter said to him, 'Explain the parable to us'.
> (Matthew 5.15)

In place of Mark's deliberate seclusion of disciples and Jesus in 'the house', Matthew has a conversation of Peter, the prince of disciples, with Jesus *within* the public scene set up at 15.10: His church and its disciples are more set in the world than Mark's. It is clear that Matthew is editing, for to get to 'the parable' in question we have to skip back awkwardly, over the intervening parables of *blind guides* and *plants* to the saying about defilement. It is a parable of the second sort in the Old Testament list (p. 9): a figurative saying or metaphor. The processes of physical digestion, eating and excreting, are seen as standing for processes of mental or spiritual digestion. The very manoeuvre of treating regulations allegorically takes away from their force: a source of anxiety to Jewish exegetes of the time (see Lauterbach, 'Ancient Jewish Allegorists', in *Jewish Quarterly Review* 1 [1910–11], pp. 301ff). Matthew can take such allegorizing of law from Mark but not his thoroughgoing, radical antinomianism. He omits Mark's 'cannot defile him' from his 15.17. He omits from the explanation of this parable Mark's note, 'Thus he declared all foods clean' (Mark 7.19). All he will allow is that 'to eat with unwashed hands does not defile a man'. The rule against defilement may be ineffectual, but it is not attacked. He is as chary of jettisoning Jewish dietary laws at a stroke as of abandoning Jewish oral tradition. This reticence has motivated his editing. That done, the *digestion* parable suits Matthew's concern with inner and outer ethics, and with the purity of heart of his beatitude (Matthew 5.8). Adjustment of Mark's more cavalier attitude to Judaism occurs again in the healing of the gentile Canaanite woman's daughter which follows. Matthew adds the saying of Jesus, 'I was sent only to the lost sheep of the house of Israel'.

The next parables occur in chapter 18 in the context of Jesus giving rules and norms of church life and discipline. There are two of them: the *lost sheep* and the *two debtors*. A long and important series of events leads up to them in Matthew 15.21—17.27, which is a version of the same series in Mark 7.24—9.32. At their centre, a famous watershed or focus, is Peter's acknowledgement of Jesus as the Christ and the visionary display of Jesus' status in the transfiguration. Predictions of suffering frame it on either side. Christology, the truth about the Gospel's central figure, is the monumental gathering point of the whole section which Matthew inherits from Mark (Matthew 16.13–20‖Mark 8.27–30). In his hands it keeps its character as focal revelation of Christ; with editorial interventions which add a parallel demonstration of the nature of the Church, lacking in Mark: Peter's acknowledgement of Jesus as Messiah is amplified by Jesus' congratulating him on being the recipient of supernatural revelation and instating him as the rock on which the Church is built, the conclusive authority on earth of the Kingdom of heaven. A further substantial addition by Matthew to Mark's narrative is at 17.24–7. Peter, asked if Jesus pays temple tax, says yes. But when he gets home first suggests that this is wrong by a little parable of *kings and their sons*: others pay tax, sons are free. Then Jesus tells Peter to go and catch a fish. The necessary money to pay tax for the two of them will be in its mouth. The parable is both Matthean and rabbinic in its use of the stock figure of the king. The message is given by its allegory. God is the king, Jesus and Peter the proto-Christian are sons, and the Jews who pay temple tax are – 'the others'. It is another brief surfacing of the theme, which preoccupies all the evangelists, of the supersession of Judaism by Christianity. The parable is based in that historical-theological transition, which it affirms with concise allegory. But the affirmation is qualified by the command to go and catch a fish with a shekel in its mouth and pay the tax. It is very like Matthew's previous ambiguity over dietary laws. What is allowed may not be convenient. Although things have been radically changed by Jesus and Christianity, and men are free of their past, it is not always politic to act on such radical truth. Perhaps there is yet a further devious twist. It must count for something that Peter is told to get the tax by such fantastic means: and whereas the fantasy of evangelists is usually informed and controlled by the prescriptions of holy Writ, here the Greek legend of Polycrates' ring is invoked. There is a light-hearted tone and feeling to it all. What matters for present purposes, however, is that the whole incident is, parabolically, about the status of the Christian Church. It is a symbolic or parabolic event (p. 18) and not just a tall story. Together with the other Peter material at 16.13–20 it has woven an ecclesiastical theme into the narrative. The teaching about church disciplines and norms in chapter 18 has been prepared for and precedented.

Matthew is using Mark in chapter 18. First is the incident of the little child whom Jesus sets in the midst of the disciples as a sort of living parable against their religious ambition to be great in the Kingdom of heaven. They must become like children to enter it. By the same token they should treat other 'little ones who believe in me' with care. The addition of 'in me' to 'believe' is Matthew's work on Mark, making entirely clear that the little ones are Christians. This is the idea which he picks up again at verse 10. It uses the current Jewish belief in guardian angels, of whom Raphael in *Tobit* is the most famous. But whereas it was Jewish tradition, based on Isaiah 6.2, that angels do not see God's face, here they emphatically do: and we have another example of Matthew's accepting and changing ancient lore, bringing out of his treasure things new and old. There follows the parable of the *lost sheep* (Matthew 18.10–14). The previous Marcan teaching is illustrated by a parable of Matthew's own. He used parables of his own in this way in chapters 13 and 15. He will do so again on a grand scale in chapters 24 and 25. Parabolic exposition of Mark is one of his specialities. Like his rabbinic counterparts he used parables to explain when explanation was needed. And the *lost sheep* parable is very much his. He likes sheep, giving them eleven mentions against two in Mark and two in Luke. There is black and white contrast between two kinds of people. The number of Matthean words is high: 25 out of 65 according to Goulder (p. 399). The setting and import are ecclesiastical. The signs of Matthew's hand are unmistakable and Jeremias agrees that he has set the parable and worked on

91

it. The converse belief that Luke was the authentic version is more doubtful and will be considered when we get to Luke.

The parable of the *two debtors* which follows straightaway at 18.21–34 is just as unmistakably Matthean in colour, structure and theology. It is about people, unsubtly characterized. There is sharp contrast, vivid exaggeration, and hell. The ecclesiastical application is emphasized by Peter's asking the question, 'How many times shall my brother sin against me and I forgive him?', to which the parable is Jesus' answer. The allegorical character of it all is obvious, with God as king (in rabbinic vein), the two servants as two kinds of Christian, the debts as sins. In the Matthean style, it all gathers to the eschatological point of judgement. Goulder counts 79 of its 214 words as Matthean and reasonably concludes that Matthean authorship of it is compelling (Goulder, p. 404). Matthew is illustrating a text: Mark 11.25. 'And whenever you stand praying, forgive, if you have anything against anyone; so that your Father also who is in heaven may forgive you your trespasses.' He has just done the same with Mark's saying about care for little ones by the parable of the *lost sheep*. He did so before with his *tares* and *net* and he will do it again. As rabbis explain their Old Testament Scripture with parables, so does Matthew his Christian Scripture, Mark. It should be noticed that neither of these parables in chapter 18 is worked out on the historical template of the transition from Judaism to Christianity. Their setting is solely Christian, confronting present conduct with ultimate judgement in the manner of Matthew's masterpiece, the *sheep and goats* at 25.31–46.

After these two parables, Matthew makes a break in his accustomed manner. 'Now when Jesus had finished these sayings (cf. 11.1, 13.53) he went away from Galilee and entered the region of Judea beyond the Jordan; and large crowds followed him' (19.1f). In the latter part of the verse he is following Mark, having Jesus turn momentously to Judea and Jordan after the revelation of his identity in the transfiguration. Luke makes yet more of this by having Jesus at this point (Luke 9.51) set out for Jerusalem itself. With Mark and Matthew the movement is less direct, first to the south-east of Judea beyond Jordan and then the approach to Jerusalem from, suggestively, the east at Mark 10.32‖Matthew 20.17. The movement of events in the preliminary journey reaches its resolution at Matthew 20.1–16 in the parable of *labourers* in the vineyard which Matthew adds to Mark as, once again, illustrative explanation.

With the *labourers* parable Matthew's concern with the relation of Christianity to Judaism in the overall pattern of history returns.

This, to him, is the context of Mark's 'first and last' saying which immediately precedes the parable at 19.30 and sums up what has been said about children, the rich man and impoverished disciples from 19.13 to 19.29. Matthew wants to justify the ways of God in favouring Christian newcomers to the historical-religious scene. The sacred heritage is represented, as Isaiah and Mark had represented it before, as God's vineyard. The divine favouring of the Christians is not unjust to the Jews. They, who have worked in God's vineyard longer, also get their agreed reward and so have nothing to resent. This contrasts with Mark's *vineyard* parable (Mark 12.1–11) where the Jewish tenants are actively wicked and then totally disinherited. Matthew will not baulk at that when the time comes to present it. History, after all, had validated it. But here his historical meditation is more affected by considerations of justice such as have occupied him in the preceding verses about proper rewards.

The allegory of the parable is accordingly painstaking. At the start of the day, representing the divine covenant which was the nation's charter, labourers are hired on set terms. As the historical day goes on, more are called, just as in sacred history God called prophets and kings to do his work. This happens three times at three-hourly intervals. The last group is enlisted at the eleventh hour, a significant break in the orderly three-hourly pattern which has prevailed so far. This group is the Christians, coming in just before the end of time. Then comes the reckoning: 'pay them their wages, beginning with the last, up to the first'. At this point the Marcan saying about first and last returns, having already stood as a caption at the start (19.31). As it does so it polarizes the four groups into the two of first and last. With deliberate management the last are paid first so that the first see them being paid the same as themselves. Their reasonable protest is overruled by divine sovereignty which, while doing no wrong, does what it chooses with its own. Is such positive goodness cause for envy? Have the grumblers lost anything they had a right to expect? The wrongness is with Jewish conservatism, not with God, and Matthew can repeat his theme triumphantly at the end. 'So the last will be first and the first last.' He has managed by his parable to interpret the aphorism on the grand historical scale while defusing the threat to divine justice which it previously implied.

There are many rabbinic parables about masters, labourers and wages. Goulder (pp. 407f) gives three of them. There is one in H. B. Green's commentary (Oxford 1975, p. 173), and there are more in A. Feldman's *The Parables and Similes of the Rabbis* (Cambridge 1927) pp. 46ff. Some of them stick to the plain justice of wages according to hours or days of work done. Thus in Sifra to Leviticus 26.9 ('And I will have respect with you') Israel gets more reward than the rest of humanity for having worked longer, and in the Midrash to Psalm 4.7 David is right to expect an exceptional reward for a lifetime's work. But in a celebrated parable about Rabbi Abun who died young it is the quality, not the quantity, of work which counts. Abun worked so well that the master (God) took him by the hand and strolled about the vineyard with him, presumably in amicable conversation. At the end of the day Abun got full wages, which made the other labourers complain, 'we have toiled through the whole day, and he toiled only two hours, yet the king gave him his wages in full'. The king replies, 'Why do you complain? This man by his diligence has done more in two hours than you in the whole day.' Disparity of lifespan here forces an adjustment of obvious calculation. Feldman (pp. 48 and 46) has two parables which go further by invoking divine freedom and grace. At *Shoher Tob* 26.4:

> Solomon said 'Our fathers toiled and received goodly reward, what merit is it that they had toiled and received payment? We are all slothful labourers, give us a goodly wage, and this will be an act of great goodness.'

The same theme is explored in the same parabolic setting at *Shoher Tob* 3.3:

> Why does scripture say, 'to the Lord our God belong mercies and forgiveness for we have rebelled against him' (Daniel 9.9)? Rather should it have said, 'for we have kept his law'. Whereupon Jonathan replied, 'Well does scripture say this. For according to the common custom, when a labourer works faithfully with his master, and the latter gives him his wages, under what obligation is the workman to his employer? But when is it that the labourer is filled with gratitude? At a time when he does not work faithfully with him, and yet the master does in no way withhold his wages, because it is written "to the Lord our God belong mercies and forgiveness for we have rebelled against him".'

None of these is an exact parallel to Matthew, but throughout them Matthew's themes are scattered. They are found in a compilation made later than Matthew. Goulder will not have it (p. 408) that 'a Nazarene heretic' could have had 'such widespread influence', and posits a common stock on which both Matthew and rabbis drew. Such a common stock is a widely accepted and highly plausible scenario. But parables do not necessarily respect the boundaries of orthodoxies. In the Old and New Testaments, tales from alien cultures have lodged and survived, whether Gilgamesh in the Noah legend or the old Egyptian story which surfaces in Luke's parable of the *rich man and Lazarus*. The decision here must be left to rabbinic scholars and critics, but the bare possibility that Matthew made a contribution to their parabolic expositions of Scripture ought to be left open as a *prima facie* possibility for them to investigate. It is difficult to believe that the flourishing of parable-making in the Gospels of their Christian neighbours made no impression on rabbis who set themselves to the same art. Hating other people is no reason for not pillaging such achievements of theirs as can be useful to yourself – with necessary adaptation. It is a widespread and venerable kind of literary poaching. The difference of Matthew from his rabbinic parallels is in the matrix and structure of his parable. Where they are interpreting Scripture in the frame of the continuity of Israel, he is interpreting history in the frame of the discontinuity caused by the coming of Christianity late (as he believed it) in the day. It is a stronger and more urgent stimulus. Once again the energy of Christian writing is seen to come from its grappling with the historical problem at its roots.

The parable of the *labourers* is followed by Jesus going up to Jerusalem. On the way he corrects the ambitions of his disciples, respectfully imputed by Matthew to their mother rather than to themselves as in Mark. He heals two blind men. Then his triumphal entry into the city puts him firmly at the centre of the public stage: 'all the city was stirred' (21.10). Matthew emphasizes the public impact of Jesus, following the expulsion of the money-changers from the Temple with assertions that Jesus did miracles of healing there, that the chief priests protested and the children were 'crying out in the temple "Hosanna to the Son of David"' – to the renewed indignation of the authorities. All this is added to Mark and followed by Mark's story of Jesus cursing the *fig tree* (cf. Jeremiah 8.13, 24), compacted into a single incident from Mark's two-episode version. The story is another acted parable or symbolic act, the fig tree representing Israel, fruitless in good works and response to God. Matthew, with Mark behind him, is exploring energetically the significance of the events of the narrative for the historical relation of Christ and Judaism. When Jesus re-enters the Temple the chief priests and elders challenge his authority. He wards off the assault by demanding their judgement on the authority of John the Baptist: an authority which they cannot affirm without inconsistency or deny without unpopularity. Their refusal to answer Jesus on this question justifies Jesus' refusal to answer *their* question. Historically this is a highly charged exchange. Nothing less is at stake than the central tenet of Christianity, the divine authority of Jesus. Yet the upshot is more a blocking, a concealing by riddles, by Jesus than an outright declaration. It all comes from Mark and is typical of the deliberate and aggressive obscurity which is a major theological theme and ploy with him. It is Matthew's habit to elucidate Mark and to do so by parables of a morally indicative sort. So here Jesus gives a parable of *two sons* told by their father to work in his vineyard. One says he will not but does, one says he will but does not (Matthew 21.28–30). The essential interpretation follows (Matthew 21.31–2). The son who professes obedience but does nothing represents the Jewish authorities. John came to them 'in the way of righteousness', to persuade them to good works, as he did at Matthew 3.10. They did not believe him. The son who refused but went to work represents the tax-collectors and harlots whose professions were their apostasy, but who did believe John and now 'go into the kingdom of God before you'. So Matthew's parabolic glossing of Mark has two points, both characteristic of him. One is a concern with good works over and above oral confessions of loyalty: better the sinner who repents than the unproductively righteous (memories of the fig tree). The other is historical, the parable explaining the momentous transfer of divine approval from orthodox Jewry to the unrespectable but responsive gathering of repentant sinners who make up the Church. The themes of vineyard and work recall the previous parable of the *labourers* from which this one derives and to which it is a pendant. The same vineyard imagery carries into the next parable of the wicked husbandmen, making a consecutive trio of three *vineyard* parables, all of them historical allegories. Isaiah 5 lies behind them all, making abundantly clear to the hearer or reader that these three parables are about God's vineyard, Israel, from which he has a right to expect fruit – or abandon it. For future reference, it is worth noting the similarity of Matthew's parable of *two sons*, one apparently righteous and the other a repentant sinner, to Luke's more famous *prodigal son*.

The *vineyard* parable of the wicked husbandmen follows immediately. It comes from Mark and has already been dealt with in chapter 3. Its historically allegorical character is obvious even to commentators who are reluctant to concede it. Matthew improves the allegory into more exact historical correspondence. The servants are the prophets. As in Mark, the fate of Jeremiah who was beaten (Jeremiah 20.2) is in the parable. The messenger who is killed is perhaps the prophet Uriah from Jeremiah 26.20–3. Matthew adds a messenger who is stoned at 21.35. He seems to be the Zechariah of 2 Chronicles 24.20 who was stoned for rebuking the people. Whereas Mark had the son of the owner first killed by the husbandmen and then thrown out of the vineyard as a corpse, Matthew has him thrown out alive and then killed – a better correspondence to Jesus' death outside the city of Jerusalem. Lest there should be any doubt of the parable's significance historically, Matthew adds his verse 43:

> Therefore I tell you, the kingdom of God will be taken away from you and given to a nation producing the fruits of it.

Fruits have been emphasized by Matthew throughout the parable: a symbol of good works which is dear to him. He has added it at verses 34 (redundantly), 41 and here at 43. At verse 41 he has also *repeated* the 'time' which he found at Mark 12.2‖Matthew 21.34, giving an extra note of historical crisis. The 'time for fruit' has been a theme of his since the preaching of John in chapter 3.

The parable of the *marriage feast* follows in more senses than one. Not only does it come straight after the *vineyard* with no more separation than 'and again Jesus spoke to them in parables, saying...'; it also takes up its themes and phrases. Jeremias noticed that 'he sent his servants' here in verse 3 is the identical phrase which was used in 21.34. Likewise 'again he sent other servants' is an exact repetition of a phrase in 21.36. The killing of the servants here in 22.6 repeats the same atrocity in 21.35. The king's retaliatory slaughter in 22.7 – 'destroyed those murderers' – is an actualization of the inevitable future of 21.41, 'he will horribly destroy those horrible men'. Jeremias further notices that the killing of the servants bringing the invitations to the banquet is 'motiveless'. That is to put it very politely indeed. But the observation is telling, as is the suggestion that the missing motive is in fact given in the previous parable where the messengers bring an unwelcome demand: a dramatic instance of the importance of reading parables *in situ*, for without having read the *vineyard* parable the *marriage feast* is not intelligible. The two belong together inextricably and where Jeremias is tentatively perceptive of this, Goulder is very bold: 'The Marriage Feast parable is nothing but a second version of the Wicked Husbandmen in terms of the Esther story, with suitable Christian glosses, and in the Matthean manner' (p. 415). What needs to be brought out more clearly than it is either by Jeremias or by Goulder is that the two parables are linked by a theme: the historical crisis whereby Judaism was condemned and Christianity authorized, the fundamental Christian historical myth. That this should come up yet again is a reminder of the importance it had for Christians

97

obsessively busy with establishing their own identity and authority, explaining how they stood first in God's favour although they came last in his plan, how authority has passed from its traditional holders to those who responded to Jesus as God's Son. It is important to notice that in both these parables the crisis is not doomsday but the fall of Jerusalem. The vineyard is handed over to other tenants who will produce its fruit: an historical community of righteousness is envisaged, not heaven. Those in the parable of the *marriage feast* who refuse their invitations and kill the messengers fall victims to royal anger by being destroyed and having 'their city' (a remarkable intrusion into the story, motivated by nothing but historical allegory) burned: after which other invitations are issued and the feast goes on, including the disciplining of the undressed guest. This crisis *within* history, followed by a new historical phase, is an important modification of straightforward eschatology which was prompted by the fall of Jerusalem, has its primary parabolic expression in Mark's *vineyard*, and gets more through expression in Luke's Gospel and parables. On the literary level, the recurrence of the historical theme of the doom of Judaism and the treatment of it by allegory shows that this is a parable in the proper biblical sense which it had for Ezekiel, performing its proper function of making events in history transparent to the divine plan behind them.

Much of the allegorical symbolism is second-hand. It usually is, and is best that way because people will understand its signals. Jesus as bridegroom and his disciples as wedding guests goes back to Mark 2.19‖Matthew 9.15. The king is God. What the burning of the city meant in terms of Jewish history could not be mistaken by anyone after AD 70. The guests who refuse their invitations are the Jews. Those who accept are Christians, 'bad and good' as Matthew knew them in his imperfect church. Likewise Wisdom had laid a banquet and invited the simple or 'foolish' (LXX) to eat it and become wise (Proverbs 9.1–6). In the background of the parable there is also the story of Esther, particularly the climactic banquet at the end of the tale where the unworthy Haman was unmasked and condemned.

There is a rabbinic parallel to this parable in the Midrash Rabbah on Ecclesiastes 9.8, 'Let your garments be always white; let not oil be lacking on your head':

> To what may the matter be likened? To a king who made a banquet to which he invited guests. He said to them, Go wash yourselves, brush up your clothes, anoint yourselves with oil, wash your garments and prepare for the banquet. But he fixed no time when they were to come to it. The wise among them

walked about by the entrance of the palace, saying, Does the king lack anything? The foolish among them paid no regard or attention to the king's command. They said, we will in due course notice when the king's banquet is to take place, for can there be a banquet without labour and company? So the plasterer went to his plaster, the potter to his clay, the smith to his charcoal, the washer to his laundry. Suddenly the king ordered, Let them come to the banquet. They hurried the guests so that some came in their splendid attire and others came in their dirty clothes. The king was pleased with the wise ones who had obeyed his command, and also because they had shown honour to his palace. The king said, Let those who have prepared for the banquet come and eat of the king's meal, but those who have not prepared themselves shall not partake of it. You might suppose that the latter were simply to depart, but the king continued, No, but the former shall recline and eat and drink, while these shall remain standing, be punished and look on and be grieved.

In the Midrash Rabbah this parable is ascribed to Rabbi Jehuda who died in 217, but the Babylonian Talmud at BT *Shab.* 153A indicates Rabbi Johanan ben Zakkai as its author, and he flourished around AD 70. So the parable appears to have been extant in a rabbinic version at the same time as Matthew wrote his Christian one. The two versions are close to one another in content as well as time, most strikingly in the unworthy guests returning to their ordinary business after being invited. They differ, however, in the way each treats the matter of proper dress. In the rabbinic parable it is built in from the start by being included in the king's invitation. In Matthew's it arises suddenly at verse 11 after the original guests have been punished for their disrespectful negligence and their places at the feast taken by the people from the streets 'both bad and good'. When the feast has thus got under way the Church has, allegorically, been established. But for Matthew that is not the end of history. Churches, once established, need to be kept in order by the prospect of doomsday and the fear of hell. The man without the wedding garment is an improper and fraudulent Christian. We are not told how he got in, but in allegory that is not obligatory. He is just there. God will judge him in the end. Matthew's version is structured to the template of his historical theme: Israel – Church – Doomsday. Johanan ben Zakkai's is structured to the template of his Jewish historical scheme without the Christian mid-point of the Church: Israel – Doomsday. For the same reason, Matthew's version contains the motif of the feast being given to celebrate the wedding of the king's son, Jesus in allegorical terms, which is absent from Johanan ben Zakkai's. Both use a common stock of images. Matthew adds to it from his Christian stock in which Jesus is bridegroom. The most significant contrast between the two versions is in their similar but different patterns of sacred history. Luke will further refine Matthew's version by clearer allegorical reference to the gentile mission of the Church which, for him, takes the place in the Christian historical scheme of Matthew's preoccupation with Church discipline.

Judgement on the Household   Matthew 24.42—25.46

We have dealt with a series of four parables about this historical relation of Judaism to Christianity. Three were set in a vineyard: the *labourers*, the *two sons*, the *vineyard*. One was set in a wedding, the *marriage feast*. These settings are symbolic and we know from our sacred reading what they mean. The vineyard stands for Israel, marriage for the coming of Christ as bridegroom. In the same way the other previous block of parables in chapter 13 had presented Jesus' confrontation with Judaism in the symbolic setting of agriculture: the *sower*, the *wheat and tares* and *mustard seed*. And now we turn to a series of parables whose symbolic setting is the household. It too contains one wedding parable. We know what the household means. It is the Christian Church. Paul at Galatians 6.10 had exhorted:

> let us do good to all men, and especially to those who are of the household of faith.

And 1 Peter 4.17, 'the time has come for judgement to begin with the household of God', has it in an eschatological setting like Matthew's. Ephesians 2.9 takes up the figure by describing Christians as 'members of the household of God'. So it becomes clear that Matthew's three major blocks of parables are themselves arranged in historical series. Chapter 13, set at the Sea of Galilee, was the turning point at which Jesus first challenged unresponsive Judaism (and then turned to his disciples). The relation of Christians to Judaism was historically explored in the three *vineyard* parables and *marriage feast* parable in 20.1—22.14. Now in these household parables of 24.42—25.30 we have parables of the Church: the *thief*, the *servant*, the *wise and foolish virgins* and the *talents.* They are capped by the grand allegory of doomsday at 25.31–46. There is a noticeable development: from a block of parables which challenged and rejected Judaism, through a block which explored historically its relation to the Christian community with reference to the fall of Jerusalem, to this block which is about the community in the face of the end of time. Each phase in Matthew's Christian vision of history has its cluster of parables to explain its significance.

The geographical setting of these parables comes from Mark and is the Mount of Olives, the hill overlooking Jerusalem from the east which Zechariah 14.4 had made the base of divine operations in the final eschatological battle. There Jesus sat, talking to his disciples privately and giving them his prophecy of the secret course of events which will usher in doomsday. For all of this Matthew draws on Mark 13, the apocalyptic climax of Jesus' teaching in the Gospel. Characteristically, he adds to it some extra reassurance to the Church in the midst of the coming catastrophes at 24.10–14 (those who endure will be saved) and some historical precedent for sudden catastrophe (Noah's flood) at 24.37–41. But his grand editorial *coup* comes at the end of Jesus' discourse where he adds the series of five parables which are our concern. It is important to see just how he joins them on. Mark 13 ends thus:

Take heed, watch; for you do not know when the time will come. It is like a man going on a journey, when he leaves home and puts his servants in charge, each with his work, and commands the doorkeeper to be on the watch. Watch therefore – for you do not know when the master of the house will come, in the evening, or at midnight, or at cockcrow, or in the morning – lest he comes suddenly and find you asleep. And what I say to you I say to all: Watch.   (Mark 13.33–7: the *servants* parable)

The parallel passage of Matthew, 24.42–4, runs:

Watch therefore, for you do not know on what day your Lord is coming. But know this, that if the householder had known in what part of the night the thief was coming, he would have watched and would not have let his house be broken into. Therefore you also must be ready; for the Son of man is coming at an hour you do not expect.   (The *thief* parable)

So Mark ends with a simile-parable about a temporarily absent householder, sandwiched between urgent injunctions to watch. Matthew delights in parables, using all that Mark provides and adding more. This one has the particular appeal of being a parable of a household: Matthew thinks of himself as church teacher as a householder (13.51f), and of God in the same figure (13.27; 20.1; and 21.33). There is the further incentive, which we have already seen Matthew responding to promptly and parabolically, of Mark's needing elucidation: exploitation is necessary. Mark's parable is a parable about not knowing and so provides nothing to hang on to other than the repeated command 'watch'. It leaves us at the edge of an abyss. This sort of unrevealing parable is typical enough of Mark, but also a major reason for editing him into something more practically useful and intelligible. This Matthew will do – parabolically yet again – by working Mark's brief simile of the temporarily absent householder into his parable of *talents* with the accent no longer on ignorance but rather on the work to be done by the servants, which he greatly expands from its short notice in Mark's parable. But that is postponed and will be the fourth of our set of five parables.

Meanwhile he takes up Mark's suggestion of a household parable as a good way of teaching Christians about their responsibilities in the face of the coming end of the world. He tells the parable of the *thief*. Its most extraordinary feature is the likening of the Lord-to-come, who must be Christ or God, to a thief. But allegory is more tolerant of incongruity than more realistic forms of narrative. Paul at 1 Thessalonians 5.2 had said that 'the day of the Lord will come like a thief in the night', so Matthew was picking up a simile made legitimate and respectable by tradition (he has already had the last trumpet of 1 Thessalonians 4.16 at 24.31). Matthew himself has spoken of thieves breaking into houses at 6.19f. With the Lord as thief, the householder has to be a Christian disciple – a meaning of it which he has already used at 13.51f. Although this parable is not from Mark, two major features of it are: the house and the waiting within it for an event of uncertain timing. The function of the parable, and of each allegorical detail in it, is to key up the Christian community for its great surprise. It is not obfuscated by notes from Mark about the duties of servants. Matthew will deal with these later and at more leisure in the *servant* and *talents* parables. As a result his *thief* parable does its single job of alerting more clearly than Mark's *servants*.

Then he passes on to deal with his suspended Marcan business, the conduct of servants within the ecclesiastical household. In Matthew 24.45–51, as in Mark 13.35f, the householder is away. He leaves one servant in charge of the others rather than giving to each his task: a sign of some elementary church hierarchy such as Matthew enjoyed in his own community. The chief character is either one man who undergoes a sudden, unexplained and total character-change from being a 'faithful and wise' servant to being 'that wicked servant' – such metamorphoses are not intolerable to allegory – or it is two characters contrasted in typically Matthean black-and-white terms. Matthew himself does not take the trouble to make it clear. The message is what matters, not the realism, as is all too plain at the end of the parable where the wicked servant is first cut in half (or, to pieces) and then put with the hypocrites: which latter, as Goulder observes, comes too late to be a punishment. But Matthew is more intent on frightening his Christian readers into attending to their duties than in nice consistency. Incidentally, the reference to drunkenness in verse 49 is a further similarity to 1 Thessalonians where also, at 5.7, it incapacitates eschatological alertness.

The contrast which Matthew fudged a little in this parable is tidy and clear in the next one, the *ten virgins*. The setting is nocturnal. The basic figure is a wedding, and particularly the arrival of the bridegroom, which since Mark 2.19f has stood for the coming of Christ: a symbolism already explored by Matthew in his *marriage feast* parable at 22.1–14. By the same token, the attendants of the bridegroom are Christians, as they were in Mark 2.19f. As in the previous parable, these are important elements sprung out of the seminal Marcan parable of the *servants* which Matthew displaced at the outset with his *thief* parable. From it comes the concluding message of the *ten virgins*, 'Watch therefore, for you know neither the day nor the hour' (leaving out 'when the lord of the house will come') from Mark 13.35. From it also comes the midnight crisis. Midnight was one of the times when the Lord might come in Mark 13.35. That Matthew chooses it as *the* time here for the bridegroom to come may well be due to Exodus 12.29. God smote the first-born of Egypt at midnight and 'there was a great cry in Egypt'. Likewise here there is a cry at midnight. Basically, all Matthew has done to make this parable is to blend the symbolism of bridegroom and attendants from Mark 2.19f, already used in the *marriage feast* at 22.1–14, with the symbolism of sudden arrival at midnight from Mark 13.35 – from which also comes the motif of sleeping; 'lest he comes suddenly and finds you asleep'. In Matthew's *ten virgins* sleeping is crucial. 'While the bridegroom delayed, they all slumbered and slept.' It did not matter, because preparedness, oil in the lamp, turned out to be what counted. That it is there at all is, therefore, due to Mark. The result is Matthean enough however, with severe contrast within the mixed body of Christians and its eschatological sorting out: features it has in common with the *servant* which immediately precedes it, and the *talents* which immediately follows it. The extreme unlikelihood of a wedding in the middle of the night seems not to matter to Matthew at all. Its symbolic significance is its justification, as so often in allegory.

The *talents* is yet a further variation of the seminal Marcan parable of the *servants* awaiting the Lord's return to his house.

> It is like a man going on a journey, when he leaves home and puts his servants in charge, each with his work.   (Mark 13.34)

Matthew's *talents* parable begins very similarly:

> It will be as when a man going on a journey called his servants and entrusted to them his property; to one he gave five talents, to another two, to another one, to each according to his ability.   (Matthew 25.14f)

The similarity is so strong as to make it clear that in the setting up of the parable Matthew is following Mark. The householder is going on a journey, leaving his servants in charge: this fundamental pattern, the matrix of all that follows, is Marcan. But Matthew changes it in a highly characteristic way. Mark's householder left his servants with 'authority' (Greek *exousia*). What, exactly, is that? Matthew is more precise. His householder leaves his servants with material goods, hefty sums of money. Nor are they, it emerges, just to sit on their benefactions. They are to make them work. This is indicated by the deliberate phrase, 'to each according to his ability' (Greek *dunamis*/power). It is a telling revision of Mark's 'in charge, each with his work', clarifying the vaguer 'charge' or 'authority' and 'work' into something very definite for them to do. This makes a subtle but significant change in the historical pattern. In Matthew there is more to be done in the historical era of the Church than there was in Mark. This is confirmed when Matthew says at verse 19 that the Lord returned 'after a long time'. This was not even implicit in Mark where the time of absence was, if anything, short. Here the crucial time for the exercise of enterprise by the servants is extensive. The Church has its own temporal space. And the metaphor of trade which is used to describe its business is apt. The Lord gives the servants sums of money to exploit, so there is continuity of the Church with Jesus in the initial gifts, development and change in the commercial increasing of them. The importance of this second aspect is clear when the third servant is condemned for failing at it. So, when another text from Mark is deployed at the end it is reinforced with extra condemnation of the third servant:

> For to him who has will more be given; and from him who has not, even what he has will be taken away.
>
> (Mark 4.25‖Matthew 25.29)

To the first clause Matthew adds, 'and he shall have abundance', but to the second clause he adds, 'and cast the worthless servant into the outer darkness; there men will weep and gnash their teeth'. Altogether, Matthew makes the ecclesiastical interim of the Lord's absence busier and more fateful than Mark did, while using Mark's pattern. In the same vein it is worth noticing that Mark 4.25 ('For to him who has . . .') comes from Mark's parable chapter and refers to the capacity, or lack of it, to understand parables. Matthew has transposed it to the realm of work. To understand is not just to be illuminated but, more practically, to do. To watch is to work. So the *light* figure from Mark was, at Matthew 5.16, amplified by, 'Let your light so shine before man that they may see your good works'. The evidence of Matthean redaction is massive and firmly attached to his ecclesiastical interest.

There is more. The worthless servant at verse 18 'went and dug in the ground and *hid* his money'. He is the reverse of the cunning man who found treasure hidden in a field and, with laudable commercial enterprise, sold all that he had to buy the field – and then, surely, dug up the treasure (13.44). Secondly, this is a parable in which three human examples are compressed into ultimate dualism, as in the *labourers* parable, where, too, several groups are fined down into ultimate contrast between the two most extreme. So here, the faithful exploiter of two talents fades before the contrast of the one with five (become ten) and the one with one which remains one. A further similarity with the *labourers* parable is the way the master throws back at the worthless servant what he already knows. There it was the agreed wage, here it is the servant's knowledge of his hardness.

The series is concluded by the grand doomsday parable of *sheep and goats*: allegorical as ever, terrifyingly focused on the end of time, using good works as the criterion of judgement, and repetition, such as we noticed in the previous parable of *talents*, to ram home justice. It closes the series by bringing it full circle. The grand topic of them all has been the coming of the Son of Man in glory and judgement (Matthew 24.30‖Mark 13.26). The context of that eschatological dénouement is the Church. Mark had suggested this by having Jesus deliver the whole of his apocalyptic teaching in chapter 13 to Peter, James, John and Andrew privately on the Mount of Olives. Matthew kept the scene and the privacy but included all the disciples as audience. Then his elaborations of Mark's one household parable of *servants* into three household parables (*thief, servant, talents*) amplified the ecclesiastical interest and reference. The inclusion of a wedding parable, the *ten virgins*, maintained the perspective on the coming of the Son of Man (= the coming of the bridegroom) by being put in the middle of the series. Now that theme comes out triumphantly and conclusively with the beginning of the *sheep and goats*.

> When the Son of man comes in his glory, and all the angels with him, then he will sit on his glorious throne. Before him will be gathered all the nations.   (Matthew 25.31f)

It is a version and a recapitulatory repeat of the saying of Jesus in Mark 13.26f:

> And then they will see the Son of man coming in clouds with great power and glory. And then he will send out the angels, and gather his elect from the four winds, from the ends of the earth to the ends of heaven.   (Mark 13.26f)

Matthew has a stronger ecclesiastical interest than Mark and it will show itself in the parable by the focus on the little ones, the least among Christ's brethren (cf. verses 40 and 45) whom we know from chapters 10 and 18 to be lowly Christians. At 10.42 Jesus had promised

> Whoever gives to one of these little ones even a cup of cold water because he is a disciple, truly I say to you, he shall not lose his reward.

Here it has happened. The sheep are those who gave to the absent Lord, by giving to his present brethren, drink when thirsty. They do not lose their reward. Chapter 18 began with Jesus setting a child in the midst of the disciples, and contained the parable of the *lost sheep* to encourage care for 'these little ones' who are erring Christians. There, as here in this parable, the least must not be left to perish.

The sources of the parable are, as usual: Mark as read by Matthew in the light of his concerns, and the Old Testament. Q is not needed. From Mark comes the basic tableau of the Son of man returning in glory to judge. Mark 8.38 is an influence:

> Whoever is ashamed of me and my words in this adulterous and sinful generation, of him will the Son of man also be ashamed, when he comes in the glory of his Father with the holy angels.

Son of man, glory, angels and judgement are all in Matthew's parable. So is the criterion of judgement, what people do or fail to do in the present. But in Mark this was a matter of 'me and my words', of being ashamed or making a brave profession. In Matthew it is still 'me', the Son of man, but good deeds done are crucial, rather than good words said. That emphasis on works done or neglected has been typical of Matthew throughout this series of parables, and notably in his revision of Mark's *servants* in the *talents*. Equally typical of Matthew is the parabolic use of

106

sheep. The figure goes back to the Old Testament and Ezekiel 34 is relevant here, verse 17 in particular:

> As for you, my flock, thus says the Lord God, Behold I judge between sheep and sheep, rams and he-goats.

This has obvious affinity to the Matthew who has already given us the parables of sorting out in *wheat and tares* and the *net*. Mark had spoken twice of sheep. At 6.34 Jesus pitied the crowds because they were as sheep without a shepherd, and at 14.27 Jesus recalled Zechariah 13.7 before his arrest: 'I will strike the shepherd and the sheep will be scattered'. Matthew has much more pastoral imagery than this. There are false prophets as wolves in sheep's clothing (7.15), the lost sheep of the house of Israel (10.6 and 15.24), disciples as sheep among wolves (10.16), a sheep in a pit (12.11), lost sheep (18.12). Sheep are always good and valuable, often at risk, and twice seen in Matthean contrast with wolves. That contrast would not work in this parable which has its base in the mixed flock of Matthew's Christian Church, so goats are substituted. Sheep could mean Israel, but here their care for 'the least of these my brethren' makes them anyone sympathetic to Christians. Which brings an oddity to light: the sheep are justified because of their pastoral work as if they were shepherds! Only allegory, and particularly allegory in an apocalyptic frame, can tolerate this sort of surrealistic metamorphosis. Realism has scarcely been the keynote of this series, in which a man cut in half has been put with the hypocrites to weep and gnash his teeth, a wedding has taken place at midnight, and servants have been lent sums beyond the dreams of avarice.

This is the last of Matthew's parables in more senses than one. It occurs at the close of his final block of parables, 24.43—25.46, a group which confronts the Church with the judgement of Christ as the parables in chapter 13 had confronted Israel, and as the intermediate group at 20.1—22.14 had explained the transition of divine authority from Israel to Church. It is about the end of all historical process at the last assize where men will be judged on their works – as John the Baptist had proclaimed in the first parables of this Gospel. It is shaped throughout by Matthean dualistic contrast, presented in allegory and finished off, as so often, with eternal punishment – only here balanced with the promise of eternal life. For all its strong apocalyptic character it confronts its hearers more unmistakably with their workaday moral duty than Mark did, by the same token putting a greater weight of emphasis on what people do in history. It is a trend which Luke will take further.

107

5 Luke

PARABLES IN LUKE

John the Baptist
3.7	Snakes	
3.9	Tree and Fruit	
3.17	Threshing	

Nazareth
4.23	Physician	**P**

Levi's House
5.31	Physician	Mark **T**
5.34–5	Bridegroom	Mark **H T**
5.36	Clothes	Mark **H T P**
5.37	Wineskins	Mark **H T**

Sermon
6.39	Blind Guide	Matt. **P**
6.40	Disciple	Matt.
6.41	Speck in Eye	Matt.
6.43–4	Trees	Matt.
6.45	Treasures	Matt.
6.47–9	Houses	Matt.

Nain (?)
7.24–5	Reed, Courtier	Matt.
7.31	Children's Games	Matt. **H**

Simon's House
7.41–2	Debtors	Eph.2 14–18
		Matt. 18.23ff **H T**

Crowd
8.4	Sower	Mark **H P**
8.9–10	Theology	Mark
8.11–15	Interpretation	Mark
8.16	Lamp	Mark **H**

108

Seventy Return
10.29–37   Good Samaritan   2 Chron.28   h

Praying Somewhere
11.5–8   Friend at Night   Matt. 25.1–13   h

Exorcisms
11.17–18   Kingdoms/Houses   Mark/Matt.   H
11.21–2   Strong Man   Mark/Matt.   H
11.24–6   Empty House   Matt.   H

Crowds
11.33–6   Lamp   Matt.   h
12.16–21   Rich Fool   Pss.; Matt. 6.19–26
                                Matt. 16.26‖Mark 8.36   h S P
12.24   Ravens   Matt.
12.27   Lilies   Matt.

Disciples
12.35–9   Servants   Matt. 24; Mark 10.45;
                                Matt. 25; John 13.4   H   Matt.   P
12.42–6   Steward   Matt. 24.45–51   H
12.47–8   Graded Penalties   H

Crowds
13.6–9   Fig Tree   Mark 11.12–21   H P
13.18–19   Mustard Seed   Mark/Matt.   H
13.20–1   Leaven or Yeast   Matt.   H

On the Way
13.24–30   Door   Matt. 7.13f; 25.10–12; Exod. 24.11;
                                Matt. 8.11–12; Matt. 19.30; 20.16   H

Pharisee's table
14.7–11   Table Places   Matt. 23.6‖Mark 12.39; Matt. 23.12;
                                Prov. 25.6   h T P
14.12–14   Ask the Poor   cf. Luke 14.16–24; 16.19–31   T
14.16–24   Banquet   Matt.   H T

Crowds
14.28–30   Tower   T?
14.31–3   Kings at War   2 Sam. 8.10   T?
14.34–5   Salt   Mark/Matt.   T?

Tax Collectors and Sinners

15.3–7	Lost Sheep	Matt.	**H** **T?**
15.8–10	Lost Coin		**H** **T?**
15.11–32	Lost (or, Prodigal) Son	Gen.27; 37—47;	
		?Matt. 23.13	**H** **S** **T?**

Disciples

16.1–8	Unjust Steward	?? 2 Kings	**h** **S** **T?**

Pharisees and Money

16.19–31	Rich Man and Lazarus	Matt. 25.31–46	**H** **T?**
		Luke 6.20–24; Deut. 30.11f	
		Trad. Egypt.	
		Plato, *Republic*, 10.614	

Disciples – Prayer

17.7–10	Master and Slave	**T?**	
18.1–8	Unjust Judge	Ecclus. 35.15f	**h** **S** **P**
18.9–14	Pharisee and Publican	Matt. 18.9; 23.12	**h** **S** **P**

Near Jerusalem

19.11–27	Pounds	Matt.; Mark 13.34f	**H** **T** **P**
		Jos., *Ant.* xvii.11.1	

Temple

20.9–18	Vineyard	Mark	**H** **S** **P**

SYMBOLS:

Mark or Matt. when there is clear parallel to Mark or Matthew, note of chapter and verse when parallel obscure.

P = Luke calls it a parable

S = Soliloquy in the parable

H = clear historical reference

h = less clear historical reference

T = Table setting
  with ? when, from 14.24—17.10, there is no declared change of scene and the last was at table.

Introduction

Luke has unique importance in the New Testament's parable tradition. So far all has been continuous. The historical allegory which the Old Testament and intertestamental literature regarded as parable *par excellence* was also the main thing, with developments, for Mark and Matthew. With Luke we meet this – and something different: unallegorical, realistic stories which are rich in homely detail and characterization. These include such famous examples as the *good Samaritan* and the *prodigal son*. For Jeremias these are parables of Jesus which need little or no form-critical restoration of the sort meted out to historical allegories. They are Jesus' own defence of his historic mission. To test that notion we will need to get as clear a view as possible of them. So we will consider them in their context right away, as a good way of opening up the study of Luke's parables.

The list of Luke's parables at the beginning of this chapter can be sorted into seven sections:

1 *3.7–17: Three figures used by John the Baptist* as in Matthew.

2 *5.31–7: Four parables told at Levi's table*. They all come from Mark and deal with the historical significance of the new gospel.

3 *6.39–49: Six parables in the Sermon on the Plain*. They all have parallels in Matthew and deal with ethics.

4 *7.24–42: Three parables told at Nain and one at Simon the Pharisee's table*. These too all have parallels in Matthew. The first three are about the historical significance of John the Baptist, the last of them (*children's games*) including Jesus too – whose patronage of sinners is defended by the *two debtors* parable told to Simon.

5 *8.4–18: Two parables told to the crowd*. They are the *sower* and the *lamp*. In Mark and Matthew they had historical significance which is maintained by Luke, though less strongly.

6 *10.29—18.14: Parables in the so-called Central Section of Jesus' Journey to Jerusalem*. This is far the biggest section, containing thirty of Luke's fifty parables and including the most famous of them. Chapters 15 and 16 are Luke's counterpart of Mark 4: his most monumental and characteristic parabolic work.

7 *19.11—20.18: Parables told near and in Jerusalem*. These are the *pounds*, parallel to Matthew's *talents* but deliberately set in a bigger historical scope by 19.11; and the *vineyard*, parallel to Mark. Both are historical allegories.

Of these sections, 1, 2, 4, 5 and 7 contain parallels which in one

111

way or another do the now familiar job of explaining the history in which they are set. Section 1 is about ethics. That leaves the crucial section 6 to be considered as the best index of Luke's way with parables in a preliminary view designed to get an outline of the Lucan landscape. Of its thirty parables the following fourteen are peculiar to Luke except the *lost sheep*, which is Matthean but included because of its close ties to the other two *lost* parables.

> The Good Samaritan
> The Friend at Night*
> The Rich Fool
> Table Places
> Tower
> Kings at War
> (The Lost Sheep)*
> The Lost Coin*
> The Lost Son (or, The Prodigal Son)*
> The Unjust Steward
> The Rich Man and Lazarus
> Master and Slave*
> The Unjust Judge*
> The Pharisee and the Publican

Those marked with an asterisk contain possible elements of allegory. The features of them which I will now pick out are their pattern, their humanity and the allegorical elements in many of them.

L parables have a characteristic shape of which the most striking feature is that the crisis happens in the middle, not, as so often in Matthew's parables, at the end. In the *good Samaritan* the crisis occurs when the traveller is left half dead at the roadside. In the *friend at night* it is rousing the neighbour. The *tower* builder and the *kings at war* exemplify failure to appreciate the mid-term crisis by being in a hurry to get to a conclusion. The *unjust steward*, on the contrary, exemplifies a determined and resourceful facing of it. The three parables of the *lost* all have the crisis in the middle, most dramatically the *prodigal son* when he is reduced to penury and famine. The *rich man* is careless of the crisis before him in Lazarus. The *unjust judge* responds better to the clamorous widow. The *publican* realizes his present need better than the *Pharisee*, much as the slave in the *master and slave* ought to realize the unworthiness of doing no more than his duty. This leaves the *rich fool*. His crisis is his death. 'They', presumably angels, require his soul 'this night'. But though this is the end of his life it is not the end of the world. His goods will pass to others. Luke has an individual eschatology of death which he uses here as in the *rich man and Lazarus* and with the penitent thief at the crucifixion. It is independent of universal eschatology (which he believes in) in that history goes on beyond it – even for the individuals concerned who have after-lives in heaven and hell where they talk, recline, or feel thirsty. So the *rich fool* is also held in the central-crisis pattern.

It is in fact a pattern familiar to students of Luke from Conzelmann's work on *die Mitte der Zeit* (1953/7 ET *The Theology of St Luke* [Faber 1960]), the mid-point of time. It shapes Luke's work as a whole. Jesus is for him the central crisis of sacred history. Before him is the Old Testament. Luke's first two chapters set him in it by being traditionally 'biblical' in language, content and events (see J. Drury, *Tradition and Design in Luke's Gospel* [Darton 1976] pp. 46–66). He also connects Jesus with the past by making him like the prince of the old prophets, Elijah (ibid., pp. 67f, etc.), a role which the previous evangelists had given to John the Baptist. Beyond Jesus is the Church. Luke adds Jesus' instructions to it to the traditional narrative of the Last Supper, he labours apostolic witness of his resurrection – and adds the vast appendix of the Acts of the Apostles. The pattern in the L parables is deeply embedded in Luke's mind. It is the pattern of the whole of his history. Jesus in his Gospel is not history's end but its turning point, setting it on a new course in which Judaism drops away and the Christian Church goes triumphantly forward.

⌐How original is this? Not entirely. Compared with Matthew it is a continuous development. Matthew was much concerned with the transference of divine authority from Judaism to Christianity. He dealt with it in the *vineyard* parables between 20.1 and 21.46: the *labourers*, the *two sons* and the Marcan *vineyard*. With these belongs the *marriage feast* at 22.1–14. In all of them there was a crisis which is not the end of the world: pay-time for the labourers, the calling of the sons to work, the transference of the vineyard to new tenants, the issuing of invitations. Only in the *marriage feast* was there a second crisis which did seem to be doomsday. This group is remarkable because Matthew was very ready to end his parables with the end of time. It was his consciousness of historical process which changed him here. He had a much more sophisticated historical sense than Mark and developed the Christian view of history in a way which proved indispensable to Luke (see Drury, op. cit., pp. 164–71). Yet neither was Matthew's view a bolt from the blue. We can trace things farther back. Mark's great *vineyard* parable had spoken of a crisis within history, the fall of Jerusalem most likely, which was an end for one set of tenants but a beginning for another. So the line of development in Christian historical narrative runs through all the Synoptic Gospels from Mark, through Matthew, to Luke. The sense of historical process which Luke shows in his parables as in his grand authorial design is not an entirely original development although it is a decisive one. He exhibits a fully articulated version of a thought latent in the first gospel narrative, given room to develop by the recession of eschatological hope.

If only by symmetry of pattern, the L parables fit perfectly into Luke's perception of the historical significance of Jesus' biography. Jeremias sees this togetherness of L parables with their narrative: they are the vindication of Jesus' ministry to the least and the lost (pp. 116–32 and *passim*), particularly of his table fellowship with sinners. A telling text to support this view is Luke 15.1f which introduces the three *lost* parables:

> Now the tax collectors and sinners were all drawing near to hear him. And the Pharisees and the scribes murmured, saying, 'This man receives sinners and eats with them'.

But this gets Jeremias into trouble with one of his major criteria for distinguishing the historical Jesus from the Church's version: that the settings of parables are likely to be 'freely handled' (pp. 39f) and even the work of the evangelist concerned. At p. 100n he says that 'Luke 15.1–3 has been thoroughly worked over by Luke.' On p. 132 the passage is considered again under a non-committal 'we are told that . . .', but it is treated as if historically dependable. By p. 227 its dependability is unquestioned. The unstable criteria and unexplained progress from possibility to certainty are unfortunately typical of the procedures which make Jeremias so hard to follow, and all too familiar in the quest for the historical Jesus generally.

A second big feature of L parables is their setting in the world of human beings. This, like Luke's historical pattern, is the result of previous development. Mark's parables in chapter 4 were about nature, but in the *vineyard* in chapter 12 he dealt with people, the emissaries of God and their persecutors. From this standpoint too, Mark's *vineyard* is a turning point in the history of the parables. When Matthew edited Mark 4 in his chapter 13 he enhanced the human element. His *wheat and tares* was a version of Mark's *seed growing secretly* in which dialogue between the farmer and his labourers predominated. To Mark's *mustard seed* he added 'a man' who sowed it. The four parables at the end of Matthew 13 were all human: 'a man' found the *treasure* and the *pearl*, fishermen divided the catch in the *net*, the Christian scribe was like a *householder*. All the longer parables which Matthew added to

Mark were about people, though many brief metaphors he drew from nature. The L parables which we have listed are all human. The *lost sheep* was in the list on p. 112 in brackets because it is Matthean. Its human content is stepped up by Luke's addition of the shepherd calling his neighbours together to celebrate. But the L parables are more human than anything in Matthew in the sense that the characters are far more subtly drawn. Instead of Matthew's black and white contrasts we get the *chiaroscuro* of ambivalent human beings: doing good out of self-interest, calculating profit and loss, finding the way home out of despair, doing no more than their duty or acknowledging their shortcomings. Often we are let in on their thinking by means of soliloquies. Mark had something of this sort when the wicked *vineyard*'s owner said 'they will respect my son', and the tenants said to one another, 'This is the heir. Come, let us kill him and the inheritance shall be ours' (Mark 12.7, followed by both Matthew and Luke). Yet again Mark's *vineyard* is a point for new departures by his revisers. Matthew used soliloquies twice more. The exorcised man at 12.44 said to himself, 'I will return to my house from which I came'. The bad servant at Matthew 24.48 said to himself, 'My master is delayed'. Luke uses both these but has more of his own, and they include elements of questioning absent from the Marcan and Matthean precedents: the rich fool, the prodigal son, the unjust steward, the unjust judge, all soliloquize.

We thus find two examples of development along the line of succession Mark – Matthew – Luke which both begin with Mark's *vineyard*. There is development of the historical pattern into a greater and more conscious emphasis on Jesus' ministry as the crucial mid-term crisis: this at the expense of close and thorough-going eschatology. First Matthew, then Luke, filled out the content of the time before the end with increasing ethical and historical substance. Secondly there is development in the roles played by people. Where Mark's disciples understood practically nothing, Matthew's understood but lacked faith (see *Tradition and Interpretation in Matthew*, Bornkamm et al. [SCM 1963] pp. 105–24). Matthew added human parables to Mark. His people were a mixture; but collectively, not individually. Within the collective the good were good and the bad were bad. Luke's human parables contain people mixed within themselves. Mark, we saw, held the strict apocalyptic view that the wicked would go on being wicked and the good being good. He was grimly predestinarian. So was Matthew, but he modified it by a temporary tolerance of the wicked which left the sorting out for doomsday. Luke's people change. They adapt in the face of the crises in front of their noses.

He picks up the teaching on repentance in his predecessors, Matthew particularly, and presents us with a rogues' gallery become a communion of saints. Zacchaeus (Luke 19.1–10) and the repentant woman in Simon the Pharisee's house (Luke 7.36–50) are the equivalents in narrative of the justified sinners in the L parables; parables which are thus narratives in a fuller and more sophisticated sense than anything by his predecessors. We shall see that Luke owes much to the Old Testament historians in his psychological acuteness. Biblically he is not original. But within the Gospels he is original with the sort of derivative originality we expect to find in works of historical imagination. Luke's people have understandable motives, they are something more interesting than sons of light or sons of darkness, and they have the limited but critical freedom of decision which we all exercise.

One last major feature of the L parables: the reader will now be sated by the emphasis in this book on allegory, and particularly historical allegory, so it will come as a relief that Luke uses it proportionately less than his predecessors; it is a reason for Dodd's and Jeremias' treatment of L parables as genuine parables of Jesus. The L parables tell themselves. We need no key; there is no code to break. People interact so intelligibly that a modest knowledge of human character is all we need to grasp them. They are wisdom parables in the older and more mundane sense of wisdom – that art of coping which the Book of Proverbs put in aphorisms. As stories they are like the Joseph saga or the court chronicles of David and Solomon. This is not the supernaturally revealed wisdom so fundamental to Paul and Mark, born of apocalyptic despair of world and man. This is the wisdom of daylight, not of nocturnal vision. It affirms commonsense and resourcefulness. So it does not *need* allegory as much as apocalyptic wisdom did. It copes with what is here in the world, because here in the world matters are decided: whereas for the apocalyptist the real decisions are made in the heavenly elsewhere. But although Luke does not need allegory as strongly as his predecessors did he is happy to use it within his historical realism. It is a fallacy to suppose that a writer, or anyone at all, intends or does one thing and one thing only. There are telling and important elements of historical allegory in the best known L parables. In *the good Samaritan* the neglect of the temple officials, priest and levite, contrast with the Samaritan's care. This chimes in with the pattern in Luke's history whereby Samaritans and Samaria, heretical brothers of orthodox Jerusalem Judaism, take up the gospel in Acts 8 in its first phase of expansion after Stephen's death. The Gospel gives a foretaste of it in the incident of the

Samaritan leper, the only one of ten cleansed to be grateful, at Luke 17.12–19. So within the parable there are major symbolic connectors with the historical narrative beyond it such as we have seen in more thoroughly and exclusively allegorical parables. Likewise in the *prodigal son* there are important elements of allegory which add to its resonance. The father stands for God, the older son is orthodox unreconstructed Judaism, and the prodigal who has put himself beyond the orthodox Jewish pale by his fornicating and swineherding is typical of the sinners and Gentiles who were welcome to Luke's Church. Each of the main characters in the tale has an allegorical connection with the wider history of Jewish unresponsiveness and the readiness of sinners and Gentiles. It is not absolutely necessary to getting the parable's point but belongs in the richness of its full contextual meaning. It is as gross a mistake to think of Luke as unallegorical or anti-allegorical as it is to think of him as uneschatological or unapocalyptic. In both instances he has other preoccupations, the present-historical and the real, which change the tale and the tales. But equally he keeps and uses and even adds both apocalyptic eschatology and allegory.

More appreciation of Luke's derivative originality can be got by looking at the Q or Matthean parables in the Journey Section. These are:

> Kingdoms/Houses
> *Strong Man*
> Empty House
> Ravens/Lilies
> *Servants*
> *Fig Tree*
> Mustard
> Yeast
> *Door*
> *Table Places*
> Banquet

Those in italics are such thorough redactions as to create markedly different parables. The others show Luke as a more conservative retailer of tradition, a man like his wine taster who says 'the old is good' (Luke 5.39).

The first of the thoroughly redacted parables is the *strong man* at Luke 11.21–3. Without changing its message Luke gives it an entirely new vocabulary, with only the word 'strong' surviving from the versions of Matthew and Mark which, by contrast, are closely similar to one another. The effect of Luke's thorough rewording is to change the vaguer 'no one' into a well set-up warlord, guarding his palace and weaponry, and then conquered by a still stronger warlord (the original strong man of Mark and Matthew) who sacks his armoury and divides his spoils. The promotion from household to palace together with the lavish military realism add colour, sharpness and grandeur to the original version. Yet its allegorical nature is unchanged: the strong man is Satan, the stronger is Jesus or God. Indeed, it is more allegorically apt to his supernatural status that Satan should be a warlord rather than a humdrum householder and that his eschatological defeat should be in terms of battle rather than burglary. A recollection of Isaiah 53.12, 'he shall divide the spoil with the strong', compounds the theological force of the allegory: a literary improvement which comes as readily to Luke as his more obvious talent for realism.

The *servants* at 12.35–40 is a hotchpotch of allusion integrated into an allegory of the Christian Church awaiting its Lord's return. Loins are girded as for passover, lamps burning as in Matthew's *wise virgins* – from which also comes the motif of marriage with its traditional christological significance. Again, both allegory and realism are improved by having the servants wait at home, in the church-household of which Matthew had said much in parables. The Lord knocks at its door and then comes in to give them supper, a close parallel to Revelation 3.20:

> Behold, I stand at the door, and knock: if any man hear my voice, and open the door, I will come in to him and will sup with him, and he with me. (AV)

There is also similarity to John 13.4f where Jesus girds himself and serves his disciples. Whether Revelation and John's Gospel are using Luke or some vanished common source, the effect here is, again, to make a parable at once vivid and allegorical. It is followed by a version of Matthew's householder watching for the *thief* (Matthew 24.43) but in Luke it is even clearer that the householder is a Christian official and not Jesus by virtue of its position as a pendant to the *servants*.

There follows, at verse 41, a question from Peter, 'Lord, are you telling this parable for us or for all?'. The question is an interjection, enhancing the element of dialogue in a way Luke prefers. It is answered by Jesus continuing and developing the *servants* parable. The question also raises the big question of Mark 4 about who parables are for: initiates or everybody? It gets, parabolically, an answer in intelligible terms of culpability and responsibility based on knowledge. First comes a fairly faithful version of Matthew's *servant* parable (Matthew 24.45–51). It was a confused parable with the servant inexplicably changing from being thoroughly good to being thoroughly bad, and so seeming to be – or being – two different people. Luke clarifies that somewhat by omitting the word 'bad' at Luke 12.45 and so making clear that we are dealing with one person capable of playing his role in different ways. Luke's hand can also be seen in the addition of slavegirls at verse 45. He allows more to women than his predecessors (see Drury, op. cit., pp. 51f). The Matthean parable answers Peter's question by saying that, for the Christian leadership which Peter represents, the preceding parable about servants watching for their Lord's return is designed to incite attention to the pastoral duties of their position. That is what the parable means for them. As for the rest, Jesus adds at verses 47 and 48 the graded penalties worked out on the basis of responsible knowledge. It is more casuistically sophisticated than Matthew's dualism of blessedness or hell, more intelligible to common sense than Mark's mysterious predestinarianism. For Luke a man can be relatively good or bad: relative, that is, to what he knows because it is in front of him and demands his response. Throughout this long and developing parable of *servants*, well articulated allegory goes hand in hand with a more commonsensical realism and justice than Luke's predecessors had managed. Their eschatological perspective remains while the needs and duties of the present are more patiently explored. Luke seems to be editing Matthew characteristically enough to exclude any real need of the Q hypothesis.

The parable of the *fig tree* at Luke 13.6–9 has already developed through two stages. At Mark 11.12–21‖Matthew 21.18–22 (but not in Luke) Jesus cursed an unfruitful fig tree. This symbolic action is then expanded as 'parable' of future history in the eschatological discourse in all three Gospels. Here is a third and more naturalistic variation which yet has essential historical significance. The vinedresser gets leave from the disappointed owner to dig around the tree. This is still the treatment recommended by gardening handbooks for unfruitful fig trees. The digging prunes the roots and stimulates fruiting. Manure will help too. If this fails then let it be cut down. This is much more realistic than the previous narrative versions. But it is also allegorical of Judaism being given a further chance of repentance after the Lord's ministry by the evangelistic activity of the apostles in Acts. Lest there be any doubt of the allegorical import (which is in any case evident from the setting in Luke 13 where the *fig tree* comes after the Galilean massacre and the fall of the tower at Siloam) the fig tree is set in a vineyard – and everyone knows what that means. It is natural enough that a fig tree should be in a vineyard, but it is *also* unmistakably symbolic. Once again, Luke has got the two together.

The parable of the *door* at Luke 13.24–30 is the crowning example of the sort of Lucan parable we are dealing with, which drastically edits the existing sources. It is a mosaic of Matthean fragments edited into a coherent eschatological historical allegory, pointed (like the *fig tree*) at Israel in its present crisis of response to Jesus' prophetic ministry. Israel in the face of its impending catastrophe and the growing Kingdom of God has been the subject of Jesus' preceding teaching. There have been warnings of doom in the Galilean massacre and the Siloam tower which were from 'mournful Calendars of true history' (Wordsworth, *Prelude* [1805] x.68) used as parable. In the healing of the bent woman (a daughter of Abraham bound by Satan) and in the parables of *mustard seed* and *leaven*, there were hints and signs of recovery and growth. Which way will Israel go? The *door* parable forces the question and is set in Jesus' journeying through towns and villages towards Jerusalem. 'And someone said to him, "Lord, will those who are saved be few?"' (Luke 13.22f). The question, 'Which way will Israel go?', is historical and eschatological; the parabolic answer is a prophetic warning consistently put in the future tense – unlike the Matthean fragments of which it is made, but characteristic of Luke's clearer temporal differentiation. It begins:

> Strive to enter by the narrow door; for many, I tell you, will seek to enter and will not be able.

This is a version of Matthew 7.13. But Matthew's 'gate' (Greek *pulē*) has become a 'door' (Greek *thura*). Beyond Matthew's gate there was a road or path. It does not figure here. So what is beyond Luke's 'door'? Presumably it gives into a house, and if so the house will probably signify as usual, the Church. Entering the house/Church had been made by Luke into the point of the traditional *lamp* metaphor at Luke 8.16 and 11.33. In the next verse the presumption is confirmed:

> When once the householder has risen up and shut the door, you will begin to stand outside and to knock at the door saying, 'Lord, open to us.' He will answer you, 'I do not know where you come from.'

The door does indeed give into a house. And it is not its narrowness that stops people getting in by it: that is a Matthean feature which Luke has copied though it turns out not to matter – and so betrayed his editorial hand. In Luke they cannot get in to the house because the door is *shut*. Another bit of Matthew has influenced Luke at this point: the crisis of the *ten virgins* parable at Matthew 25.10f, when the foolish virgins return from shopping to find the door shut. 'Lord, Lord, open to us!', they call. But the Lord answers from within, 'Truly I say to you, I do not know you.' The shut door, the call to be let in and the dusty answer in Luke's *door* parable are all from Matthew's *ten virgins*. Then Luke gives the rejoinder:

> We ate and drank in your presence, and you taught in our streets.

This is something like the protest of the damned at Matthew 7.22, 'Lord, Lord, did we not prophesy in your name, and cast out demons in your name, and do many mighty works in your name?' But the similarity is not close. 'We ate and drank in your presence' is rather an echo of Exodus 24.11, where at Sinai God 'did not lay his hand on the chief men of the people of Israel; they beheld God and ate and drank'. For the source of 'you taught in our streets', we need go no further than the introduction to this parable with its note that Jesus was on his way through towns and villages, teaching. Two divine visitations of Israel are thus invoked: Sinai and the ministry of Jesus. So the speakers are Jews. They attempt proprietary claims on God and Jesus – in vain because too late. The master of the house repeats his 'I do not know you', and adds from Matthew 7.23 (we have just seen a slight relation to Matthew 7.22) the curse 'depart from me, all you workers of iniquity'. Piling on the Matthean agony Luke's next verses, 28 and 29, read:

> There you will weep and gnash your teeth, when you see Abraham and Isaac and Jacob and all the prophets in the kingdom of God and you yourselves thrust out.
> And men will come from east and west, and from north and south, and sit at table in the kingdom of God.

The source is Matthew 8.11 and 12, the healing of the gentile centurion's servant:

> I tell you, many will come from east and west and sit at table with Abraham, Isaac, and Jacob in the kingdom of heaven, while the sons of the kingdom will be thrown into the outer darkness; there men will weep and gnash their teeth.

Luke alters Matthew's order to suit his patterning of history. Where Matthew had people from east and west coming to sit at table in the Kingdom of heaven followed by the ejection of the Jews, Luke has the Jews cast out first and then seeing from outside, first the heroes of the old order in the Kingdom of God and then men from all four points of the compass (rather than Matthew's two) at table in the Kingdom. So Matthew had a characteristically eschatological ejection. Luke transposes it into historical process and the time after the Lord has risen. The excluded Jews, set in the post-resurrection era of the Church, observe the past era of the Old Testament and the present Christian 'time of the gentiles'. The Jews are outside (historically) and not in 'outer darkness' as with Matthew (eschatologically). The international table fellowship takes the place of hell as a concluding climax. So the allegory is fitted to the vision of history. It ends with the Matthean aphorism of the first being last and the last first from Matthew 20.16‖Mark 10.31.

So the parable is a patchwork of Matthean texts, but patchwork of a highly integrated order thanks to the commanding dominance of Luke's historical sense and scheme. As Jeremias says (p. 95f), 'We can actually watch the process by which a new parable has arisen out of the fusion of the conclusion of a parable with certain similes.' In fact the conclusions of two parables are used, the *ten virgins* (the dusty answer from beyond the closed door) and the *labourers* (first last, etc.) and the similes are metaphors. But the note of excitement in Jeremias at this point is unmistakable and justified. Although Jeremias took this discovery no further, it is welcome evidence that we can indeed trace out here the genesis of a new parable. 'A new parable has come into existence: the parable of the Closed Door' (ibid.). But immediately the happy sense of discovery is dropped and Jeremias concludes: 'If the attempt to discover the original meaning of the parables is to succeed, we must discard all these secondary connections.' For Jeremias that 'original meaning', which alone matters, has to be Jesus' and not Luke's. It is a momentous little crisis for Jeremias. He makes a first-rate discovery, then drops it because it does not help his theory. For our different theory, however, it is welcome evidence of Luke making the sort of historical parable, including allegory, which he inherits as normative. Let us consider two points in conclusion. First, we do not need to imagine that Luke looked up each of the bits of Matthew that make his *door* parable: Matthew's metaphors and aphorisms are highly memorable and indeed easier to remember than to place. Second, the Q hypothesis has not been needed here. Instead, knowledge of Luke's historical pattern-making has enabled us to discover him editing Matthew according to his own observable predilections.

Luke 14.7–11 (*table places*) is deceptively simple. Apparently Jesus is giving prudential advice in social etiquette. Dining with a ruler of the Pharisees, he warns those whom he sees going for the places of honour of the social embarrassment they could incur. But there are signs that there is more to it than that. It is called 'a parable', which usually implies significance beyond the particular and obvious instance. Its climax is a quotation of Matthew 23.12 about the humbling of the exalted and the exaltation of the humble. In Matthew it follows upon a criticism of Pharisaical social climbing and an injunction to his disciples to behave otherwise, to be brethren in service. Pharisaical norms are superseded by Christian. If we further notice that Jesus is here using the theology of reversal announced in the Magnificat at 1.52f – the mighty unseated and the low exalted, the hungry filled and the rich sent away empty – we have enough hints that Luke's grand historical plan is showing itself again. It was, after all, around the issue of table fellowship that, according to Acts and Galatians in their different ways, the issue of Christian identity was decided. There is sufficient reason to think that something more than manners is referred to by this parable, that Luke's everyday realism is again combined with a wider historical reference allowed by tacit elements of allegory.

The *banquet* follows and is the last in this group of thoroughly edited parables. It is a version of Matthew's *marriage feast* with big differences. Its allegorical significance is diminished by Luke's substitution of a man giving a banquet, for Matthew's king (God) giving a marriage feast for his son (Christ). But allegory is increased by the second and third rounds of invitations: to the poor of the 'city' and then to people in 'highways and hedges', signifying, as many commentators agree, the Church's missions to disregarded Jews and to Gentiles. The setting of the parable also makes clear that here, more definitely than in the preceding instruction about places at table, something beyond etiquette is signified:

> When one of those who sat at table with him heard this, he said to him, 'Blessed is he who shall eat bread in the kingdom of God!' But he said to him . . .

Then the parable makes clear that the blessed state enthusiastically referred to is conditional on responding positively to the invitation. Eternal happiness has historical conditions. On the other hand Luke omits, as well as Matthew's king's son's marriage, the demolition of the city of the unresponsive at Matthew 22.7 with its clear reference to the fall of Jerusalem. This could well be because, for all its historical appeal, it is too fantastic a feature of the parable for one who likes his parables to be realistic. It is certainly not because Luke does not care about the catastrophe. He also omits the ejection and killing of the improperly dressed guest; for the same probable reason. The result is a more unified and likely story. But it is not obviously, as Creed believes (*The*

Gospel According to St Luke [Macmillan 1930] p. 191) a simpler one. If Matthew's bloodthirsty interludes go, Luke has a more complex and vivid set of three excuses with scriptural backing in Deuteronomy 20. He also has the three deliberately allegorical rounds of invitations. That there are fewer jolts along the line of Luke's story than Matthew's is more demonstrably due to his greater narrative skill than to primitive simplicity. 'Luke does not allegorize', says Creed (ibid.), but then commenting on verse 21 allows the significance that 'the Pharisees and the religious leaders having rejected their opportunity, they are replaced by the publicans and sinners'. Jeremias is similarly inconsistent. Goulder, too, having asserted that 'Luke shows a marked aversion from allegory' (p. 59), says that 'Luke's secondariness is made certain by the added allegory of the gentile mission' (p. 418). Such confusion can be avoided by simply dropping the *a priori* assumption that Luke is unallegorical. His text shows that he can handle both the simply realistic and the allegorical. This parable in comparison with Matthew's version shows him combining both well. He cuts allegorical ornaments in the interest of the narrative line – and adds them elsewhere. It is not that Luke eschews allegory but that he has other ways of telling parables as well: realistic ways which can happily include and bear allegorical significance. Here in the *banquet* parable his redistribution of the allegorical weight is done to the template of his overall historical pattern. Matthew's improperly dressed guest and his fate brought the curtain down on doomsday as the decisive crisis. Luke's insertion of the gentile mission, like his more detailed excuses, shifts the crisis back from the end and into history itself as the decisive arena.

We have considered two sets of parables in Luke's journey section. The L parables gave a clear insight into Luke's methods: his historical patterning, his human interest, his continuance of the long allegorical parabolic tradition which he inherited in addition to his own more realistic narrative interests. The same features were found in the second set, those parables in the journey section which use materials found in the other two Synoptic Gospels, mostly Matthew. There too his people behaved more ordinarily and intelligibly than Mark's or Matthew's, they acted within his middle-of-time historical pattern, and often their deeds and characters had allegorical significance. In view of this similarity of the two sets, L parables and Q parables in the journey section, is the Q hypothesis necessary? One of its features is the notion that Luke has the simpler and more primitive – and so more Q – version of parables. After unravelling the complexities of Luke's *servants* and *door* parables that notion no longer looks plausible:

particularly since their complexities were integrated and given a certain unified coherence (which could be called simplicity) *by Luke's own ideas and methods*. His *banquet*, so often held up as a simpler and unallegorical Q predecessor of Matthew's *marriage feast*, has emerged as a version with its own detail and allegory – and intelligibly Lucan. The Q hypothesis has flourished on critics' knowing Matthew's obtrusive editorial ways well, but having much less appreciation of Luke's, which are subtler. As Luke's methods are understood the necessity for Q diminishes.

Parables before the Journey Section

Now that we have some acquaintance with Luke's ways and means as an evangelist we can better examine his work as an editor of existing parables in that part of his book which comes before Jesus sets out on his journey to Jerusalem.

He begins with a faithful and conservative copying of the metaphors used by John the Baptist in his preaching at Matthew 3.7–10‖Luke 3.7–9. He changes the audience from Matthew's Pharisees and Sadducees to 'the multitudes that came out to be baptized by him'. So he gets a wider historical scope of the sort adumbrated by the international dating with which chapter 3 began. John's figurative preaching is given word for word as it is in Matthew: vipers, fruit, stones, axe, trees and fire. The same applies, with very slight modification, to the metaphor of winnowing at Luke 3.17‖Matthew 3.12. It is worth noticing that in verse 16 he betrays knowledge of Mark as well, having his 'there comes' (Greek *erchetai*) instead of Matthew's 'he who comes' (Greek *erchomenos*), and Mark's loosing his sandal's latchet instead of Matthew's bearing of sandals. So this is not a pure Q passage and presents problems to holders of that theory which they have to solve by positing overlap between Mark and Q which obfuscates their theory and makes it, at this point at least, redundant.

Luke follows Mark when he gives his first series of Jesus' parables, Section 2 in the list on p. 111. Jesus is at table in the house of his new disciple Levi the tax collector. Like Matthew at the same point, he omits Mark's introductory 'and John's disciples and the Pharisees were fasting' because this information is contained in the question, Why do Jesus' disciples not fast?, or as Luke prefers it, Why do they 'eat and drink'? Luke follows Mark in the metaphor of the *bridegroom* and sons of the bridechamber with which Jesus answers. It is an appeal to the exceptional historical nature of his ministry and death. The 'sons' fast in verse 34 as in Mark 2.19. They do not 'mourn' as in the parallel Matthew

9.15. Luke's 'while' in the same verse is Mark's Greek *en hō*, not Matthew's Greek *eph hoson*. Yet Luke agrees with Matthew in omitting the redundant second half of Mark 2.19. Here is editorial complexity to muddy the waters of any simple source theory. The Q hypothesis does not clear them. What is clear however is the simple fact that Luke is using a traditional allegory of the historic significance of Jesus and his disciples which has its vantage point on the other side of Jesus' passion.

In the next metaphor of *clothes* and patches Luke is energetic in making changes to Mark's version. For comparison, the two read:

> No one sews a piece of unshrunk cloth on an old garment; if he does, the patch tears (literally, 'takes', Greek *airei*) away from it, the new from the old, and a worse tear (Greek, *schisma*) is made. (Mark 2.21)

> He told them a parable also: 'No one tears (or 'divides' Greek *schisas*) a piece from a new garment and puts it upon an old garment; if he does, he will tear (or 'divide' Greek *schisei*) the new, and the piece from the new will not match (or 'agree with' Greek *sumphōnēsei*) the old'. (Luke 5.36)

The first thing Luke does is to substitute 'a piece from a new garment' for Mark's 'piece of unshrunk cloth'. It is a momentous change. 'New' for 'unshrunk' takes away the whole force of Mark's metaphor. But Luke has something else in mind. He adds a second and 'new' garment. This changes the outcome. In Mark it was a worse tear in the old garment disfigured by an inharmonious patch. Why? Clues are given by two verbs which Luke uses in his version although they are not in Mark's or Matthew's. The first is the Greek *schizo*, which is translated 'tear' in its two instances in our RSV translation. That is a possible translation; all the synoptic evangelists use *schizo* of the tearing or splitting of the temple veil at Jesus' death. John uses it of the dividing of Jesus' robe at the crucifixion and the splitting of the net in the miraculous catch of fish. So 'divide' and 'split' are equally allowable translations. It is a versatile word. In the Johannine instances it is used in contexts which are most probably symbolic. The splitting of the net, for example, signifies the threat to the unity of the Church posed by its missionary success. *Schizo* lends itself to symbolism by having another and less material use: the intellectual or religious dividing of a body of people. Luke uses it at Acts 14.4. ·

> The people of the city were divided; some sided with the Jews, and some with the apostles.

And at Acts 23.7 the council is split between Pharisees and

Sadducees on resurrection. The noun *schisma* which figures in Mark's and Matthew's version of the parable, and so is the source of Luke's use of the verb *schizo*, is used in this way of divisions among the Jews in John's Gospel (7.43; 9.16; 10.19) and of divisions among Christians in 1 Corinthians (1.10; 11.18; 12.25). It emerges that 'divide' could be a better translation of *schizo* than 'tear' if the meaning of division in a body of people is allegorically present in this parable.

The second verb shows that it is. *Sumphōneo*, which is translated as 'match' in the RSV, signifies agreement between people in all the other uses of it in the New Testament. Matthew has it of the agreement of Christians at 18.19, and of the master with the *labourers* at 20.2 and 13. Luke uses it in Acts of the collusion of Ananias and Sapphira and of the agreement of the prophets of the Old Testament to the admission of Gentiles into the Church at Acts 15.15. The word is much, and symbolically, deployed in Hermas, *Vis.* III.ii–v. This is a parabolic vision of the Church as, surrealistically, a tower built on water (i.e. baptism) by angels. *Sumphōneo* is used throughout of the fitting together of the stones which symbolize the 'apostles, bishops, teachers and deacons' who 'always agreed [the same verb] among themselves'. In the Septuagint *sumphōneo* is always used of people.

With *schizo* meaning the dividing of material objects or of a group of people and *sumphōneo* meaning the agreeing of people, and only symbolically the agreeing of things like stones or pieces of cloth, it is clear that the trouble Luke takes to recast the parable is in aid of heightening its symbolic reference to the human world. He is interested in the human world as a Christian historian, recording the emergence of a new religious body over against the old one. The parable reads well if we suppose that the two garments represent those two bodies: Church and Judaism. In Acts the Church causes the Jews to disagree. It is of the utmost importance to Luke that the Church should not be similarly divided. His account of the ecclesiastical council at Jerusalem is his most conspicuous effort to this end. So the parable is an historical allegory apt to his grand narrative design. He introduces it with a deliberately added note that it is a parable. And so it is in two major traditional ways. It is an allegory of history, as such improving on its source. And it has a twist of riddling absurdity: who would divide a new garment to patch up an old one with which it does not 'agree'?

Last in the Marcan series is the metaphor of *wineskins*. Like the two previous ones it stands in Mark as an historical signpost. Matthew had improved on Mark by not having the new wine destroyed along with the old wineskins. The wine is not destroyed or lost but released. The change is from *apolluō*, I destroy or lose, to *apoluō*, I release or let go: a difference of only one letter which puts right the unfortunate implication in Mark that the Christian gospel comes to nothing. Luke agrees with Matthew in making it within this Marcan context. He also adds the complacently traditionalist Jewish drinker who, as a lover of old wine, does not want new for, he says, 'the old is good'. The addition both fills out the historical reference and symmetrically matches the old garment of the previous parable which would not 'agree' with the new patch.

The series *bridegroom*, *clothes*, *wineskins* not only shows Luke taking up Mark's historically symbolic metaphors. It also shows him enhancing their range and precision of allegorical reference in the last two instances. It has, after all, long been known that Luke is a versatile stylist.

Luke's Sermon on the Plain is shorter than Matthew's Sermon on the Mount. It begins like it with blessings and ends like it with the parable of *two houses*. By adding woes to blessings Luke gets contrast at the beginning of the Sermon to match the contrast-parable at its end. And between the two the Sermon divides into a first half about goodness and a second half which contrasts it with badness. It is a sermon about basic ethics and as such can afford to lose the details of piety and the casuistry in Matthew's version. Four Matthean/Q parables occur in the second part of the sermon.

First is the *blind guide*. He is in the conditional at Matthew 15.14 ('if the blind . . .') and in the interrogative, by which Luke particularly likes to introduce parables, at Luke 6.39 ('can the blind . . .?'). Luke prefixes the note, 'He also told them a parable'. Consistently with the similar prefix to the *clothes* and *wineskins* he understands parables as including functional elements of the absurd. The *speck in the eye* at 6.41f follows Matthew 7.3–5 closely. Creed (op. cit., p. 97) notices that it is less well placed than in Matthew and in better Greek: the latter a good reason for believing it to be secondary to Matthew's version. The *trees* at 6.43f combine two of Matthew's three versions of this metaphor: Matthew 7.16–18 and 12.33. The mixing is much more likely to have happened loosely in the back of the mind than painstakingly by comparison of texts.

Only with the closing parable of the Sermon, the *two houses*, does Luke exert himself editorially. Most obviously, he makes it more realistic. Matthew's house built on a rock is a far less usual thing that Luke's house built on well dug foundations. Matthew's house gets the sort of apocalyptic battering from the weather that John Martin would have liked to paint: rain, flood, and winds. For Luke the flood is enough. After all, it is in fact more inevitably damaging to a house than the other two. Matthew's second builder built, crazily, on sand. Luke's builds 'without a foundation' which is more like jerry-building. We have, however, already noticed that Luke is capable of increasing realism and allegorical signification simultaneously: the mark of a seasoned literary craftsman. He does it here. The foundation which he emphasizes so deliberately is not just good building practice. It is also a stock image among early Christian writers. The first to use it is Paul at 1 Corinthians 3.10–11 (see p. 32) where the apostle makes the laying of a foundation ('which is Jesus Christ') the metaphor of his own evangelistic work. People are free to build on it as they will, but the judgement of fire, like the judgement of water in our parable, will test it. The pattern of foundation and catastrophe is the same as in our parable and the foundation is avowedly symbolic. It is picked up in Colossians 1.23 where Christians are exhorted to 'continue in the faith, founded and steadfast' and at Ephesians 2.20 in a more hierarchical vein, the Church being 'the household of God, built upon the foundation of the apostles and prophets, Christ Jesus himself being the chief cornerstone'. The Pastor uses it in a typical appeal to complacent self-interest at 1 Timothy 6.18f where the rich are advised to do good deeds 'thus laying up for themselves a good foundation in the future'. At 2 Timothy 2.19 the complacency is theological and institutional. The heretics will fail because 'God's firm foundation stands'. I have argued elsewhere (op. cit. pp. 15–25; see also S. G. Wilson, *Luke and the Pastoral Epistles* [SPCK 1979]) that Luke is contemporary with the writing of Ephesians and the Pastoral Letters. Their symbolic use of foundations is common ground with Luke.

The healing of the gentile centurion's servant follows Luke's Sermon at 7.1–10‖Matthew 8.5–13. There is thematic continuity with the *two houses* parable. The centurion is an apt example of a good builder. Materially he had, according to the delegation of Jewish elders who speak for him in Luke, 'built us our synagogue' out of generous love (the topic of the first part of Luke's Sermon) for the alien nation – even the love of enemies which was twice enjoined in Luke's Sermon as against Matthew's once. Spiritually he has faith in the word of Jesus: 'say the word only and my servant shall be healed'. Luke takes extraordinary pains to keep the centurion off-stage. This is dictated by his strict historical plan whereby Gentiles have their time in Acts. Cornelius there is his *alter ego*. He cannot *appear* in the Gospel any more than the Syro-

Phoenician woman from Mark. The raising from death of the widow's son at Nain comes next, a greater miracle which shows Jesus in his role of Elijah *redivivus*. In 1 Kings 17.8–24 Elijah met a widow 'at the gate of the city', who gave him food. Later her son died. Elijah revived him and 'delivered him to his mother'. So in Luke 7.11–17 Jesus meets a widow at 'the gate of the city', revives him and gives him to his mother. The bystanders, lest the reader has missed the significance of the episode, exclaim 'A great prophet has arisen among us!'. To make Jesus so firmly the antitype of Elijah, a role which Luke's predecessors gave to John the Baptist, raises the question of who John, then, is. It is dealt with in the next section, Luke 7.18–35∥Matthew 11.2–19. Two parables occur in it, the *reed* and the *children's games*. The *reed* is word for word the same as Matthew, the *children's games* only slightly spruced up in its grammar. It is, as we have seen, a little historical allegory of John's asceticism, Jesus' conviviality, and the failure of either to get the positive attention of 'this generation'. Luke is not only content with it, he once again boosts the allegorical significance by his preceding additional note at 7.29–30 that

> all the people and the tax collectors justified God, having been baptized with the baptism of John; but the Pharisees and the lawyers rejected the purpose (Greek *boulē*) of God for themselves, not having been baptized by him.

Next Luke provides, as is his wont, a vivid example of Pharisaic mugwumpery and the positive response of the disreputable. To this end he adapts the scene of Jesus' anointing by a woman from Mark 14.3–9∥Matthew 26.6–13, making the Simon of the story a Pharisee instead of a leper and the woman into a sinner. Simon's unspoken soliloquy, in which he sees the incident as contradicting the claim that Jesus is a prophet, is miraculously perceived by Jesus and answered with a parable of *two debtors*. It is both like Matthew's parable of *two debtors* at Matthew 18.23–35 and different from it. Here both debtors owe to the same lender instead of one to a third party and one to the other. The sums of money are more reasonable and everyday, but still work symbolically. A well-behaved Pharisee has less 'debt' to God than a badly behaved woman. Therefore divine forgiveness excites less love of God in him than in her. The two debtors, and the two kinds of people they stand for, are both under judgement as in the L parable of the *Pharisee and publican* at Luke 18.9–14. From Matthew's parable come the key words 'not having' and 'to repay' in verse 42. There are six Lucan words in the two verses. So vocabulary confirms what the comparison of the parables suggests, that this is a Matthean parable very thoroughly edited by Luke. It is allegorical, the lender being God and the two debtors, Pharisees and sinners: characters which for Luke are bound up into the emergence of Christianity over Judaism. The theme of female ministration to Jesus is taken up in the next verses where, at 8.2, women whom Jesus had exorcized and healed provide for Jesus out of their means. Parable and narrative support one another.

At 8.4 Luke begins the parable of the *sower*, and a stretch of editing Mark which goes on until 9.50. For the previous chapter and a half he has used Matthew freely, and he keeps his freedom here. He transposes a passage in Mark so that the *sower*, having been preceded by the note about ministering women, is followed by Jesus' rejection of his mother and brothers in favour of disciples. He keeps an eye on Matthew, agreeing with him in omitting the following phrases: Mark 4.26 'he said in his teaching', the 'it happened' in Mark 4.2, 'it did not give fruit' in Mark 4.7, and 'growing up and increasing' in Mark 4.8. Along with these four coincidences of omission Luke agrees with Matthew at 8.8 in having a participle instead of the present indicative for 'he who has ears'. The marine setting which Matthew kept forgetting disappears completely in Luke. Instead Jesus addresses city people. Luke's version is both simpler and more rhythmical than Mark's. His major editorial stroke concerns the seed on stony ground at verse 6. It becomes 'the rock', and the seed on it did not shoot up immediately but 'withered away because it had no moisture': which is decidedly more natural.

He also takes hints from Matthew in dealing with the troublesome Mark 4.10–12, omitting with him Mark's 'when he was alone', the redundant 'see' as well as 'look' (Luke 8.10‖Matthew 13.13), and the offensive 'lest they should turn and be forgiven'. The passage is not rejected but softened. Luke achieves this by abbreviation, rather than by the addition of explanatory material such as Matthew's 'to him who has shall be given', or the text from Isaiah about hard hearts and deaf ears at Matthew 13.15.

In the interpretation of the parable too Luke uses Matthew's editing, omitting with him both 'how then will you understand all the parables?' (Mark 4.13) and the phrase in the middle of Mark 4.19 'cares for other things enter in'. His main concern is to interpret the parable as being about belief and in a longer perspective than Mark's. He adds believing at verses 12 and 13. He extends the perspective by adding 'of God' to 'the word' at verse 11, which awakens echoes of Old Testament prophecy, and by adding 'in patience' to the fruit-bearing at verse 15. He also adds

131

the notion of perfection at verse 14 and the good heart at verse 15. The effect of these little changes is to adjust the interpretation towards a more general intelligibility than Mark's. Perennial problems of belief are set in a long historical view and in the motivations of the heart. This is just what we would expect of Luke. A couple of important verbs which he alone uses here are listed as characteristic by Hawkins: 'receive' and 'fall away' in verse 13. And there is the unique (to the New Testament) 'bring to perfection' (Greek *telesphorousin*) at verse 14.

Only the parable of the *lamp* remains from the other parables which cluster around the *sower* in Mark and Matthew. In Mark the lamp mysteriously 'comes'. In Matthew people light it and place it. Luke has 'no one after lighting a lamp...'. The metaphor has been steadily humanized. Matthew's light emerged to be the good works of disciples (Matthew 5.16). Luke's, here as at 11.33, is put 'so that those who enter may see the light'. It is a guide to the Church's converts. Each version is instructively characteristic of each evangelist. Luke's shows him to be as ready to use the symbolism of allegory, in the frame of his own historical vision, as either of his predecessors were – a readiness to which his version of the *sower* and its interpretation also testify.

Parables in the Journey Section

We looked at some of these in the introductory part of this chapter in order to get the preliminary view of Luke's preferences necessary for coping with the dauntingly large collection of parables which Luke presents. They exhibit, for example, his 'middle of time' pattern, their micro-shape coinciding with the macro-shape of Luke-Acts. Their crises are turning-points not ends: a development which we traced from Mark's *vineyard* parable, through Matthew's *vineyard* parables to Luke. In their concentration on the human they also capitalized on Matthew's parabolic work. Thirdly, we noticed in them a diminution of allegory, edged off by narrative realism, but not excluded: an edging off similar to Luke's postponement, not cancellation, of eschatology. Some parables in the Journey Section were considered in enough detail in that introduction to make it unnecessary to look at them again: the *strong man*, the *servants*, the *fig tree*, the *door* and the *banquet*. But that still leaves for detailed inspection Luke's greatest parables: among them, the *good Samaritan*, the *prodigal son* and the *unjust steward*, to name but three of a dozen or so. We will take them in order.

The *good Samaritan* is set in dialogue, as the *two debtors* of

Luke 7.41f was set in the argument with Simon the Pharisee about sinners and forgiveness. Here the argument, less heated and more amicable, is with a lawyer. The source for this preliminary dialogue is Matthew 22.34–40, where it is not preliminary but complete in itself. The source is not the parallel Mark 12.28–31. Luke's preference for Matthew's version is made evident by: the lawyer (Luke 10.25‖Matthew 22.35), not the scribe of Mark 12.28; the omission, as by Matthew, of the exordium to the commandments, 'the first is, Hear O Israel, the Lord our God, the Lord is One', at Mark 12.29; the omission, again as by Matthew, of 'there is none other commandment greater than these' at Mark 12.30. Yet Luke betrays memory of Mark by the 'strength' with which God should be loved in Mark 12.30‖Luke 10.27, absent from Matthew 22.37. It is awkward for the Q hypothesis that Matthew and Luke should agree so resoundingly together in a Marcan narrative context. Q, to survive, has to resort to the additional unverifiable theory of overlap with Mark. Further, there is development from Matthew to Luke here. Luke increases the element of dialogue by having the lawyer begin with the question, 'What shall I do to inherit eternal life?' (ex Mark 10.17). Then Jesus asks him, in turn, how he reads in the law. So he, not Jesus, recites the double commandment. Jesus congratulates him and he asks Jesus, 'Who is my neighbour?' – the occasion for the parable. In place of the single question and single answer in Matthew, Luke has three questions and two answers, *plus* the parable which forms the third answer. There is more dialogue after the parable. Adding dialogue is an editorial habit of Luke's which can also be seen in the *pounds* (19.25) and the *vineyard* (20.13 and 16f). For Matthew, Jesus' single answer sufficed; 'on these two commandments depend all the law and the prophets'. What more could be said? Luke holds with the law (Luke 16.17). He is not as emphatic about it as Matthew. Rather, he takes it in his Christian stride. The lawyer's answer from the law is emphatically right. More, it recalls the emphasis in Luke's Sermon on the Plain on the law as generous philanthropy. So there is nothing here to contradict but rather much to exploit and explore. What more could be said? A parable could be told and a realistic Lucan story-parable at that, to expound the favourite Lucan theme of philanthropy.

So here is a parable of people: a man in crucial need, two representatives of central Judaism and one of its fringe – a Samaritan. For Luke the Temple is (or was) as central to Judaism as law. Jesus went there as a boy as well as teaching there at the end of his life. At the beginning of Acts the apostles frequent the Temple. Here the two official Jews are temple officials. The parable is shaped by the *crux* in the middle of it when the Samaritan does what the Jewish clergy had neglected: after which life, restored and mended, goes on. The basic pattern – Christianity going on beyond the failure of Judaism – lies behind it. There is, as so often in L parables, an emphasis on money which owes something to Matthew (Mark had no money in his parables such as Matthew did in his *talents* and *labourers*), but it is done with more care for everyday realism. The parable contains twelve words which occur only here in the New Testament: a usual feature of L parables, attributable to their richness of detail. Creed sees it as one of a group of parables, a close family not scattered throughout the Gospels but confined to Luke's, which

> are not parables in the usual sense of that word in the gospels. The usual parable describes one natural process or happening in social life which presents an analogy to a spiritual truth; the point of the parable lies in the analogy . . . In the case, however, of these illustrative stories, the story itself conveys the moral. (op. cit., pp. 150f)

'Illustrative stories' is good. So is the perception that story and moral form a self-contained whole and Creed's modest implication that here is something new in the tradition of gospel parables. Yet it is not entirely new. As we have seen, realistic stories as vehicles of ethics and theology were an older genre in the Old Testament than the historical-allegorical parables of Ezekiel. The Joseph and David sagas are examples. Esther and Judith show the genre flourishing in post-exilic Judaism. And from post-exilic Judaism comes the source of this *good Samaritan* story, a narrative in 2 Chronicles 28. Ahaz, King of Judah, was captured by Syria in divine retribution for liturgical apostasy, the Chronicler's bugbear. Israel joined in the punishment of Judah gleefully, killing and taking prisoners. The prophet Oded denounced this fratricidal cruelty and the chief men of Samaria took his part by refusing entry to the triumphant Israelites.

> So the armed men left the captives and the spoil before the princes and all the assembly. And the men who have been mentioned by name ['men of Ephraim', sc. Samaritans] rose and took the captives, and with the spoil they clothed all that were naked among them; they clothed them, gave them sandals, provided them with food and drink and anointed them; and carrying all the feeble among them on asses, they brought them to their kinsfolk in Jericho, the city of palm trees. Then they returned to Samaria. (2 Chronicles 28.14f)

134

Clothing the naked, anointing, provision of food and drink (at an inn in Luke), carrying on asses and Jericho: all are there in Luke's story without exact verbal correspondences, suggesting strongly that the *good Samaritan* story in Luke draws on memory of the original good Samaritans story in 2 Chronicles. We cannot tell whether Jesus told it. Luke certainly did, and he was an apt pupil and imitator of the Old Testament historians.

From the good life as works Luke turns, in his story of Martha and Mary, to the good life as listening and then prayer. Jesus teaches his disciples to say, 'Father, hallowed be thy name', and then gives as an example of praying the story of the *friend at night*. Its advice to be importunate makes it one of a pair with the *unjust judge* at Luke 18.1–8. It begins with Luke's favourite interrogative phrase, 'Which of you?'. The calling up in the night and the shut door may be some reminiscence of Mark's *servants* at 13.35 or of Matthew's *ten virgins*, but it is slight. The substance of the story is very much Luke's. The concern with provisions was part of the first L parable, the *good Samaritan*, and returns here to remind us of the part played by eating in Luke's theology, from the Magnificat (Luke 1.53) through the hungry (not 'after righteousness' as Matthew) of the Sermon at 6.21, and the table scenes, to these L parables which include a banquet for the *prodigal son*, the *rich man's* sumptuous fare and the servant waiting on his master at table (17.7ff).

The shape is Lucan, a crisis arising in the course of ordinary life which, once dealt with, sets life off again on a better tack. Here the crisis is relieved not out of pure compassion, as in the *good Samaritan*, but for the sake of sleep and peace. The request is shameless, even impudent, the response grumpy as befits someone woken in the night. Both the realism and the positive use of negative human reactions are common in the L parables, the latter most famously in the *unjust steward* and the *unjust judge*. Journeys, too, figure in the L parables. There is a friend on a journey here. The *good Samaritan* and the *prodigal son* are much on the road. Luke's fondness for travel was shared with contemporary writers of romances and blooms in Acts. The man in bed does not have a soliloquy such as occurs in several L parables but we are told his motivation for getting up and supplying his neighbour's need. There is a slight allegorical element, the asker standing for the Christian at prayer and the giver for God. The fact that the giver is not entirely laudable in his motive is something which does not trouble evangelists so much as dainty modern commentators, as witness Mark's likening of the coming of the Lord to a nocturnal burglar. For Luke, jolts to the ordinary moral sense give the sense of surprise which Mark, less whimsically, got by his riddles and his doctrine of secrecy.

It is worth noticing a rabbinic parallel to the *friend at night* and the *unjust judge* which shows the same bold attitude to prayer. It is a comment on the barreness of Hannah before she bore Samuel (1 Samuel 1):

> Said Hannah before the Holy One, Blessed be He: 'Sovereign of the Universe, of all the hosts and hosts that thou hast created in Thy world, is it so hard in Thine eyes to give me a Son?' A parable: to what is the matter like? to a king who made a feast for his Servants, and a poor man came and stood by the door and said to him 'Give me a bite!' And no one took any notice of him. So he forced his way into the presence of the king and said to him, 'Your majesty, out of all the feast which thou hast made is it so hard in thine eyes to give me one bite?'   (*Ber.* 192)

There are three parables in the Beelezebub controversy which follows. The first is of *divided kingdom/house*. Luke 11.17 takes the phrase 'kingdom against itself' (Greek, *basileia eph 'eauton*) from Mark, not Matthew. But from Matthew he takes 'brought to desolation' (RSV 'laid waste') which is not in Mark. Luke's 'house falls upon house' is his own free version, apparently envisaging a street of houses. We have already noticed his free redaction of the metaphor of the *strong man* (p. 117). By contrast, he treats Matthew's *empty house* conservatively, even slavishly. It would seem to be allegory of Jewish history such as he would be inclined to respect and welcome as it stands. The *lamp* metaphor at 11.33 is allegorized as it was before at Luke 8.16: the light guides those who enter, the converts to Christianity.

With the *rich fool* at Luke 12.13–21 we are back with the L parables. It is about their favourite theme of material goods and contains a soliloquy: 'What shall I do?', he wonders, like the unjust steward and the lord of the vineyard at Luke 20.13 (Luke's addition to Mark). It is an exemplary tale: this time in the negative form of warning against the obsession with riches displayed by the one from the crowd who asks, 'Teacher, bid my brother divide the inheritance with me'. Like the *good Samaritan*, this parable draws substantially on the Old Testament. The man is a fool in the sense used by the Psalmists: he reckons neither with God nor time. The use of Ecclesiasticus 11.18f confirms the 'wisdom' character of it:

> There is a man who grows rich through his diligence and self-denial, and this is the reward allotted to him: when he says 'I have found rest and now I shall enjoy my goods!' he does not

know how much time will pass until he leaves them to others and dies.

The story of Tobit is also in the background. At Tobit 7 Tobias and his angelic companion arrive at the house of his uncle Raguel. Raguel's daughter Sarah is a *femme fatale*: the young men who marry her die on their wedding nights, killed by a jealous demon which is in love with her. Tobias' angel plans to drive off the demon so that Tobias can survive where others have failed. Before the dangerous night Raguel says to Tobias,

> Eat, drink and be merry; for it is right for you to take my child. But let me explain the true situation to you. I have given my daughter seven husbands, and when each came to her, he died in the night. But for the present be merry.   (Tobit 7.9–11)

So Ecclesiasticus gives Luke conventional wisdom which suits his favourite narrative shape: after the crisis of a man's death life goes on without him and his goods go to others. Tobit gives him 'eat, drink and be merry' on the eve of a night which looks like being Tobias' last. The phrase is also at Ecclesiastes 2.24 and Greek examples in Creed, op. cit., p. 173 – this was a widespread *parabolē* in our first Old Testament sense of 'saying')'. There is no allegory in this story at all. It is an incident in the ordinary world, the moral force of which is intelligible to common sense.

Matthew's metaphor of birds from the Sermon on the Mount (Matthew 6.26) follows very aptly. The birds are exemplary, as L parables are. Luke makes them ravens – with scriptural point, since at Job 38.41 and Psalm 147.9 the young ravens are fed by divine providence. Instead of Matthew's 'they do not gather into barns' Luke has 'they have no storehouse or barn', which could be reckoned a little less weird. The companion *lilies* are left by Luke much as they are in Matthew.

The extended *servant* parable at 12.35–48 has already been considered (p. 117). So has the *fig tree* at 13.6–9. The *mustard seed* at 13.18–19 is another conflation by Luke, probably using memory as well as texts, of Mark and Matthew. It starts with a double question,

> What is the kingdom of God like?
> And to what shall I compare it?

Compare Mark 4.30:

> With what can we compare the kingdom of God,
> or what parable shall we use for it?

By contrast Matthew 13.31 is a simple and single narrative

statement, 'he told them another parable'. A man sows the seed – in his garden according to Luke, and contrary to Jewish law which he does not know as well as Matthew. He uses the verb 'grow' as Matthew does but not Mark who prefers 'go up'. It becomes a tree in both Luke and Matthew but not Mark. We have seen that Matthew's parable was a version of Mark's. Goulder agrees with Butler (p. 370) in seeing the parable as 'classic for the dispensability of the Q theory'. The *leaven* which pairs with it follows Matthew faithfully. The three measures of meal in which the leaven is hidden could be symbolic of the three days of Jonah in the fish's belly at Matthew 12.40. Why these two parables follow upon the healing of the bent woman is obscure.

The parable of the *door* has been considered at pp. 119ff and the *banquet* with the directions about sitting at table and invitations at pp. 123f. So we can go on to the parables of *tower*, *kings at war* and *salt* at Luke 14.28–35. They are about discipleship, adding to Matthew's stern teaching of leaving family and taking up the cross. They are typically Lucan exemplary parables: practical, prudential and realistic. A leap into the dark is transmuted into common sense. Luke's version of Matthew's house-builder could be a source for the first of them, the *tower*. Here as there, foundation is mentioned. It is introduced with Luke's formula 'Which of you?', and in its two verses contains two words found only here in the New Testament ('cost' and 'completion', Greek *dapanē* and *apartismon*). Such *hapax legomena* are typical of Luke and an aspect of his detailed naturalism.

The *kings at war* (Luke 14.31f) is an exact pair to the *tower*, as the *lost coin* will be to the *lost sheep* in chapter 15. It too is prudential and commonsensical. It too revolves around a mid-term crisis. An Old Testament influence on it might be King Toi of Hamath sending an embassy to David with gifts at 2 Samuel 8.10. A nearer historical influence may well be the catastrophe of AD 70: if only Jewish nationalists had come to terms with Rome, had agreed with the adversary quickly (Matthew 5.25)! That this is a thought in Luke's mind, whether or not it informs this parable, is witnessed by Jesus' lament over Jerusalem, only in Luke and at 19.41–4:

Would that even today you knew the things that make for peace! But now they are hid from your eyes. For the days shall come upon you, when your enemies will cast up a bank about you and surround you, and hem you in on every side, and dash you to the ground, you and your children within you, and they will not leave one stone upon another in you; because you did not know the time of your visitation.

The parable is about discipleship by virtue of its association with sayings on this theme. It is typical of Luke to deal with the theme prudentially and in figures drawn from the public stage. Of the vocabulary, 'and if not' (Greek *ei de mēge*) is in Hawkins' list along with *pros* (*eirēnen*/'peace') at the end of the parable. *Sunbalein*, translated as 'encounter' in the RSV, occurs only in Luke-Acts in the New Testament – seven times; *bouleuomai* occurs thrice in Luke-Acts and elsewhere only in John (2) and 1 Corinthians (1). Altogether, it looks like Luke's work.

Last in this group of three comes *salt*. It has had a previous history more certainly traceable than the preceding two. We have seen Matthew making Mark's confused version into something clearer (p. 75). It is Matthew's version which Luke uses here, along with its Matthean motif of throwing out useless salt. But he keeps Mark's 'salt is good'. We have seen that such composite editing, probably using memory, is typical of him. This is a parable of the riddle type beloved of Mark. Salt does not lose its savour. Luke compounds the absurdity, in a vein of rather plodding realism, by pointing out that it is useless even as manure.

The parables of Luke 15 and 16.1–8 are Luke's *pièce de résistance*, equivalent as such to Mark 4, which he reduced to something of a shadow of its former self, or Matthew 25. It includes that parable of parables to modern minds, the *prodigal son*, which has been turned into ballet, opera and numerous pictures and sculptures. On either side of it come other parables about the restoration of loss: the *sheep* and the *coin* before it and the notorious *unjust steward* after it. We shall see Luke at his best here, deploying all his favourite themes and techniques with a freshness and vigour which survive endless readings and interpretations.

The section is set up in a clear historical context. We have examined it on p. 114. Tax-collectors and sinners gather round Jesus to hear him. Pharisees and scribes complain that he receives sinners and eats with them. So there is a sharp division between Jesus and sinners on one side, Pharisees and scribes on the other. Such is the context and the first parable is called a parable, presumably because it is an allegory of the historical situation so lucidly presented.

Luke's *lost sheep* is an amplified version of Matthew's at 18.12–14. About a quarter of Matthew's original survives in its vocabulary, most of it in the beginning at Luke 15.4: the man, his ninety-nine safe sheep and one lost, his looking for the lost. In the next verse the key verbs from Matthew survive, finding and rejoicing. Verse 6 has no words from Matthew. The final verse 7 has only

Matthew's heaven, and his ninety-nine and one again. So Matthew provides the basic materials. But Luke has altered the setting from ecclesiastical pastoralia to the world at large. This is not a simple sign of historical accuracy, since the setting of the Christian gospel in the historical world at large is as major, obvious and continuous a theological concern of Luke's as the Church was for Matthew. Luke has also added his verse 6: the return to the house, the gathering of friends and neighbours, the celebration and the little speech. We are told in the next verse that these signify the joy in heaven when a sinner repents, a more vivid and concrete little apocalyptic scene (happy apocalyptic!) than Matthew's 'it is not the will of my father in heaven that one of these little ones should perish'. We get a glimpse of celestial celebration. It comes out of Matthew's more laconic 'he rejoices over it'. Luke has three words of rejoicing (*chairein*: characteristic of him in Hawkins' list), in contrast to Matthew's three uses of going astray. And the sheep has taken over the centre of interest from the shepherd: a sign of what is to come in the *prodigal son*. The Lucan shape of mid-term crux asserts itself over Matthew's final crux, mainly by the party in the house having space to itself after the recovery. And the human element is amplified. Once again Luke shows himself able to combine allegory with natural vividness: the sheep is any sinner rather than Matthew's erring Christian, the friends and neighbours are presumably angels, the shepherd is Jesus whereas in Matthew he was a Christian pastor. (This identification has precedent in Mark 6.34 where Jesus pities the crowd for being like sheep without a shepherd so he feeds them; and perhaps Mark 14.27 where Jesus is the stricken shepherd of Zechariah 13.7.) Not everything in the parable is allegorical, but enough to make it less than a self-contained realistic unity: it refers to the historical world of Jesus' ministry and to the heavenly realm. As for the leading theme of this and the three subsequent parables, as Creed judiciously observes, 'the glad tidings of God's love for the penitent sinner proclaimed by Jesus is *the evangelist*'s favourite theme, and into this parable that theme is concentrated' (p. 196, my italics).

Creed's judgement is supported by the next parable of the *lost coin*. There is no need to posit Q or any other source than the *lost sheep*. The reader will have no difficulty in making up any number of variations on it himself: the lost child, the lost letter, the lost bicycle – and the reader may well be a less able storyteller than Luke. That Luke made up the *lost coin* is further and strongly suggested by its being about a coin, for we have seen his care for money in the *good Samaritan* and elsewhere. It is about a woman, and we have seen his interest in women at 8.2f; also in the prominence of Mary and Elizabeth in his infancy stories and in the Martha and Mary incident at 10.38–41. This, too, is not unprecedented. Women are the witnesses of the resurrection in Mark. Once again there is some allegory in the naturalism: Jesus is the housewife, the sinner is the coin, the angels are, overtly now, the friends and neighbours. But the allegory is giving trouble. It is failing to fit at the crucial point. At the end of both parables the 'one sinner who repents' was declared to be its point. But there was no equivalent for such repentance in the parable itself. Neither the sheep nor the coin repented. Such oversight is, according to the normal practice of gospel criticism, a sign of editing. So it is unlikely that Luke has a primitive Q version here. He is doing his own work. But more important than this is Luke's problem and his solution of it. The allegorical structure of these two parables has given him a sheep and a coin as equivalents not just of the sinner – that might have been all right – but of the sinner *who repents.* What could a sheep be got to do that would represent repentance; still more awkwardly, a coin? Repentance is decidedly a human act. Luke's solution is to leave the symbolic treatment of the sheep and the coin for the direct treatment of a human being. Only that will do full justice to the theme. At this fascinating turning-point we can see Luke's revolution in the making and use of parables: the transition from symbolism to realism. It is not a merely literary experiment; it is driven and required by Luke's fundamental conviction that theology is realized in the material historical world of people. The theology of the Deuteronomic historians and the commonsensical wisdom school takes over at this point from the apocalyptists' other-worldly wisdom which could not but emerge in symbols and allegories. Luke cannot do what he most wants to do in the old parabolic way. The story of the *lost and found son* follows upon the stories of *lost and found sheep* and *coin* and is born of them; yet born of their limitations, and the overcoming of them, as much as of their positive power to suggest and stimulate. This is some reason for the unequalled quality of the *lost son.* In it something happens to the traditional parable form such as Mozart did to traditional opera: a new depth of human realism revives and renews an old genre.

Jeremias is serenely confident that this is a parable of Jesus. He refers throughout to Jesus as its author, does none of the restoration which he does on parables which he believes to have suffered later editing, and is happy simply to explain it as Jesus' own vindication of his message and method.

There are about 380 words in the parable of which 36 are in

Hawkins' list of characteristically Lucan words and phrases. It is worth adding again that the wealth of detail in the tale, its rich circumstantiality, bring in many words so rare in the Gospels that they would slip through any statistical net. So we have about a tenth of the words characteristically Lucan, or 36 words in 22 verses: a slightly higher count of verbal *spécialités de la maison* than we got with Mark's *sower*. They also come in a very fair overall spread.

For syntax I refer to Plummer (ICC Commentary lxii f) and Cadbury (*The Making of Luke–Acts* [SPCK 1927] pp. 213–38), who mention the following usages which occur in this parable:

11	The indefinite 'a certain' (Greek *tis*)
12	Participle with the article: 'the due share' (*to epiballon meros*)
13, 31	The use of 'all' (*pan*)
14, 17 20, 21	Frequent use of the personal pronoun (*autos*)
24, 29 30, 32	Emphatic words (*houtos, oudepote, tosauta*)
25	Combination of cognate words: 'as coming he approached' (*erchomenos engisen*)
20	'While' constructions
24	'Begin' in a week sense
28	'so . . . and' (*de . . . kai*)

Cadbury (op. cit., chapter 16) notices some major features of Luke's style, three of which occur in this parable. There is the invention of speeches for the actors in styles appropriate to each, which Luke could have learned from Greek historians (from Jewish too, the David history being full of this). There is the use of parallel and contrasting pairs of which the two brothers here are as good an example as any. There is 'the sense of suspense and the quality of pathos' which pervades this whole parable. More could be added: the interest in goods and property in a middle-class setting, the reversal of fortunes, repentance, fondness for journeys, the soliloquy, fondness for the dinner table and the pervasive background in Old Testament story and in Deuteronomy, the use of 'biblical' (i.e. Old Testament) style in the prodigal son's confession. These last two features will come up again in considering the wider cultural setting. Anyhow, enough has been said and found to land us in the preposterous position that if Jesus is the author of this parable then it must follow that there is a case for his authorship of Luke's Gospel.

It is worth looking back from this peak of Luke's work over the preceding terrain again and with a longer perspective. The *prodigal son* is the climax of a theme of repentance which has been running and growing strongly throughout the central section of this book and particularly from the beginning of chapter 13. It is not only, or just, the repentance of individuals which is at stake but that of the Jewish nation at large as it walks blindfold towards the catastrophe of AD 70. And it is presented by means of a narrative pointed up, and even dominated, by wisdom parables (that is, parables about common sense and coping) which are sometimes derivative from Matthew/Q and sometimes original. Chapter 13 started with the discussion of two ostensibly historical incidents used parabolically to instil the need of repentance: the massacre of Galileans and the disaster at Siloam. Then came something which was an historical incident in Mark but which Luke turns into a parable with similar purpose but more temporal spaciousness: the *fig tree*. The healing of the bent woman had a more than individual purport if as 'daughter of Abraham' she refers to a bent nation. The national interest came into the open with Jesus' prophetic lament over Jerusalem at 13.31–5. Chapter 14 began with a miracle, the healing of a dropsical man on the sabbath, which invited rethinking of sabbath customs and became a chapter about thinking and thinking again in the context of the reversal of fortunes historically – both ways. So to the definitive handling of repentance in chapter 15: first with the *lost sheep* from Matthew/ Q, then with the *lost coin* which is built on the same plan, then with this parable of the *prodigal son* which brings in the human characters necessary to a handling of repentance and its opposite. Luke's creative abilities, particularly in the invention of parables from other sources, have been growing all the time and are now running high, carrying over into that most provocative of wisdom parables, the *unjust steward*. It hardly needs saying that, as well as fastening what has gone before, these great repentance parables point to what is coming. As Jesus tells them, he is on his minatory and ominous way to Jerusalem to present the capital city with its last call to change.

These four parables in 15.3—16.9 thus occupy a momentous point in Luke's narrative and are imbued with his view of history. It contrasts vividly with Mark's. Mark's *sower* was driven by the apocalyptic world view with its deterministic, and mostly pessimistic, view of human nature and history aptly symbolised by the inexorable and mysterious processes of nature. It is all very different with Luke. He believes in a fundamental capacity of human nature to change for the better and is a qualified historical optimist. He had learned his attitude from an older Old Testament school of historiography than the apocalyptists who shaped Mark's thinking. Before the collapse of confidence in the human moral scene as the place where things could come out right because it was a place within which God could work, there was a time when it held and flourished. Between Solomon and the Deuteronomic historians, it attained a scope and sophistication for which there was no parallel in contemporary historiography. Because the Deuteronomic historians did so magisterial a job of editing existing historical materials into a vast continuum, it is difficult to be at all precise about what went before – though the very achievement argues for considerable precedent. E. W. Heaton (*Solomon's New Men* [Thames and Hudson 1974]) has put the start of it with Solomon's scribes, trained Egyptian-style in practical realistic wisdom such as the arts of surviving and succeeding at court. They gave something to the Jewish tradition of far more interest than the customary chronicles and lists: such subtly realistic wisdom narratives as the stories of Joseph and of David's last years. Heaton compares their secular humanism and their realism to that of the European novelists of the eighteenth century and their *tableau de moeurs seculaires*. Already we are being reminded of the *prodigal son*. And we can be more precise. It is a parable to excite repentance, like Nathan's to David (2 Samuel 12) and is similarly realistic. It is also full of echoes of the Joseph story. It too begins with the younger son who goes down to a far county where he is neary caught by a harlot (Potiphar's wife), and where there was famine. It ends similarly. In Genesis 45 the son Joseph rushes to meet his approaching father Israel and falls on his neck: Luke's roles reversed. To the famine which occupies the middle of both tales the protagonists react differently – both shrewdly, but Joseph by provident administration and Luke's man be smelling roast veal from afar and 'coming to himself'. Pharaoh at Genesis 41.42 'took his signet ring from his hand and put it on Joseph's hand, and arrayed him in garments of fine linen'. So here at 15.22 the father says, 'Bring quickly the best robe and put it on him, and put a ring on his hand.' We are in the same world, or world-view. Here God worked in and through the human causality of the tale so implicitly as to be hidden in its continuum. It was resolved in the here and now, not the hereafter. Morality and history work together here in ways that are both predictable and, more, subtly unpredictable. The all-important twists and surprises come when a man copes with disaster by putting his mind to it, thinking again about himself and his historical situation, which is also and at the same time his situation before God. Likewise

144

David when he had committed adultery and murder, repented and was granted the continuity of his dynasty.

The *prodigal son* has sibling rivalry as a constituent theme. It was a favourite trope of Old Testament narrative. Deuteronomy dealt with it straightforwardly. Deuteronomy 21.15–17 defended the right of inheritance of the first-born son, even if his mother were a hated wife, against a younger son, even if his mother were a beloved wife. As for the 'stubborn and rebellious son' like this prodigal who is 'a riotous liver and a drunkard', he is to be stoned. Such is law. Things were very different, more complicated and more tolerant in the stories. There is a sneaking distrust of older brothers and fondness for the younger, even when less meritorious. It gave the excitement of reversal to many tales – and more scope to God. Of Cain and Abel, God preferred the younger. Younger Jacob/Israel supplanted senior Esau. There is an echo of that classic tale of sibling rivalry in the *prodigal son*. The elder son was 'in the field' when he heard of his young brother's return. Esau was a man of the field. When Jacob disguised himself as Esau to get his father's blessing he did it so well that the blind old man exclaimed: 'See, the smell of my son is as the smell of a field which the Lord has blessed.' Tales of younger brothers getting the better of elder were of great and practical appeal to the Christians as they argued their superiority to senior traditional Judaism. Paul at Galatians 4.21–31 invoked Ishmael and Isaac to this end.

There are still more Old Testament echoes in our parable. When, at the outset, the father divides his goods between his two sons, he flouts the sound advice of ben Sirach (Ecclesiasticus 33.19–23) to do no such thing before death because it puts a man in jeopardy. (King Lear and his daughters are the grandest example of such foolishness.) There are Old Testament echoes in the prodigal's soliloquy:

I will arise and go to my father, and I will say to him, 'Father, I have sinned against heaven and before you; I am no longer worthy to be called your son.'

Similarly Solomon in his great prayer at 1 Kings 8.47ff imagines prisoners of war:

If they shall bethink themselves in the land whither they are carried away captive, and turn and make supplication unto thee ... saying, we have sinned and done perversely ... if they return unto thee ... then hear thou their prayer.

There is further parallel to the prodigal's soliloquy at Exodus 10.16 where Pharaoh says to Moses, 'I have sinned against the Lord your

God and against you'; and in Hosea's prodigal wife who says to herself in her abandonment, 'I will go and return to my first husband; for then it was better with me than now' (Hosea 2.7). The elder brother's protest at the welcoming of his brother 'who has devoured your living with harlots' recalls Proverbs 29.3:

> whoso loveth wisdom rejoiceth his father, but he that keepeth company with harlots wasteth his substance.

Luke's greatest parable is a mosaic of Old Testament reminiscences. Old Testament stories provide its structure and pattern too. For they dealt with crises in the middle of time rather than at the apocalyptic end of all tales ever. The crises turn within the human mind and heart.

From there, via that momentous hinge of action and by repentance or resourceful coping with disaster, the narrative sets off on a new but continuous course. Luke's positive view of human history makes this a parable with a life of its own, and a very vigorous life of its own it has had, walking with ease out of its context in Luke's Gospel into all sorts of other places. It has come to mean so much. But what did it mean to Luke? Some judicious words of Creed's provide the clue:

> Luke's interpretation of the parable is given by his opening verse [sc. Luke 15.1f]: the younger son represents the publicans and sinners, and the elder brother the self-righteous Pharisees. And this no doubt is true of the mind and attitude of Jesus. It was a natural extension of the original idea that the younger son should be taken to mean the converted pagans and the elder brother the Jews.   (op. cit., p. 197)

'This no doubt is true of the mind and attitude of Jesus.' Very probably. It is also true of the function of biblical parables as we have discovered it all along this inquiry, that they should refer to the historical world of their origin. And this world contained many people and many parable tellers beside Jesus. This parable shows several signs of referring to the wider crisis 'precipitated by Jesus' of the schism between gentile Christianity and traditional Judiasm. The elder son speaks for Pharisaism when he says, 'these many years have I served you and I never disobeyed your command'. It is the voice of the Pharisee in the *Pharisee and the publican* parable of Luke 18.9–14, of Simon the Pharisee at Luke 7.39. The younger son in his far country with harlots and pigs is practically a Gentile – as Creed says, that is 'a natural extension'. We have seen that Luke is careful to postpone Gentiles until Acts. But he has got far away, geographically, morally and ritually, from orthodox Judaism. He is an archetype of the riff-raff on its fringe who mean so much to Luke in his Gospel. And the father cannot but represent God. Remembering what has been said about the placing of this parable in the narrative as a climax of Jesus' pleading with his compatriots to repent before it is too late, we can see that it has precise contemporary historical reference. Allegorical elements deeply embedded in its structure connect with it. It is continuous with the two preceding parables which were allegorical and as such posed a problem about repentance. Here the allegory is more apt and is easily carried by the story's captivating realism. But it is there. The historical context is pervasive: the origin of Christianity within Judaism at the point of Jesus' prophetic mission to his nation, and its imminent spread to the gentile world.

The *prodigal son* has elements of allegory. They matter for a full appreciation of its significance, particularly its historical significance. But they are optional in the sense that the story can be read without them; whereas the two previous parables of *lost sheep* and *lost coin* could not. The trend away from allegory becomes still more marked with the *unjust steward*. It is about a steward and a household, both of which are used in the epistles as figures of the church officer and the church. Paul at 1 Corinthians 4.1f had spoken of himself and others as 'stewards of the mysteries of God' who had to be 'found trustworthy'; and at 1 Corinthians 9.17 he had described himself as one entrusted with an *oikonomia* or stewardship. These figures were taken up in the Pauline and deutero-Pauline epistles. Titus 1.7 says that a bishop is God's steward. In Ephesians *oikonomia* is expanded into a wider significance which includes the whole of God's historical providence and grace (Ephesians 1.10; 3.9f). But any attempt to find this common symbolism in the *unjust steward* is unconvincing. It cannot plausibly be read as advice to church leaders. This remains true in spite of the parable's slight possible connection with Matthew 24.45–51‖Luke 12.42–6; the ambiguous parable of the faithful and wise servant who suddenly becomes 'that wicked servant'. Luke made him a steward and clarified Matthew's muddle somewhat by omitting the 'wicked'. The similarities with the *unjust steward* are in the two features of a head servant dealing with subordinates and the sudden visitation of the Lord finding everything in order or disorder. Allegorical deployment of the figures of steward and household was thus available to Luke, who had already used them in 12.42–6 in an ecclesiastical context. So it is very striking that here he uses the figure in a frame which is not allegorical but, as in the *prodigal son* but more so, narrative with a naturalism and vigour which need no symbolic assistance. So through the series of parables, *lost sheep – lost coin – prodigal son – unjust steward*, there is a progressive decline of the allegorical references which had once, and so recently, been constitutive of the parable, and a congruently progressive rise of the purely human and realistic narrative.

The *unjust steward* would be better called the 'crafty steward'. It commends shrewdness and cunning, favourite qualities of the earthy or realistic wisdom tradition of the Old Testament as opposed to the apocalyptic. Moral principles take a back seat. The art of coping is supreme. It takes tricks and even lies in its stride. The great thing is to get by, to come through: a theme far more suitable to spicy narrative than universalizable ethical generalization. It had enlivened many Old Testament stories of cunning escapes: of patriarchs pretending their wives were their sisters, of the numerous successful dirty tricks of Jacob/Israel the nation's father, of David whose moral ambivalence assisted his wonderful capacity for survival.

A story with particular resemblances to our steward is at 2 Kings 7. The Syrians were besieging Samaria, reducing its inhabitants to starvation. Four Samaritan lepers who were sitting in the gate decided that they had nothing to lose. 'Why sit we here until we die? If we say, we will enter into the city, then the famine is in the city and we shall die there: and if we sit still here, we die also.' So they fixed on a bold move. They would go out to the Syrians. They could only be killed by them, which was their likely fate in any case, and they just might be taken prisoner and so survive. When they got to the Syrian camp they found it deserted. God had frightened them away by miraculous military sound-effects. The lepers helped themselves to food, drink and booty. They hid a quantity of valuable spoil.

> Then they said to one another, 'We are not doing right. This day is a day of good news [LXX *euangelia*, 'gospels']; if we are silent and wait until the morning light, punishment will overtake us; now therefore come, let us go and tell the king's household.'

Notice that 'not doing right' is here more prudential than abstractly ethical: they stood to get into trouble with their compatriots. In the event, their report was believed after some hesitation. Luke, who knew his Old Testament well, would have been particularly attracted to this tale. It was about Samaritans. It was about lepers. And he has the only Samaritan leper in the Gospels (17.12ff). It was about a city under siege, and Luke was vividly aware of the siege of Jerusalem (21.20–4, particularly his additions). It mentioned *euangelia*, good news, which could not but be a magnet to the eye of the Christian historian and evangelist. It was about material goods. Above all it showed the sort of quick-footedness which Luke approved and which is the great point of the story. The *prodigal son* had just exhibited this very quality. Zacchaeus (only in Luke, 19.1–10) shows it too, together with a readiness to make amends with those whom he had defrauded.

However odd the *unjust steward* may seem to the morally nice reader, it is very much at home in Luke's Gospel, not least in its imitation of Old Testament narrative precedents. It is, indeed, exemplary of Luke's particular parabolic ways and means. The central character is both good and bad in a much more intelligible manner than Matthew's head servant. He has a soliloquy as he confronts his mid-term crisis. Money plays an indispensable part and the setting is prosperous. It contains some twenty Lucan words or phrases including nine of the *hapax legomena* which are common in Lucan parables. Altogether, it looks very much like Luke's work. But that is not to say that it is an utterly original tale born of his own unassisted ingenuity. We have seen how much it owes to his discipleship of Old Testament historical narrative, and how much to themes which he has already developed and explored. His powers are certainly running strong, warmed up by the preceding parables and particularly the *prodigal son*, but they owe much to the (probably unconscious) tapping of sources. One more of them ought to be mentioned. Jeremias says (p. 180f) that the *unjust steward* is 'closely connected' with Matthew 5.25f:

> Make friends quickly with your accuser, while you are going with him to court, lest your accuser hand you over to the judge, and the judge to the guard, and you be put in prison; truly, I say to you, you will never get out till you have paid the last penny.

The accuser seems, as Jeremias says, to be a creditor. Here, as in the *unjust steward*, there is strong incitement to respond with 'resolute action' to 'the challenge of the hour'. Jeremias explains the similarity by ascribing both passages to Jesus. In the absence of criteria which could decide for or against that hypothesis, there is room for the alternative suggestion that Matthew's instance of an effectively patched up agreement averting crisis in a financial setting has influenced this story, which is Luke's.

The parable of the *rich man and Lazarus* follows after eight verses of rather miscellaneous and disjointed teaching. It has connections with another L parable, *the rich fool* of 12.16–21. He too enjoyed his material goods without a thought for death: 'Fool, this night they are asking your soul of you.' 'They' are the angels,

which, in this parable, are actually shown taking a soul (Lazarus')
to heaven. According to Luke souls go to their eternal destinies,
Hades or paradise, at the moment of death without waiting in
limbo for a general resurrection: Jesus' promise to the penitent
thief (a very Lucan character and only in Luke) at 23.43 is a
further instance of it. Loisy (*Les Evangiles Synoptiques* [1908] II,
p. 174) notices that this is a Lucan kind of eschatology which was
not Jesus', if the testimony of Mark and Matthew – and Luke
himself elsewhere – is to be believed: 'He announced the coming
of the Kingdom of God on earth, not the carrying of the poor into
Abraham's bosom.' Certainly it is only in Luke among the
evangelists that we get such eschatology, realized in the course of
time by death.

Like the *prodigal son*, this parable has a second part in which
the implications of the catastrophe (using the word in its literal and
literary sense) are explored. Reasons were given there for the
extravagant celebrations over the returned prodigal, and here the
reversal of fortunes is justified by Abraham. It is a kind of
interpretation, held within the tale and put in the mouth of one of
its characters, instead of being given *ab extra*, obviously apt to
Luke's greater narrative skill and more narrative theology. Loisy
(ibid.) is right in seeing allegory in it.

> These five brothers, who 'have Moses and the prophets' (sc. the
> Old Testament) in their hands, represent Judaism; they do not
> hear Moses and the prophets, because they do not know how to
> find Christ there; and it is foreseen that the resurrection of a
> dead man will not move them either, because they were
> indifferent to the resurrection of Jesus. So the parable becomes
> an allegory explaining the reprobation of the Jews, and this
> allegory, perfectly intelligible as the thinking of Christian
> tradition, makes no sense in the mouth of Jesus because it
> presupposes the death and resurrection of the Saviour, the
> obduracy of Judaism towards the new faith, and the controversy
> between Jews and Christians about the messianic prophecies.

Loisy's case rests firmly on two major features of Luke-Acts. First,
the messianic-Christian nature of the Scriptures, 'Moses and the
prophets', is made much of in Jesus' post-resurrection appearances
at Emmaus (24.27) and to the eleven (24.44). Second, in Acts
Paul's central difference with traditional Judaism is not about law,
as in Galatians and Romans, but about resurrection (Acts 23 and
24): he cannot convince his Jewish hearers of it, even the Pharisees
who are meant to believe in resurrection.

The parable is based on a very old legend. Creed (pp. 209ff)

150

gives an ancient Egyptian version from Gressmann, in which a rich man fares ill in the after-life because of his wickedness and a poor man fares well because of his goodness. There are rabbinic versions too (see Creed, p. 260). So the story was in circulation before and during the time of early Christianity. Whether an intermediate version of it by Jesus himself underlies the thorough Lucan redaction which we possess is, as ever, not determinable. As with other L parables we can lay our hands on previous stories which could have been sources or influences and on the version in the Gospels. Jesus' version is not available, supposing it to have existed. The decidedly Lucan character of the version we have is evidenced by the 35 instances of Lucan words and *hapax legomena* (either to the Gospels or the New Testament) which occur in its 22 verses. Together with the Lucan theological motifs which we have noticed (to which can be added the reversal of fortunes as part of Luke's 'Magnificat' theology, the table setting, the realism and the pathos) they make a persuasive case for Lucan authorship: though, once again, this is not authorship of a wholly original kind.

It is, finally, worth reverting to the allegorical nature of this parable, on which Loisy was persuasive. It marks the return of allegory after its progressive eclipse in the previous parables. Luke has shown there that he can do without allegory. Now he shows that he can do with it too. Indeed, when it comes to his grand overall theme of the transference of religious initiative and authority from the Jews to the Christians, he uses anything that works and helps. The allegorical elements in both the *prodigal son* and the *rich man and Lazarus* refer to it and illustrate it.

After six verses of teaching about forgiveness and faith comes the curious little parable of *master and slave*. The slave does no more than his duty if, after a hard day's agricultural work, he serves supper to his master before having it himself. The parable sees the relation of God and man hierarchically. Most of Luke's parables do, and get much of their vivacity from adventurous handling of hierarchical relationships: father and son, steward and lord, plaintiff and judge, master and servants. The events of the parables put various kinds of strain on the relations involved, insubordination being brought into play against subordination, but do not break them. This is slightly odd because we have often noted the reversal of fortunes, and so of positions, as a theme of Luke's theology, which has a revolutionary streak running right through it, and particularly through its primary theme of the supersession of Judaism by Christianity. But revolution has its limits and humankind cannot bear very much of it without wanting order again: the knowledge of what to expect and whom to please.

So, if Luke's is the Gospel which is most explicit at some points about the revolutionary character of Christianity, at many others it is the most conservative and orderly-minded of Christian writings. Paul's, and Mark's, head-on confrontation with the law is avoided, the apostles are enhanced both as people and as officials, functionaries of the Roman Empire are given a good press. Moreover, Luke's style and forms of thought are deliberately old-fashioned in their frequent imitation of Old Testament Scripture. He is more of a bourgeois, at home in the world's order, than one of the dispossessed seeking to overturn it. But then even Paul was decidedly conservative politically, and Luke's conservatism holds and contains vivid sparks of insubordination and egalitarianism. In this quasi-political area thorough-going consistency is hard to come by and not always welcome when found.

Another aspect of this little parable is worth noticing for its general application. It is decidedly Lucan with its beginning, 'Which of you . . .?', its table setting in a well-to-do household, and its realistic commonsensical wisdom. Yet its placing is apparently random. 'There appears to be no connexion with what precedes', as Creed says (p.215). Luke can do much better than this, even in the rambling Journey Section. But it suggests forcibly that the parables can be older than their settings in the particular book. Whether we should therefore attribute them all to Jesus is another, and (it must be said yet again) unresolvable, question. They have, in principle, the whole of the past to draw upon and their origins can be as old as the Old Testament or as recent as Luke's own activity as a Christian teacher before he wrote his Gospel. In this instance the latter looks the more likely.

The next parable, the *unjust judge*, is better set. It comes after a passage of teaching about the suddenness of doomsday and would, as Creed says (p. 222), 'lose its main force' without its element of eschatology. It is, however, eschatology with an element of delay, such as Matthew began to develop out of Mark's more immediate sort and which Luke takes further still. It is not just eschatology but delayed eschatology which informs both parable and interpretation: and once more parable and interpretation are unified. The *unjust judge* has connections with two other L parables. It is very like the *friend at night* (11.5–8) in its conviction that insistent asking overcomes reluctance to give by imposing a stronger pressure of inconvenience. In both parables Luke is happy to portray God as the giver under pressure – an example of fresh vitality working within an accepted hierarchical frame. The beseeching woman here matches the beseeching man there, much as the shepherd and the housewife made a pair in the *lost sheep* and *coin* of 15.3–10. Secondly, this parable is also linked to the immediately subsequent one of *Pharisee and publican*: not as much by shape this time as by topic, which is prayer.

Ecclesiasticus 35.13–18 contains so much of the drama and theology of the *unjust judge* that it looks like a very probable source for it.

> He [the Lord] will listen to the prayer of one who is wronged.
> He will not ignore the supplication of the fatherless,
>   nor the widow when she pours out her story.
> Do not the tears of the widow run down her cheek
>   as she cries out against him who has caused her to fall?
> He whose service is pleasing to the Lord will be accepted
>   and his prayer will reach to the clouds.
> The prayer of the humble pierces the clouds,
>   and he will not be consoled until it reaches the Lord;
> he will not desist until the Most High visits him
>   and does justice for the righteous, and executes judgement.
> And the Lord will not delay...

The wronged but vocal widow, the Lord who will vindicate speedily for all the appearance of delay, the high and energetic theology of petitionary prayer: they are all there. Luke's parable is an improvement on ben Sirach's repetitive disquisition. Once again, it is decidedly Lucan. As well as the similarities with the other L parable of the *friend at night* there is the setting in a city, the characteristic Lucan phrase of (not) 'fearing God', and the judge's soliloquy. It is dominated by two themes of Luke's particular theology: the power of petitionary prayer, and the delayed, but certain and dependable, eschatology. There is also the moral ambivalence or liquidity which we are accustomed to find in L parables and is so different from the crisp dichotomies of Matthew. This is, in addition, very much an historian's parable. It refers to, and makes sense of, that tense penultimate phase in God's great historical plan in which the elect await their divine vindication. It is the situation which gave birth to apocalyptic. Luke's hand can turn as readily to apocalyptic as to so many other kinds of literary art (see 10.18 and 21.24–6, his work). But how cool he is here, at the very point where apocalyptic fantasy could ignite, and just after the prophecies of 17.22–37! The parable is earthy and commonsensical, and only slightly allegorical since the woman represents the elect while God is both something like, but much more unlike, the lazy judge: if he gives justice reluctantly, will not God give it readily?

The *Pharisee and publican* which follows also refers to a phase of history, the constantly pondered change-over from Judaism to Christianity. Pharisaical confidence gives place to the sinner's humble penitence, the grand theme of the *lost* parables of chapter 15. The Pharisee is reminiscent of the elder brother, the publican of the prodigal son. Whereas the *unjust judge* turned upon futurist eschatology, here heaven is a constant presence, always there in parallel with earthly goings on as it was in the *lost sheep* and *coin*. Luke's eschatology comes both realized and futurist. All this shows the parable's Lucan character, but yet again it is not an utterly original product of Luke's creativity. There is Pauline theology here.

> God chose what is low and despised in the world, even things that are not, to bring to nothing things that are, so that no human being might boast in the present of God.
>
> (1 Corinthians 1.28)

It is the Paul of Corinthians to whom Luke has affinity; not the Paul of Galatians and Romans. He has Paul's insistence on the utter dependence of men on God, without Paul's other insistence on the supersession of the law. Luke is not a thorough disciple of Paul. He has learned much from Matthew who forcibly denied Paul's doctine of the redundancy of the law, and preferred the notion of a more radical obedience to it than its devotees practised. Luke held the revolutionary newness of Christianity within the frame of the law. Matthew's tag,

> everyone who exalts himself shall be humbled, but he who humbles himself shall be exalted   (Matthew 23.12)

is the parable's triumphant conclusion. Behind it, too, stands Matthew's warning to the Pharisees,

> Truly I say to you, the tax collectors and the harlots go into the kingdom of God before you.   (Matthew 21.31)

Matthew's charge against the Pharisees was that their interpretation of the law was out of proportion: 'tithing mint and dill and cummin and neglecting the weightier matters of the law, justice, mercy and faith' (23.23). Likewise here, the Pharisee betrays himself by his confidence in his accomplishment of the details of legal observance which differentiates him from 'other men'.

This is the last of Luke's 'illustrative stories' (Creed, p. 222), that great collection of examplary tales whereby he turned the whole genre of parable from allegorical suservience of other realities into the autonomous tale which consumes its own smoke and has a naturalistic life of its own in which the meaning is

154

digested and absorbed. It is not surprising that modern critics, unconsciously but decisively influenced by realistic Bible pictures like Holman Hunt's and by the host of novels since the eighteenth century which obey much the same laws as Luke's parables, should have seized on them as normative and primary. Historically, however, it is the other way about. The allegorical parable was the norm, and the rabbis stuck to it. Luke's achievement was to make a new sort of parable by bringing in to the genre the kind of realism, moral ambivalence, excitement and common sense which he learned from Old Testament storytellers. So this was not an unprecedented achievement. But it was a fine one big with consequences for art, literature, drama and theology in Christendom and beyond it – not to mention the exegesis of the gospel parables in the twentieth century.

The last two parables in the Gospel are a return to the old kind of parable, the historical allegory. The *pounds* is paralleled in Matthew, the *vineyard* in Mark. They make clear that the great L parables are, for all our affection and admiration for them, something of a loop or detour in the line of parable tradition. Luke himself returns to the old way and nothing like the L parables is to appear again in Christian literature for a very long time.

The *pounds* figured in Matthew as the *talents* among the parables which he added to Mark's apocalyptic chapter 13 to explain what watching entailed. It had an ecclesiastical setting and reference. Luke puts it after Jesus' encounter with Zacchaeus in Jericho. Zacchaeus the publican had done well out of his business and was able to give half his goods to the poor as well as restoring fourfold to those whom he had swindled: something like the two servants in the parable who increase their capital by enterprise. The parable is firmly attached to the Zacchaeus story by the first half of its introductory verse, 19.11:

As they heard these things [what Jesus said about Zacchaeus] he proceeded to tell a parable...

The second half of the same verse gives it a wider historical context:

... because he was near to Jerusalem, and because they supposed that the kingdom of God was to appear immediately.

So the parable is attached to two major markers of Luke's overall historiography: the end of Jesus' earthly ministry with 'his departure which he was to accomplish at Jerusalem' (9.31), and the subsequent period in which the Kingdom does not come immediately but – instead of the restoration of the kingdom to Israel (Acts 1.6) – there is an era of Church and mission, of

155

preaching and response. Matthew's ecclesiastical setting of the parable gets historicized in the sense of being given a more precise placing in a longer temporal perspective. Which is just what we would expect of Luke.

Luke's main difference from Matthew is his mixing in of an added story of a nobleman: who goes away to receive a kingdom, is opposed by his citizens and returns to take vengeance on them. It is very obviously an addition to the primary story of the exploitation of capital sums which we have in Matthew. It can be removed and a clearer and more unified parable results. So why did Luke add it? It copes allegorically with the delay of the second coming, as has often been noticed. There are two more reasons, both germane to his methods. In the first place the nobleman is a reflection of actual history: the relation of the Herodian quislings to Rome and their unpopularity at home. The story of Archelaus in Josephus, *Antiquities* xvii.11.1, is the closest parallel. In the second place this secondary story is, as Creed says, 'an allegorical expansion designed to relate and interpret the rejection of Jesus by the Jews and the downfall of Jerusalem' (p. 232). All that needs to be added is that the allegorical expansion is well synchronized to Luke's historical scheme. Jesus' departure from the worldly scene was, according to Peter's sermon at Pentecost (Acts 2) in order to sit at God's right hand as a super-Davidic messianic king. The refusal of the Jews to accept him as such runs throughout Acts up to its vitriolic ending. 'We will not have this man to reign over us' (Luke 19.14) has a long theological resonance.

The added story brings with it an increase in both allegorical significance and historical realism. It is interesting, and confirms our view of Luke, to see him doing both these things at once. The casualty here is the story-line, which is a little obfuscated: even Luke cannot do everything at once. There is, further, some confusion about the number of servants. Ten are called at verse 13, but when the man returns as king he only reckons with three of them. An editorial stitch has been dropped. On the other hand, it is arguably an editorial improvement to have each of them given ten pounds, equal sums which enhance the point of unequal success in increasing them. It is also an advantage, and characteristic of Luke's materialism, that the successful get something more material than congratulations and promises – cities. Luke is particularly fond of cities and as rewards they set the parable more firmly in the real world of administration. It is characteristic of Luke that the dialogue is enhanced: 'I will condemn you out of your own mouth' (verse 22) and 'Lord, he has ten pounds' (verse 25). Luke did the same with the Matthean introduction to the *good*

Samaritan. The end of the parable is historicized: a judicial massacre instead of Matthew's casting into outer darkness. It has often been noticed that Luke's sums of money are more everyday and plausible than Matthew's fabulous talents. Luke's unadventurous servant wraps his money in a handkerchief instead of going to the Matthean lengths of burying it. Though this parable does not show Luke's redaction at its best, it shows a combination of the realistic and the allegorical which withstands simplistic exegesis. And it shows the secondariness of his work in relation to Matthew's.

Luke's version of the *vineyard* at 20.9–19 is also secondary. The bits of it which do not figure in Mark's version or Matthew's are unmistakably his work. The owner goes away 'for a long time', allegorically apt to Luke's eschatology. The owner is given a soliloquy as in Mark and Matthew, but three times as long by the addition of 'What shall I do? I will send my beloved son'. The *rich fool* and the *unjust steward* both asked this question, 'What shall I do?', of themselves and variously answered it. The plan to send the beloved son is taken out of the narrative and put into the speech. In the *pounds* and the *good Samaritan* we noticed Luke making, as here, more dialogue. So here in verses 16 and 17 'they' exclaim 'God forbid!' at the destruction of the tenants and the transference of their rights. Jesus 'looked upon them' – as, balefully and memorably, he will look at Peter at 22.61 – before presenting them with the text about the stone.

In this parable, as in others of which we have versions in each of the Synoptic Gospels, Luke's has features in common with both Mark's and Matthew's. As in Mark the owner is just 'a man' at verse 9 and not also a householder as in Matthew. Verse 10 is also parallel to Mark rather than Matthew: one servant, who is beaten and sent away empty. On the other hand Luke has the son first expelled then killed at verse 15: an allegorical improvement which Matthew had made on Mark. Like Matthew he has the additional text of Isaiah about the stone breaking those on whom it falls, which is absent from Mark. And as in Matthew the chief priests and scribes (Matthew, 'Pharisees') seek to arrest him instead of Mark's 'they'. The most economical theory to cope with this is that Luke knew both versions. The Q hypothesis has no advantage over it.

Finally, Luke's concern with time emerges again in the added note at verse 19 that the authorities wanted to arrest him 'in that very hour', a phrase paralleled at 7.21; 10.21; and 13.31: all peculiar to Luke. It is an imperious reminder of the importance of understanding the parables in their precise narrative contexts.

6 Epilogue – John

Readers who pass from the Synoptic Gospels to John's sense that they are entering a different world. The traditions and findings of New Testament research confirm the impression. Here is a Jesus who talks of himself rather than of the Kingdom of God and does so in long discourses, unlike anything in the earlier Gospels, which present a doctrine of religious perception and faith centring on a mystical coinherence of Jesus, the Father and the believers. Eternal reality has the upper hand over temporal events, giving a stately and static air to the whole book. It is as if John had noticed the problem of a Christianity too tightly tied to the particularity of history and answered it with a gospel of a Jesus for now and always; and a Christology in which everything in the past, present and future comes to rest. The straight line of history seems to have been bent into a circle around the central figure. He was before Abraham (8.58). Eschatological expectation is collapsed and concentrated into him, who was previously the harbinger of the end. He is as available to the believer in any century as he was in the days of his flesh. All historical moments are equidistant from him. In the first ending of John's work, Thomas believes because he has seen and touched the risen Jesus. Jesus' final words, connecting that temporal moment to any present, are:

> Have you believed because you have seen me? Blessed are those who have not seen and yet believe. (John 20.29)

Jesus, the light, is always there at the centre of existence: as life for the believers and as judgement for the rest. He is not borne away in time's ever-rolling stream. Rather, time finds its meaning and fulfilment in him.

John's achievement is dazzling, even hypnotic. Yet, like all such achievements, it reaps from the labours of others (4.38). It relates to the Synoptics. H. F. D. Sparks' *Synopsis of the Gospels*, volume 2, rightly and helpfully includes it with them. It is not an entirely different animal. Two important observations will make that clear. The first is that John's Gospel is in the form of narrative like the other three. There are four Gospels. For all John's perception of the eternal, his long speeches floating over the historical narrative, his grounding beyond history of the one who utters them – it still tells a story. And it tells it with articulate care and management. Second, the three Synoptic Gospels are themselves by no means an entirely homogeneous group. Matthew's legislating Christ is different from Mark's enigmatic wanderer, Luke's wise and philanthropic prophet different from both of them. Recent studies of the particular theologies of the evangelists have increased our awareness of these differences, and we have seen them vividly in the parables which present those theologies and are so much part and parcel of them, so indigenous to each. John, like the others, is a theologian and a narrator. And if he is both in his own distinctive way, so were they.

John's difference from, and similarity to, the other three Gospels is very evident in the matter of parables. The word *parabolē* does not occur in his book. It contains what we can only consider to be parables, but he prefers the label *paroimia* usually translated 'figure'. The significance of this is hard to assess because the difference is not clear. Figures are included in the first two categories of our list of meanings of *mashal* in the Old Testament (p. 9), the saying or proverb and the figurative saying or metaphor. The only other occurrence of *paroimia* in the New Testament is at 2 Peter 2.22:

It has happened to them according to the true proverb (*paroimia*). The dog turns back to his vomit, and the sow is washed only to wallow in the mire.

It looks as if John is preferring a more modest word than *parabolē*, but the suggestion does not hold. For ben Sirach *parabolē* and *paroimia* could be synonyms. His wise man seeks out the *apokrupha*, the hidden things, of figures (*paroimion*), and in the enigmas of parables he knows his way about. In the event John goes much further than the figure, metaphorical or plain. With his *shepherd* at 10.1–30 and his *vine* at 15.1–7 he draws on parables of Ezekiel (34 and 15) and makes parables of his own which belong with the third and grandest category in the Old Testament list, the fully articulated allegory. He does it in his own way. The *vine* is without historical reference and not at all enigmatic. The previous *shepherd* however does contain both enigmatic and historical elements. For all his apparent reticence about parables (he is reticent about sacraments too), John's cautious entrance into the genre by way of the figure takes him irresistibly into the elaborate allegory. In his hands it comes to a crystalline translucency and stability which it has not had before. But as well as his well-known creativity, he shows solidarity with the tradition which we have

159

been following. So this investigation should not close without taking some brief account of him.

His first three chapters contain some metaphors which are familiar from the Synoptic Gospels. Knowledge of what they signified there helps with understanding their meaning here.

In the calling of Nathanael there is mention of a *fig tree*. Jesus, by supernatural knowledge, saw Nathanael sitting under it before he came to him, and tells him that he did. Nathanael immediately acknowledges him as Son of God and King of Israel.

> Jesus answered him, 'Because I said to you, I saw you under the fig tree, do you believe? You shall see greater things than these.' And he said to him, 'Truly, truly I say to you, you will see heaven opened, and the angels of God ascending and descending upon the Son of man.' (John 1.50f)

The fig tree matters and signifies. According to Zechariah 6.10 Israelites will sit under fig trees on the day of restitution. In the Synoptics the fig tree stood for Israel. This was integral both to the cursing of the unfruitful fig tree at Mark 11.13f and Matthew 21.18f, and to the parable of the *fig tree* at Luke 13.6–9 which derived from the cursing incident. Here is a further variation on the same theme, with the tree bearing the same significance. Nathanael was 'an Israelite indeed' (1.47). He acknowledged Jesus as 'King of Israel'. The deliberate timescale in John's narrative confirms this meaning. The fig tree belongs to the old order and to the end of Nathanael's pre-Christian life. The past, when he sat under it as a true Israelite, is superseded first by the present in which he acknowledges Jesus' divine status, and then by the future in which he will see him as the mediating focus of divinity. The whole passage is obviously Johannine, building memories of Jesus' baptism in the Synoptics (the open heaven, the ascending and descending) into its own fabric. Jesus' divine knowledge, the stability whereby disciples come to him rather than he collecting them as he goes along (Mark 1.16–20), confession coming out of true perception and leading to greater perception – all these are typical of John and combine to create his distinctive atmosphere, settled and august. But within that there is narrative movement, a distinction of times between before Christ and after, such as is also basic in the Synoptics. And this movement is signalled by the synoptic figure of the fig tree.

At 3.19 the synoptic metaphor of *light* appears, having already played so impressive a role in the prologue as to make us forget its humbler synoptic parabolic precedents. In Mark, Matthew and Luke, light went through variations of significance. It was the mystery of the gospel in Mark 4.21f, the good works of disciples in Matthew 5.15f, a guide to those entering the house at Luke 8.16 and 11.13. Each was typical of the writer concerned. Just as typical is John's concentration of all theological symbols into Jesus himself, making him (8.12; 12.46) the eternal light which comes into the world as judgement or salvation. John the Baptist at 5.35 is a lesser and temporary light or lamp.

In the Synoptic Gospels the intermediary function of the Baptist was the occasion for historical reflection. At Mark 2.18–20 disciples of John the Baptist come to Jesus and ask him why his disciples are not fasting. Jesus answers them with the parable of the *bridegroom*. At John 3.29 John himself, rather than his disciples, uses the same figure to explain his historical relation to Jesus – the same intention as in the synoptic tradition.

> I am not the Christ, but I have been sent before him. He who has the bride is the bridegroom; the friend of the bridegroom, who stands and hears him, rejoices greatly at the bridegroom's voice; therefore this joy of mine is now full. He must increase, but I must decrease. (John 3.28–30)

The introduction of a best man, meaning John the Baptist, and of a bride, meaning the Church, is new. But the basic metaphor, the allegorical form and the overall historical reference to the change of times, are all shared with the synoptic tradition. John's parable-making is his own yet continuous with the main stream.

It is the same with the *harvest* parable at 4.35–8:

> Do you not say, 'There are yet four months, then comes the harvest'? I tell you, lift up your eyes, and see how the fields are already white for harvest. He who reaps receives wages, and gathers fruit for eternal life, so that sower and reaper may rejoice together. For here the saying holds true, 'One sows and another reaps.' I sent you to reap that for which you did not labour; others have laboured, and you have entered into their labour.

It begins with a *mashal* of the first category in the Old Testament list, a popular saying. It includes another, called a *logos*, towards the end. But the first saying is uttered only to be contradicted by Jesus' 'I tell you . . .'. The truth of popular realism is immediately overwhelmed by the truth of vision, 'the fields are already white for harvest'. It becomes an historical parable, reflecting on the significance of time in Johannine Christian terms. It is clearly allegorical: fruit is 'for eternal life', the harvest is the fulfilment of time, the labourers are Christian disciples divided into the sowers and reapers of two Christian generations. So here too John works within the main parabolic stream, and does so in his own way, which brings the different times into one. Jesus' 'I sent you to reap that for which you did not labour' is, as Bultmann says (*The Gospel of John* [Blackwell 1971] p. 200) 'spoken from the standpoint of later missionary work where every missionary could look back on some predecessor in the field'. Yet in the end the differences fade. Sowers and reapers coincide in a common joy. History is an organic whole, turning around the eternal revelation in and through Jesus. Within that scheme John uses major symbols from synoptic parables, most obviously the agricultural parables, including Mark's *sower*, as collected in Matthew 13. Later, at 12.24, the synoptic tradition of seed parables is concentrated into Christ himself as the grain of wheat which falls into the ground and dies to bear much fruit.

John's two major parables are the *shepherd* at 10.1–8 and the *vine* at 15.1–7. Both are allegorical, but in other ways they differ. The earlier *shepherd* is set in polemic. It follows upon the heated debates around the healing of the man born blind, and issues in 'division among the Jews' (10.19), some saying that Jesus is mad and some not. It thus has a divisive function similar to that of chapter 13 in Matthew's Gospel. It is obscure, not plain or open. It is noted at 10.6 that 'this figure (*paroimia*) Jesus used with them, but they did not understand what he was saying to them'. And the Jews complain at 10.24: 'Tell us plainly.' The *shepherd* speaks of the sheep, who stand for Christian disciples, in the third person – 'they'. Christianity is thus at a remove from the discourse. It is all quite different with the *vine*. There the disciples are in the second person – 'you' and there is neither contention nor obscurity. Its context and character are clear and settled. This movement from the problematic to the plain is paralleled in Mark. There too the *sower* was obscure, the *vineyard* all too intelligible. So here lucidity supravenes when the story is in sight of its goal, but a lucidity less historical and more stable than Mark's.

The setting of the *shepherd* is, as we have seen, fraught. It occurs in the last discourse which Jesus addresses to the public at large, speaking in figures. Such revelation-in-obscurity by means of historical allegory takes us back to the roots of the New Testament's parabolic tradition: to Ezekiel, in fact, whose allegory of true and false shepherds in chapter 34 is a fundamental source. As in John, Ezekiel's false shepherds kill the sheep, leaving them scattered and exposed to predators. God, as true shepherd, unites, protects and feeds them. None of the synoptic evangelists made such thorough use of Ezekiel's allegory. They took from it only the motif of lost sheep (Ezekiel 34.16), and possibly the judgement between sheep and sheep at Ezekiel 34.22 as a source for Matthew's parable of *sheep and goats*. John, on the other hand, exploits the whole scheme of Ezekiel 34 and makes a complex allegorical parable with wide historical reference.

Ezekiel himself had given his Christian interpreter a cue for his work. Having spoken of God himself as Israel's shepherd, at verse 24 he introduced a subsidiary agent.

I, the Lord, will be their God, and my servant David shall be prince among them.

John is fully aware of the synoptic tradition of Christ as son of David.

Has not the scripture said that the Christ is descended from David and comes from Bethlehem, the village where David was? (John 7.42)

Ezekiel's messianic hint, coming late in his parable and as a prelude to the vision of pastoral security at its end, is the dominant motif in John's. Throughout, Jesus is the good shepherd. Both God's work and David's are his. John's habitual christological concentration also produces a sudden and surreal metamorphosis in his parable, such as is endemic to allegory and the result of the pressure upon it of theology. At one moment Jesus is the door of the sheep (10.7, 9 – perhaps recalling the *door* parable of Luke 13.24–30). Then suddenly at 10.11 he is the shepherd. For John, Jesus is everything. If the story-line is distorted by the weight of this doctrine laid upon it, John is as unlikely as his predecessors in the making of allegorical parables to be concerned. It is an easily acceptable price to pay for his achievement of a Christian parabolic *midrash* of Ezekiel's parable.

The kind of parable deployed remains the same and survives the christening. It is allegorical rather than realistic: Ezekiel can speak of a flock scattered all over the world, John of a human door. It is historical: Ezekiel's parable is set in government before the exile and depends entirely on divine control of history, John's in the transition from Judaism to Christianity with history turning around the sacrifice of Christ (10.11,17 and 18) which is written into its structure. Before it there were only thieves and robbers (10.8). After it there will be unity (10.16), and the parable's resolution is in the Christian Church as the fulfilment of divine historical providence – a familiar theme. Jesus is the point of transition from Ezekiel's world and parable to John's world and parable.

The *shepherd* is uttered before that transition has been accomplished. It tells of what is yet to be, and is appropriately dark and uncomprehended. The parable of the *vine* is part of Jesus' farewell discourse to his disciples in which everything is as if the transition had happened. It is told 'that your joy may be full' (15.11).

Bultmann says that 'there is no comparison here, or allegory' (op. cit., p. 529). He justifies this by 'the absence of any article of comparison' and by the assertion that 'placing "I am" at the beginning is at once contrary to the form of allegory'. Such legislation is misconceived. Allegories do not have to have articles of comparison, and there is no reason why one should not begin with 'I am'. But there is good reason for Bultmann's aberration. This is an allegory of unusual transparency and simplicity. It presents no problems and needs no interpretation (nor did Mark's *vineyard*). The lucidity suits the context. But it does not stop its being an allegory. Indeed, Ezekiel's allegory of the vine in chapter 15 is a source for it. Ezekiel speaks there of Israel as a vine which has been burned and become useless. John speaks here of the burning of unfruitful branches. He owes it to Ezekiel, but it is also sound viticultural practice and has a Matthean tinge in the connection of fire with judgement. The sources of John's image are multiple. They span Hosea's 'Israel is a luxuriant vine that yields its fruit' (10.1), Isaiah's song of the vineyard (5.1ff), Jeremiah's 'I planted you a choice vine . . . How then . . . have you become a wild vine?' (2.21) and the synoptic *vineyard* parables. But all this has been thoroughly digested. The result is a quintessentially Johannine allegorical parable: not of historical process but of the abiding coinherence of Jesus and disciples within the Father's care. Like all the parables we have seen, it is fitted to the theology of the evangelist who has it, and to its particular place in his story. But it is also a point at which the dominance of historical process and change over parable-making is loosened, leaving an assurance transcending time at the centre of Christianity. With John an era of Christian historiography, of Christianity as popular narrative, ceases. A great age of Christian doctrine begins. Stories will yield to creeds.

Bibliography

Abrahams, I., *Studies in Pharisaism and the Gospels*. Cambridge 1917, 1924.

Bornkamm, G., Barth, G, and Held, H. J., *Tradition and Interpretation in Matthew*. ET by P. Scott, SCM 1963.

Black, M., 'The Parables as Allegory', *Bulletin of the John Rylands Library* XLII 1959–60.

Bowker, J., 'Mystery and Parable:' Mark IV. 1–20, in *Journal of Theological Studies* XXV October 1974.

Braunde, W. G., tr., *Midrash on Psalms*. 25 vols, Yale 1959.

Brown, R. E., 'Parable and Allegory Reconsidered', *Novum Testamentum* V 1962.

Bultmann, R., *The Gospel of John*. ET by Beasley-Murray, Hoare and Riches, Blackwell 1971.

Cadbury, H. J., *The Making of Luke–Acts*. SPCK 1958.

— *The Style and Literary Method of Luke I*. Harvard 1919.

Cadoux, A. T., *The Parables of Jesus: their Art and Use*. James Clarke n.d.

Carlston, C. E., *The Parables of the Triple Tradition*. Philadelphia 1975.

Charles, R. H., *Apocrypha and Pseudepigrapha of the Old Testament*. Oxford 1913.

Conzelmann, H., *The Theology of St Luke*. ET by G. Buswell, Faber 1960.

Creed, J. M., *The Gospel According to St. Luke*. Macmillan 1930.

Crossan, J. D., *In Parables: the Challenge of the Historical Jesus*. New York 1973.

Danby, H., ed., *Mishnah*. Oxford 1933.

Daube, D., *The New Testament and Rabbinic Judaism*. London 1956.

— *Ancient Hebrew Fables*. Oxford 1973.

Derrett, J. D. M., 'Allegory and the wicked Vinedressers', *Journal of Theological Studies* XXV October 1974.

— *Law in the New Testament*. Darton, Longman & Todd 1970.

Dodd, C. H., *The Parables of the Kingdom*. Nisbet 1961.

Drury, J. H., *Tradition and Design in Luke's Gospel: A Study in Early Christian Historiography*. Darton, Longman & Todd 1976.

165

Eissfeldt, O., *Der Maschal im Alten Testament*. Beiheft zur Zeitschrift für die Alttestamentliche Wissenschaft XXIV, 1913.

Epstein, E., ed., *The Babylonian Talmud*. London (previously published in Haarlem) 1935–48.

Feldman, A., *The Parables and Similes of the Rabbis, Agricultural and Pastoral*. Cambridge 1927.

Fiebig, P., *Altjüdische Gleichnisse und die Gleichnisse Jesu*. Tübingen, J. C. B. Mohr, 1904.

— *Die Gleichnisreden Jesu in Lichte der rabbinischen Gleichnisse des neutestamentlichen Zeitalters*. Tübingen, J. C. B. Mohr, 1912.

Freeman, H. and Simon, M., eds., *Midrash Rabbah*. Soncino Press 1939.

Funk, R. W., *Language, Hermeneutic and the Word of God*. New York 1966.

Goodenough, E. R., *By Light, Light*. New Haven 1935.

Goulder, M. D., 'Characteristics of the Parables in the several Gospels', *Journal of Theological Studies* April 1968.

— *Midrash and Lection in Matthew*. SPCK 1974.

Grant F. C., *The Economic Background of the Gospels*. Oxford 1926.

Green, H. B., *The Gospel According to Matthew*. Oxford 1975.

Hauck, F., 'Parabole', in G. Kittel, ed., *Theological Dictionary of the New Testament*. Grand Rapids 1964.

Hawkins, Sir J. C., *Horae Synopticae*. Oxford 1909.

Hengel, M., *Judaism and Hellenism*. 2 vols. ET by John Bowden, SCM 1974.

Hermaniuk, M., *La Parabole Evangelique*. Louvain, Bibliotheca Alfonsiana, 1947.

Jeremias, J., *The Parables of Jesus*. ET of 6th German edn by S. H. Hooke, SCM 1963.

Jülicher, A., *Die Gleichnisreden Jesu*. 2 vols. Tübingen 1910.

Kilpatrick, G. D., *The Origins of the Gospel according to St Matthew*. Oxford 1950.

Kingsbury, J. D., *The Parables of Jesus in Matthew 13*. SPCK 1969.

Lagrange M.-J., 'La Parabole en dehors de l'Evangile', in *Revue Biblique* 1909.

Lauterbach, J. Z. ('JZL'), 'Parable', in *Jewish Encyclopaedia*. New York 1901.

— 'Ancient Jewish Allegorists', in *Jewish Quarterly Review* I 1910–11.

—, ed., *Mekilta de Rabbi Israel*. Philadelphia 1933.

Lightfoot, R. H., *The Gospel Message of Mark*. Oxford 1950.

Lohmeyer, E., *Das Evangelium des Markus*. Göttingen 1937.

Loisy, A., *Les Evangiles Synoptiques*. 2 vols. Paris 1907.

Michaelis, W., *Die Gleichnisse Jesu*. Hamburg, Furche Verlag, 1956.

Milik, J. T., *The Books of Enoch, Aramaic Fragments of Qumran Cave 4*. Oxford 1976.

Momigilano, A., 'Time in Ancient Historiography', *Quarto contributo alla Storia degli studi Classici e del Mondo Antico*. Rome 1975.

Mortley, R., *Connaissance Religieuse et Herméneutique chez Clement d'Alexandrie*. Leiden 1973.

Moule, C. F. D., 'Mark 4, 1–20 yet once more', in *Neotestamentica et Semitica: Studies in honour of Principal Matthew Black*. Alec R. Allenson Inc. 1969.

Nineham, D. E., *The Gospel of St Mark*. Pelican 1968.

Osterley, W. O. E., *The Gospel Parables in the Light of their Jewish Background*. SPCK 1936.

Piper, O. A., 'The Mystery of the Kingdom of God', in *Interpretation* I, 1947.

Plummer, A., *A Critical and Exegetical Commentary on the Gospel according to St. Luke*. ICC 1896.

Pryke, E. J., *Redactional Style in the Marcan Gospel*. Cambridge 1978.

Rabenau, K. von, 'Die Form des Rätsels in Buche Hesekiel', in *Gottes ist der Orient: Festschrift für O. Eissfeldt*. Berlin 1957.

Robinson, J. M., *The Problem of History in Mark*. SCM Press 1957.

Siegfried, C., *Philo von Alexandria als Ausleger des Alten Testaments*. Jena 1875.

Smith, B. T. D., *The Parables of the Synoptic Gospels*. Cambridge 1937.

Stendahl, K., *The School of St. Matthew*. Uppsala, Almqvist & Wiksells, 1954.

Stone, M., *Scriptures, Sects and Visions*. Blackwell 1982.

Strecker, G., *Der Weg der Gerechtigkeit*. Göttingen, Vandenhoeck und Ruprecht, 1962.

Trench, R. C., *Notes on the Parables of Our Lord*. London 1841.

Via, D. O., *The Parables: their Literary and Existential Dimension*. Philadelphia 1967.

Wellhausen, J., *Das Evangelium Marci*. Berlin 1903.

Index of Names

INDEX OF NAMES

Index of Gospel Parables

INDEX OF GOSPEL PARABLES

PARABLES IN LUKE

PARABLES IN JOHN

Index of Biblical Passages

NEW TESTAMENT

176

INDEX OF BIBLICAL PASSAGES

178

Index of
Other Ancient Literature